AHMANSON · MURPHY
FINE ARTS IMPRINT

THE AHMANSON FOUNDATION
has endowed this imprint
to honor the memory of
FRANKLIN D. MURPHY
who for half a century
served arts and letters,
beauty and learning, in
equal measure by shaping
with a brilliant devotion
those institutions upon
which they rely.

Published with the assistance of the Getty Grant Program.

The publisher gratefully acknowledges the generous contribution to this book provided by the Art Endowment of the University of California Press Associates, which is supported by a major gift from the Ahmanson Foundation.

EXPERIENCE FLUXUS

UNIVERSITY OF CALIFORNIA PRESS *Berkeley Los Angeles London*

EXPERIENCE FLUXUS

University of California Press
Berkeley and Los Angeles, California

University of California Press, Ltd.
London, England

Library of Congress Cataloging-in-Publication Data

Higgins, Hannah, 1964–.
Fluxus experience / Hannah Higgins.
p. cm.
Includes bibliographical references and index.
ISBN 978-0-520-22867-2 (pbk. : alk. paper)
1. Fluxus (Group of artists). 2. Art, Modern–20th century.
3. Avant-garde (Aesthetics). I. Title.

N6494.F55 H54 2002
700'.9'045–dc21 2001006514

Manufactured in the United States of America
11 10 09 08
10 9 8 7 6 5 4

The paper used in this publication meets the minimum requirements of ANSI/NISO Z39.48-1992 (R 1997) (*Permanence of Paper*). ⊗

For my mother and father, bean and bear.

CONTENTS

ACKNOWLEDGMENTS

This project has passed through me, but is not of me. The many voices of consent and dissent, personal, professional, and all manner of in-between, make it impossible to feel that it is, strictly speaking, mine. I am the author because, by good fortune, I found a way to articulate a view of Fluxus that could finally be heard, first by my dissertation committee at the University of Chicago, then by my mother and father, and finally by the greater community of Fluxus artists and scholars, without whom this project would have been, literally, unimaginable.

On that committee, I benefited from the patient eyes of Reinhold Heller of the University of Chicago and Charles Harrison of the Open University, whose complex perspectives on modernism let me assume nothing. At the other end of the philosophical spectrum, another mentor and friend at the University of Chicago, W. J. T. Mitchell, dutifully attended Fluxus Events in Chicago and beyond, becoming an amateur expert on Fluxus on my behalf. I have deeply appreciated his commitment and constant feedback over the course of the past decade. To him I am profoundly in debt, as to Simon Anderson at the School of the Art Institute of Chicago, also my friend, colleague, and sometime co-conspirator on things Fluxus in the Midwest. Perhaps most important of all, however, early in the life of this project, I had the extreme good fortune to meet and share memorable evenings (always too short!) with Kristine Stiles, a performance historian and artist at Duke University. Reading drafts closely time and again, she has been my staunchest critic, dearest colleague, and most valuable ally in the daunting task that this book represents.

Beyond this world of colleagues-become-friends, there is, of course, the world of Fluxus itself, where personal friendships have become professional in myriad ways. My closest friends in Fluxus have come to me through my parents, Dick Higgins and Alison Knowles, both Fluxus artists. Among those friends I count Eric Andersen and Geoffrey Hendricks, Ken Friedman, Joe Jones, Jackson Mac Low, Larry Miller, Benjamin Patterson, Takako Saito, Carolee Schneemann, Wolf Vostell, and Emmett Williams—and many others. I owe a particular debt to Eric Andersen, who saw fit to invite me twice to European festivals, in 1984 as a co-performer and in 1992 as a resident critic. Those occasions formed my professional commitment to and perspective on these artists and also introduced me to the world of Fluxus critics, curators, and collectors. On a generous grant from the DAAD (Deutscher Akademischer Austauschdienst) in 1992–93, I got to know two of the great German collectors of Fluxus, Hermann Braun, generous and supportive, and the late Hans Sohm, whose collection, now in the Staatsgalerie Stuttgart, is overseen by Dr. Ina Conzen-Meairs. In 1993 I received a Getty Collections Resources Grant to see the Jean Brown Archives at the Getty Center for the Humanities. My memories of Ms. Brown are fond ones, and it was a pleasure to utilize that amazing archive. While in Santa Monica I finally got to know the great scholar of West Coast Fluxus, Karen Moss, who directed me to little-known materials in that archive that I might otherwise have missed. Finally, because of the generosity of the Smart Museum at the University of Chicago, I was able to study the voluminous holdings of the Gilbert and Lila Silverman Fluxus Collection Archive in New York City. Without that collection, this would be a nearly pictureless book, and I am deeply grateful to it and its curator, Jon Hendricks, for consistently generous support, even though we have different perspectives on what Fluxus is and how its story should be told.

Finally, there are the contributions of my friends and family. My husband, Joe Reinstein, has supported me with wit and patience. My father read my dissertation twice for errors and found several. Because of his untimely death in 1998, he never saw the final flowering of that text as a book. But my mother read this manuscript twice and helped me keep the faith in what follows.

PREFACE

Since Fluxus artists never seem to agree on anything, Fluxus has become "a pain in art's ass," in the words of Fluxus artist Ben Vautier. Neither the style nor the substance or significance of what they do produces consensus among the artists. Production ranges from minimal performances, called Events, to full-scale operas, and from graphics and boxed multiples called Fluxkits to paintings on canvas. The artists come from almost every industrialized nation, they span several generations, and many even dislike each other. Accurately portraying Fluxus therefore requires thinking about art in a way that forgoes the normally definitive terms of style, medium, and political sensibility. As the historian Owen Smith puts it, "For anyone seeking to learn . . . about the historical nature of Fluxus and its conceptual framework it might more readily seem to be just plain frustrating rather than radical."[1]

Smith's book *Fluxus: The History of an Attitude* presents a broad-based periodic history of Fluxus in the

United States, Europe, and Japan from the 1950s to the present. His survey is exemplary, and it went far toward filling an informational vacuum on the Fluxus project. Smith's book was concerned primarily with making sense of the immensely complex histories of Fluxus at various places and times, including the "non-hierarchical density of experience" that was central to it.[2] My book, *Fluxus Experience,* can be understood as an extension of Smith's groundbreaking work, for it attempts to assess how this "non-hierarchical density of experience" came to pass and to describe how the principle of experience operates within Fluxus.

Fluxus Experience is admittedly partial to the forms of Fluxus that are experiential in nature. It is one person's account of how several key Fluxus works have generated what the American philosopher John Dewey describes as "active and alert commerce with the world... complete interpenetration of self and the world of objects and events."[3] *Experience,* as I use the word, refers specifically to this transactional, interpenetrative framework and its capacity to create a sense of continuity with the world. In this sense, experience is neither ahistorical nor uncontextual; rather, experience is simultaneously embedded in human consciousness and in the situation that makes a specific experience possible.

Although what makes an experience possible is necessarily historically specific, the audience remains largely unaware of that context.[4] Interpretations may be subsequently attached to an experience, thus deepening or augmenting the interpenetrative capacities of later experiences and reports on them. But because any attempt to describe *an* experience moves the individual and shared meanings around in various, often unpredictable ways, the "non-hierarchical density of experience" of Fluxus is structurally ill suited to strict interpretation, which would privilege discrete elements of the experience as worthy of analysis (rendering them hierarchical) and limit the possible domains of analysis (making the experience less dense).

In what follows, I have emphasized the informational structure of Fluxus experience itself, as opposed to offering a string of interpretations of individual works or clusters of works, which are ultimately bound to a given experiencer. This study is therefore concerned with the mechanics of particular Fluxus experiences rather than with their possible meanings.[5] Nevertheless, I hope that topical analyses of individual Fluxus experiences will be forthcoming as understanding of the movement evolves.

My qualifications in this undertaking include the significant fact that I am the daughter of Fluxus artists Dick Higgins and Alison Knowles. It was a privilege to grow up in their presence and that of their many wonderful friends.[6] With my twin sister, Jessica, I explored Fluxus objects that sat in our living room; attended Fluxus concerts and Happenings; and shared dinners, demonstrations, and avant-garde festivals with these people. In short, I experienced fine art and experimental music not in the way most of the world does, as specialized products unique to elite culture, made only by experts in esoterics, but as part of life. The process of writing this book has brought me closer to these early experiences than I thought possible (or desirable).

What began as a study of the complex relationship between Fluxus and the historic avant-garde changed, as I worked on this book, into development of a framework for how the objects and performances of Fluxus affirmed and formed my humanity, drew out my curiosity, and engaged me at all levels then and now: the original project's fraternal twin.[7] My own experiential knowledge of the movement no doubt plays a part in my conviction that Fluxus is experiential in nature. Still, I have checked myself at every turn. *Fluxus Experience* is rooted in the words and writings of Fluxus artists, as well as in the objects and performances themselves. The account that follows, therefore, is not merely subjective but takes its lead from a collective instinct and intuition. Insofar as all intellectual endeavor does precisely that, this particular project is unremarkable.

INTRODUCTION

Fluxus has survived for more than forty years in part because of its experimental and educational origins. Many of the thirty or so Fluxus artists met each other in the late 1950s in situations linked to experiments in musical education. The most important of these was a 1957–59 class in musical composition offered by experimental composer John Cage at the New School for Social Research in New York. The 1958–59 class included Fluxus artists and associates George Brecht, Al Hansen, Dick Higgins, Scott Hyde, Allan Kaprow, and Florence Tarlow, with frequent visits by the Fluxus poet Jackson Mac Low and occasional visits by other artists (Harvey Gross, George Segal, Jim Dine, Larry Poons, and LaMonte Young).

In an interview with the progressive theater journal *Tulane Drama Review* (TDR, later called the *Drama Review*), Cage described his approach to the class: "I wasn't concerned with a teaching situation that involved a body of material to be transmitted by me to them."[1] Instead the students conducted experiments using chance operations in a variety of formats, including music, performance, and poetry. These were presented to the class using available objects or existing instruments located in a small music closet attached to the room. Discussion of the philosophical and practical implications of each piece followed.

The most durable innovation to emerge from that classroom was George Brecht's Event score, a performance technique that has been used extensively by virtually every Fluxus artist with varying degrees of success. In the Event, everyday actions are framed as minimalistic performances or, occasionally, as imaginary and impossible experiments with everyday situations. An early handwritten example, *Keyhole Event* (1962), framed the goings-on on the other side of a door through a keyhole (Fig. 1). Another Event involved arranging one vessel to capture the drips of another (Fig. 2). Events like these were typeset and published as Fluxus editions beginning in 1963. The first was called *Water Yam* (Fig. 3). Indeed, it might be argued that subsequent Fluxus multiples, which typically contain printed cards, take their lead from the early Event cards and the everyday artifacts associated with this deceptively simple performance structure (Figs. 4 and 5).

Cage's class was central to Fluxus work. The poet Jackson Mac Low read his chance-generated poems there and subsequently wrote and performed Fluxus poetry. Some of his concrete poems, called *Gathas* (Fig. 6), can be read in any direction. Similarly, Al Hansen produced for the class the process experiments that culminated in his Happenings and now famous Hershey bar collages (Fig. 7). The term *Happening* was itself invented in the context of the class in 1958 by Allan Kaprow, who used it to describe his experimental, multimedia form of theater.[2]

After the class officially ended, artists who would later be identified with Fluxus (as well as Happenings, pop art, experimental film and theater, and dance) continued their experiments informally. Significant for Fluxus, in 1959–60 Hansen and Higgins founded the New York Audiovisual Group, and Mac Low and Young began *Beatitude East* as an extension of a West Coast experimental musical notation magazine, *Beatitude West.* The idea was to make experimental notations more widely available. This appeared as *An Anthology* in 1961. That same year two performance series, one at Yoko Ono's loft in lower Manhattan and the other at George Maciunas's AG Gallery on Madison Avenue, expanded on and developed an audience for the

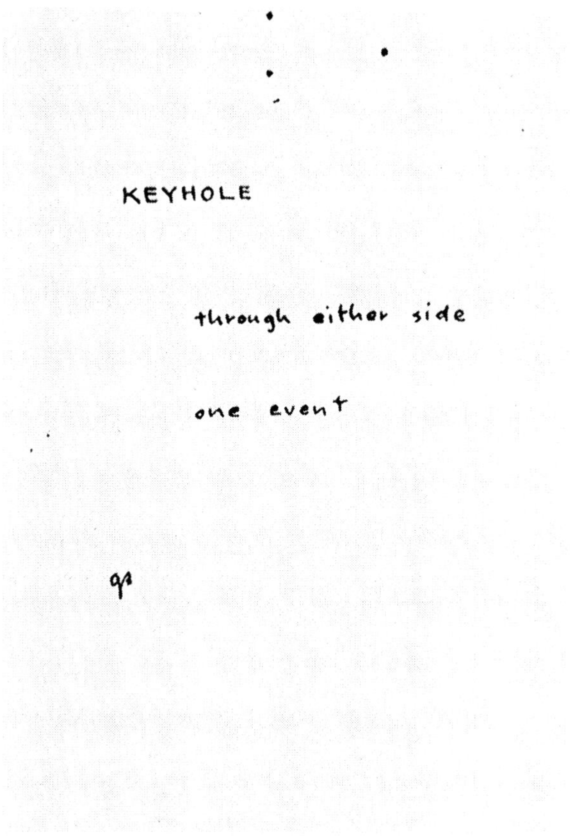

KEYHOLE

through either side

one event

1 George Brecht, Keyhole Event, 1962. Handwritten Event card, $4\frac{1}{4} \times 5\frac{1}{2}$ in. Courtesy of the Gilbert and Lila Silverman Fluxus Collection, Detroit.

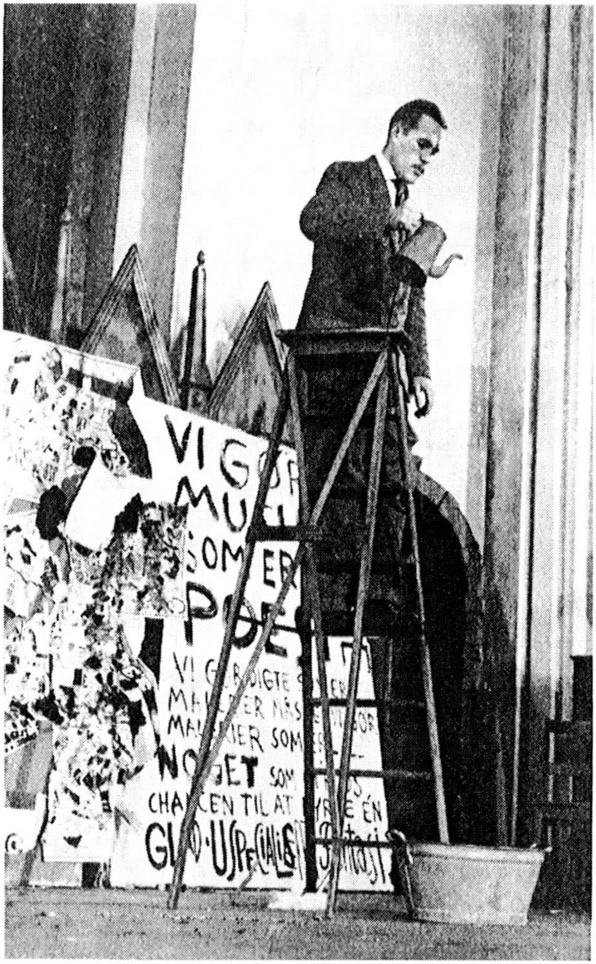

2 George Brecht, *Drip Music*, 1962. Performed by Dick Higgins at the Fluxus Festival, Nikolai Church, Copenhagen. Photo by Sisse Jarner; courtesy of Eric Andersen.

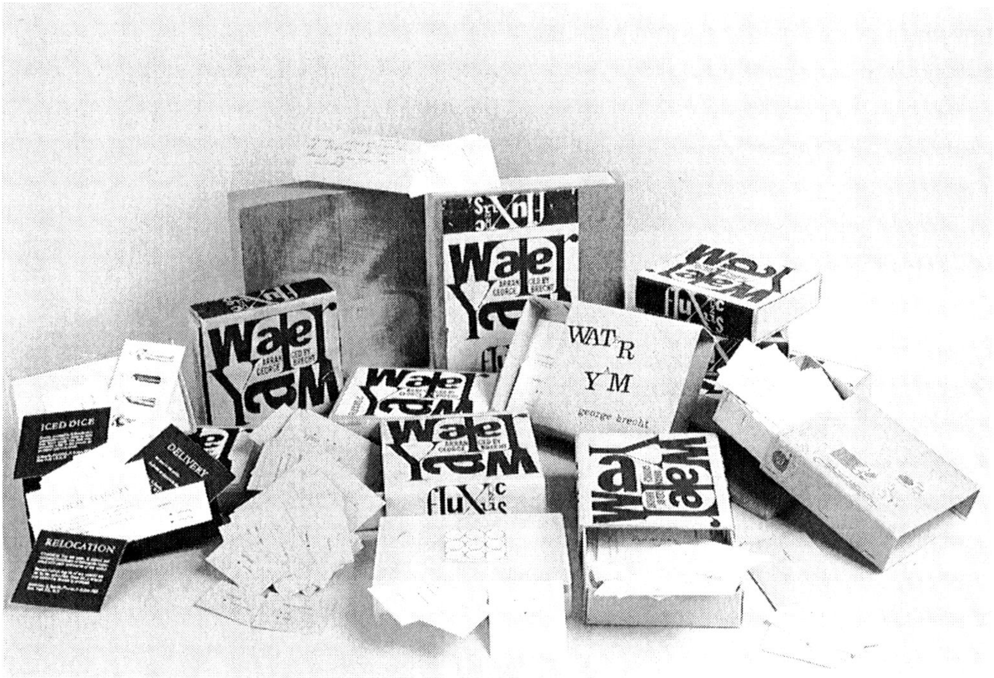

3 George Brecht, *Water Yam*, boxed Event cards, 1963–ca. 1970; designed by George Maciunas. The two examples middle and right with unique typography show collage covers by Brecht. Sizes vary; individual cards offset on paper. Photograph by Brad Iverson; courtesy of the Gilbert and Lila Silverman Fluxus Collection, Detroit.

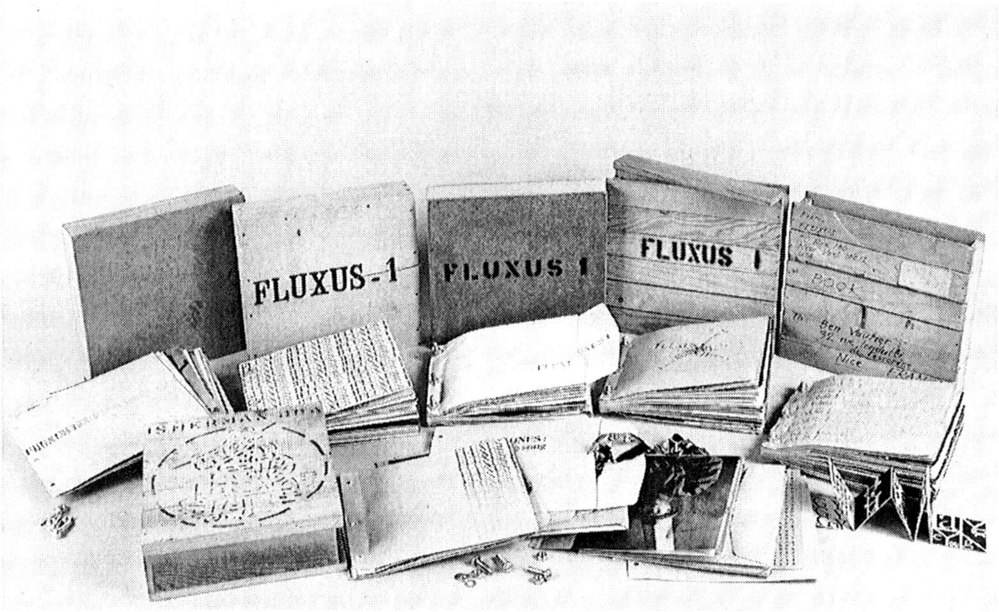

4 Various artists, *Fluxus 1,* 1964–1976; designed and edited by George Maciunas. Wooden boxes with mixed media inside bolt-bound envelopes. Sizes vary. Photo by Brad Iverson; courtesy of the Gilbert and Lila Silverman Fluxus Collection, Detroit.

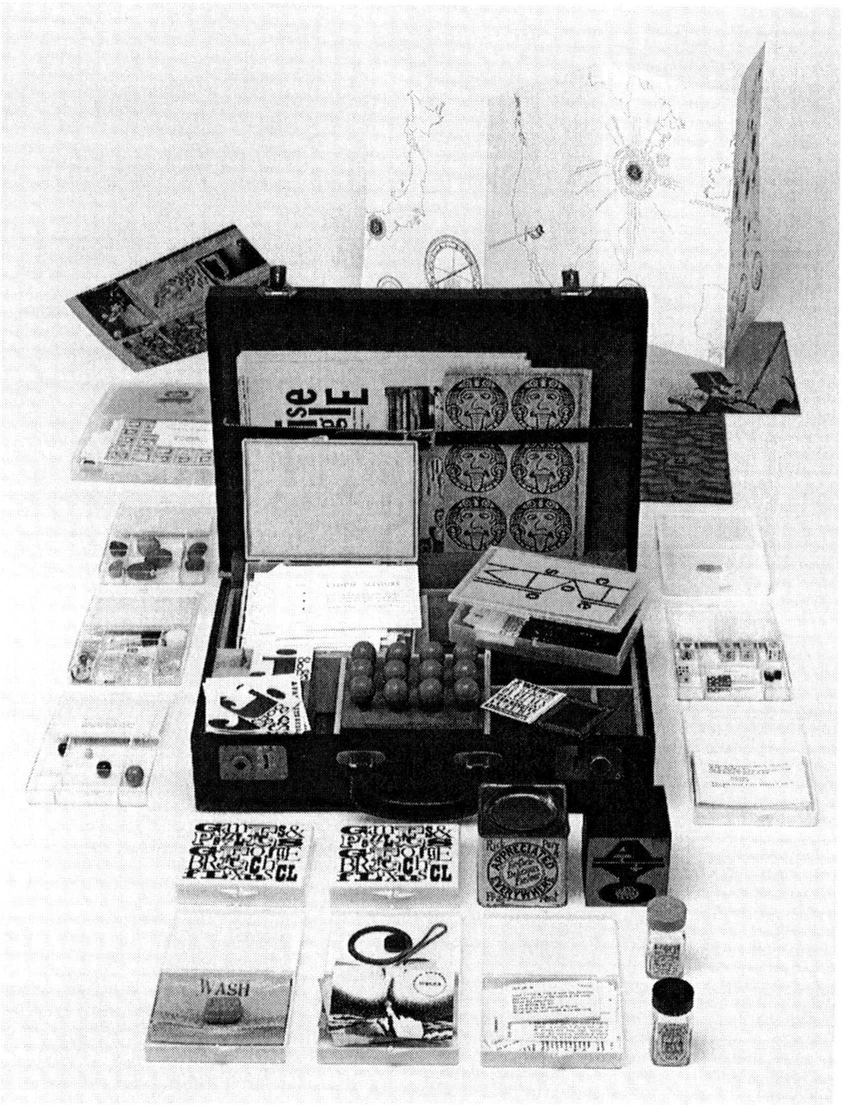

5 Various artists, *Fluxkits*, ca. 1964; designed and assembled by George Maciunas. Vinyl case with mixed media, 12 × 17½ × 5 in. overall. Other kit sizes vary. Photo by the Walker Art Center, Minneapolis; courtesy of the Gilbert and Lila Silverman Fluxus Collection, Detroit.

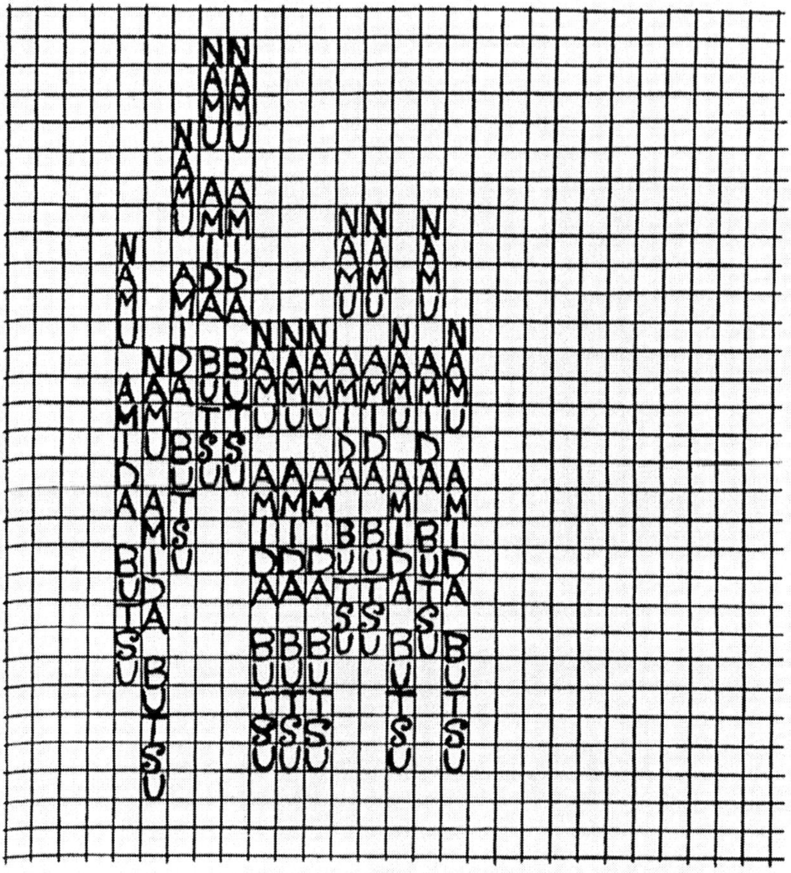

6 Jackson Mac Low, *2nd Gatha*, 1961. © Jackson Mac Low 2000. Published in the *Anthology of Concrete Poetry*, ed. Emmett Williams and Jackson Mac Low (New York: Something Else Press, 1967). Courtesy of the Estate of Dick Higgins and the poet.

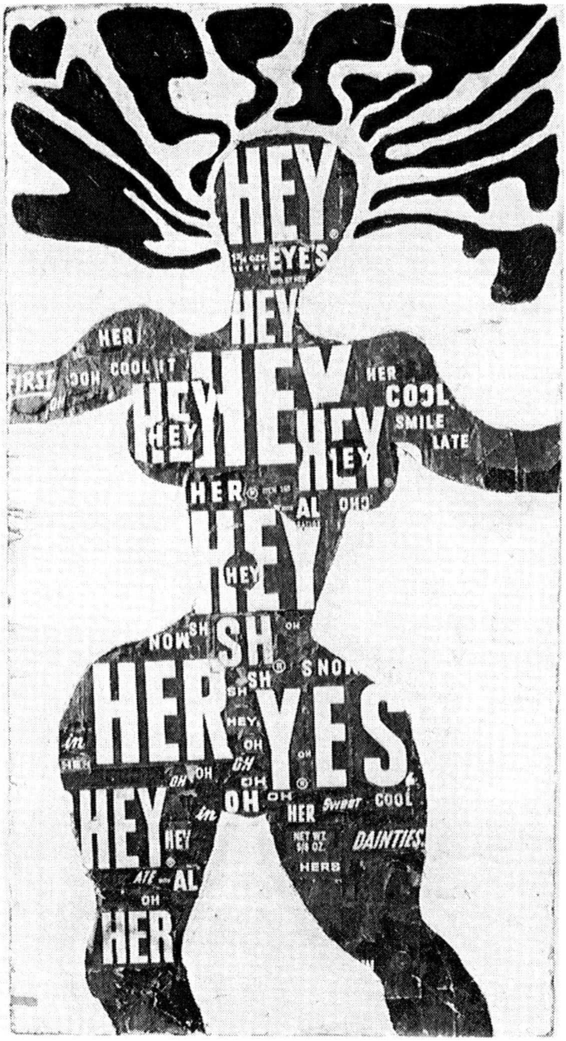

7 Al Hansen, *Miss Stuff,* 1967. Hershey wrapper Venus with paint, 16¼ × 8¾ in. Courtesy of Gracie Mansion Gallery and Bibbe Hansen.

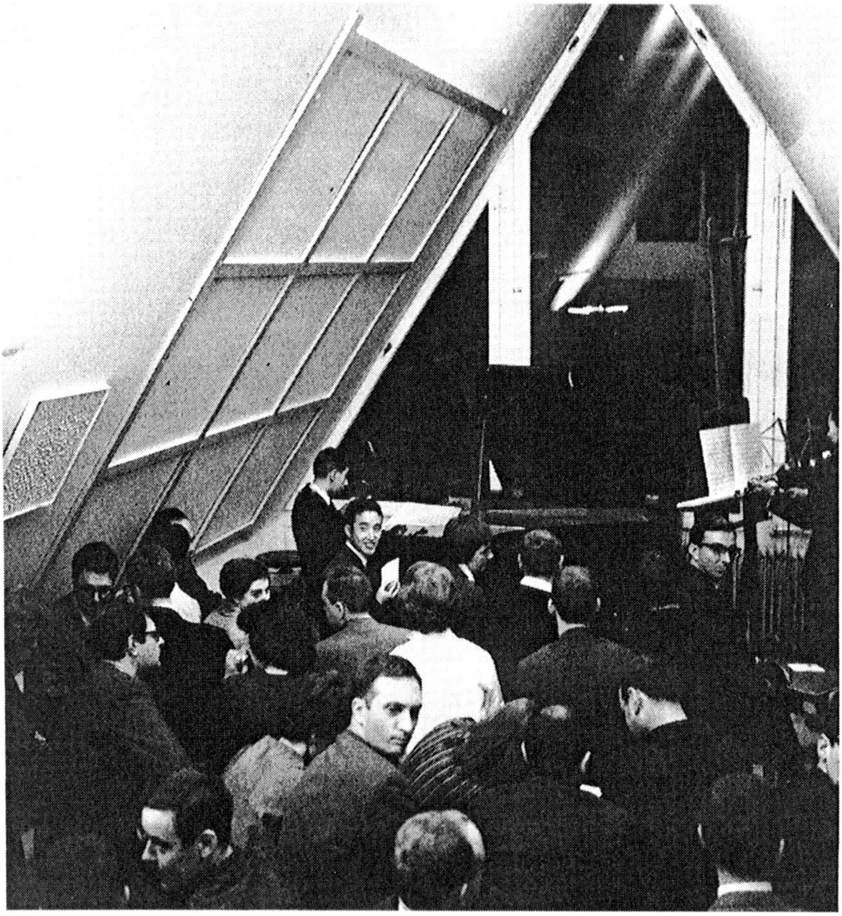

8 Mary Bauermeister Atelier, 1961. Facing the camera is Nam June Paik. Photo by Peter Fürst; courtesy of the photographer.

experimental formats associated with Brecht's Events and the Cage class generally. Clearly, the open-ended classroom experience had created an experimental (as opposed to programmatic) foundation for Fluxus and other avant-garde art of the time.

Fluxus in Europe had similar beginnings. Since the early 1950s the German serialist composer Karlheinz Stockhausen had been at the center of vanguard music in Germany. His Ferienkurs in Darmstadt, attended by Fluxus artists LaMonte Young (1958) and Nam June Paik of Korea (1957–58), shared an orbit with the experimental Darmstadt Circle of poetry and theater that in the late 1950s included Fluxus artist Emmett Williams. From 1958 to 1963 Stockhausen also worked (with Paik) in the electronic music studio of West German Radio (WDR) in Cologne, as well as in the influential performance atelier of his wife, the painter Mary Bauermeister, also in Cologne.[3] An international array of artists later associated with Fluxus circulated through this remarkable atelier, including Paik, Williams, the German Wolf Vostell, and the American Benjamin Patterson. In 1960–61, Events written for John Cage's composition class at the New School were presented at Bauermeister's atelier (Fig. 8). They were then performed at the Contre Festival, a music festival held in June 1961 in Cologne to protest the conservative International Society for New Music (IGNM). The four-day Contre series included works by Cage, Brecht, and LaMonte Young, as well as works by Paik and Patterson from Darmstadt and Cologne. Because of these concerts, the Bauermeister atelier has been called a "Proto-Fluxus in Cologne."[4] The experimental Cage, Stockhausen, and Bauermeister milieu was one of shared ideas and work across national boundaries.

Both Cage's class and the Cologne atelier can be described as comparatively nonhierarchical exchanges of information across national, disciplinary, and age boundaries, since the class and atelier were basically free exchanges among many kinds of artists. It comes as no surprise that the Fluxus movement evolving from these situations was also international, interdisciplinary, and generationally broad (with artists of three generations from the United States, every Western and Eastern European country, and Korea and Japan working in sound, text, performance, and new media).

With few exceptions, however, two formats have played important roles at all locations and in all subgroups of Fluxus artists: the Event performance and the Fluxkit multiple. Invented by Fluxus, these constitute the common denominator of Fluxus practice, although Fluxus artists have also explored other formats, such as music and graphic and painted work.[5] As Brecht's *Keyhole Event* illustrates, the Event performance typically consists of simple, everyday actions such as viewing a chance occurrence through a keyhole or polishing a violin. Fluxkit multiples generally consist of everyday objects or cheaply printed cards assembled in a box for the often private explorations of a viewer, as in *Fluxus 1* (see Fig. 4).

The minimal and prosaic basis of both the Fluxkit and the Event may initially seem puzzling. Why were such utterly simple gestures considered important enough to depart the classroom at the New School as a performance art form with a given name: Event? Why did Cage, arguably the most important American composer of the past fifty years, consider these Events interesting enough to perform later at the Bauermeister atelier? What is the relationship between the Event and the Fluxkit? These experiments must have mattered to some degree for the artists and audiences who saw them, but how? And why? I will argue that the answer lies in the immediate quality of the experience offered by both.

The first chapter of this book, "Information and Experience," analyzes how vision works in Fluxus generally, and establishes an experiential basis for Fluxus through Events and kits. In addition, it explores how Fluxus reverberates with the predominantly visual model of traditional art history, which assumes the controlled gaze of single-point perspective. In the traditional visual model, the viewer is idealized as a disembodied, single eye that is presented with an illusion. In contrast, experiential models of vision and perception, such as those proposed by James Gibson in *The Ecological Approach to Visual Perception* (1979) and David Michael Levin in *The Body's Recollection of Being* (1985), argue for an ecological, or experientially integrated, understanding of human vision and sensation. Operating within this mode, Fluxus works create a diverse experiential framework, one characterized by the dissolution of boundaries dear to Western epistemology, including the traditional distinction between subject and object on which much of Western philosophy was historically based. The result is Smith's "nonhierarchical density of experience."

The second chapter, "Charting Fluxus: Picturing History," relates Fluxus experience to the social formation of Fluxus as a group of artists persistently, but not programmatically, committed to the production of experimental work. Here, I describe the social cohesion of Fluxus as based on shared experience—and decidedly not unified by a specific interpretation of that experience, or by a coherent political or aesthetic program. To demonstrate the elasticity of this social formation, I look at two disputes that addressed the problem of linking the artistic practice of Fluxus artists to a single political or aesthetic program. The first occurred around a 1963 concert of Karlheinz Stockhausen, the second around a 1964 newsletter with programmatic intentions. Both provide sociological justifications for defining Fluxus practice as either ideologically narrow, politically broad, or apolitical. Out of each situation emerged a cluster of participants who defined Fluxus in terms consistent with or opposing these events and then drafted charts and written testimonials of their viewpoints on Fluxus.

The third and fourth chapters, "Experience in Context: Fluxus, Happenings, Conceptual and Pop Art" and "Great Expectations: A Reception Typology," explore some problems posed by Fluxus experiences in the context of related art movements, curatorial strategies, and editorial practices. These chapters ask, What do Fluxus experiences mean *as art?* In "Experience in Context," the omission of Fluxus from discussions of related movements is shown to speak volumes about both those movements and, equally important, the perspectives of their proponents. For to introduce experience as art considerably muddies our understanding of these related movements, and of Fluxus as well. For example, whereas Happenings tended to be acclaimed as action oriented, exciting, and youthful, Fluxus Events and kits were criticized as boring at best, neo-dadaesque antipainting at worst. With few exceptions, therefore, the experiential dimensions of Fluxus creations have been seen as mere negative dialectic (against painting) instead of as their own category of experientially affirmative art.

Of particular importance for this argument is the relationship between Happenings and American Action Painting, with Happenings receiving accolades, and Fluxus receiving criticism, expressly because of the positive terms applied to Action Painting. Where there is Fluxus, however, things are not so simple. Many Fluxus artists have deep debts to Action Painting—which was formulated as free gesture in the specialized framework of art criticism—as well as to the greater context of Happenings. What's more, Happenings artists like Jean Jacques Lebel, Allan Kaprow, and Carolee Schneemann (in particular) occasionally shared the program with Fluxus artists. This suggests a useful reversal of the divisive mode of art-historical categories, where movements are painstakingly pried apart. The proximity of these artists' groups to each other produced useful cross-fertilizations of ideas for both. As I will show, parallels can be made between the historiography of Fluxus and that of conceptual and pop art. "Experience in Context" thus moves Fluxus experiences out of the narrow situation of friends working with primary information and toward a greater context of art. Beginning with the Event and Fluxkit as defining elements in the generation of a Fluxus experience, this chapter initiates what promises to be a long-term project of reconciling those experiences to an art world whose sophisticated critical apparatus, largely unable to accommodate the extralinguistic aspects of experience, ignored Fluxus. It is the systematic basis of this rejection and the subsequent misunderstandings of Fluxus that constitute the subject matter of Chapter 4, "Great Expectations."

Chapter 5, "Teaching and Learning as Art Forms: Toward a Fluxus-Inspired Pedagogy," stands in the place of a conclusion but without offering any tidy summation. It addresses the question, Why should we care about Fluxus experience outside the world of art? And conversely, Why does it matter that Fluxus has been left out of art histories? Maybe it is just bad art and has been ignored the past forty years for good reason. But obviously I do not think so. Rather, the absence of Fluxus from recent art history, I believe, is grounded in a nearly culture-wide predilection for processed, secondary forms of information and so-called objective analysis and mediation, which has alienated people from one another and resulted in theoretical specialization and hyperliteracy, meaning an overdetermination of verbal elements in the arts. "Teaching and Learning as Art Forms" takes its lead from the French Fluxus artist Robert Filliou, whose *Teaching and Learning as Performing Arts,* inspired by Fluxus and related performance and poetic movements of the 1960s, argues for an experientially charged rethinking of higher education.[6] He contends, as I will too, that an experiential, and therefore unspecialized, pedagogy is central to human survival, to creating a sense of kinship across both disciplines and life experiences.

Fluxus Experience explores Fluxus first through a phenomenology of the Fluxkit and Event, then in progressively wider circles that move from this experience to the society of Fluxus artists, the creative milieu of related movements, and finally the lessons learned from Fluxus experience that can be applied to pedagogy generally.

INFORMATION AND EXPERIENCE

1

Fluxus Vision (Blink)

During a brief encounter with Fluxus in the mid-1960s, John Cavanaugh produced a film called *Flicker*.[1] Included in the 1966 program of Fluxfilms assembled by George Maciunas, *Flicker* consists of alternating frames of black and clear celluloid that, when projected, assault the eye with a battery of flickers in extremely bright white and pure black (Fig. 9). After a few seconds of this flickering, the eye becomes fatigued. Vision fades into a temporary blindness characterized by slowly moving, pulsating, colorless blobs that hover over the continuous flash of film, a response due to the inability of the optic nerve to register the flickering frames.

In *Flux Year Box 2* from 1968, a handheld projector was included with the films for manual operation (Fig. 10). With it the viewer, blinking while watching the film at variable speeds, slows the pace of the flickering frames, just as rapid blinking slows the pace of the flickering spokes

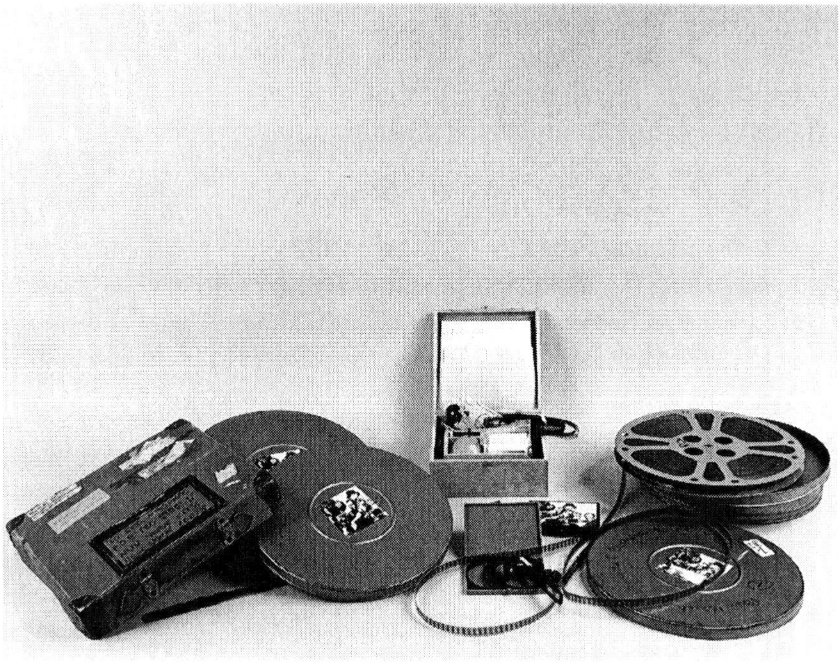

9 Various artists, *Fluxfilms*, 1966–67; assembled by George Maciunas. Photo by Brad Iverson; courtesy of the Gilbert and Lila Silverman Fluxus Collection, Detroit.

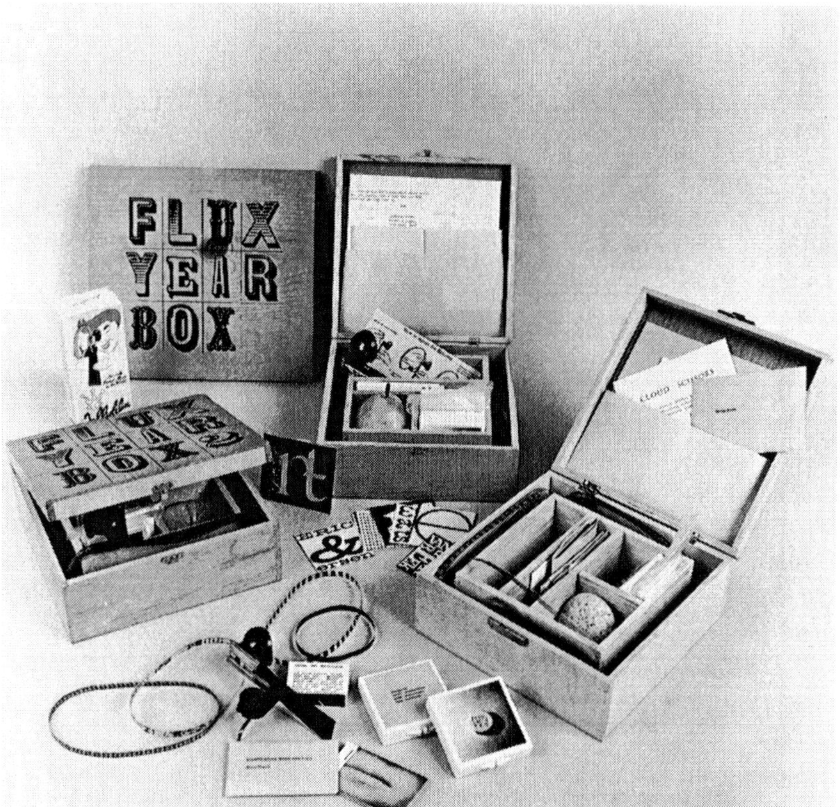

10 Various artists, *Flux Year Box 2,* 1968; assembled and designed by George Maciunas. Wooden box with mixed media, 8 × 8 × 3⅜ in.; includes handheld projector. Photo by Brad Iverson; courtesy of the Gilbert and Lila Silverman Fluxus Collection, Detroit.

of a spinning bicycle wheel. Blinking lessens the fatigue of the optic nerve, which may recover sufficiently to take in some part of the flicker again—that is, until the muscles around the eye grow fatigued as well, rendering the rapid, rhythmic blink physically impossible. In the end, the eye is simply too tired to continue its futile effort to race the mechanical projector, or to coordinate with the uneven rhythm of the handheld one.

Staring or blinking or manipulating the film's projection exposes the physical limits of the viewer's eyes. The viewer experiences the limitations of both the visible (what is seen in the world) and the optical (how humans see these things). There is neither a tangible object that corresponds to the colorless blob that hovers over the flicker, nor an objective framework that determines the precise form the blob takes. In this manner *Flicker* creates an optical experience that lies beyond the realm of the visible, where *visible* refers to an objective world of things "out there" that can be perceived or observed by the eye "in here."

An optical experience beyond the realm of the visible may seem self-contradictory. How can something that is not objectively there be seen? The answer, it seems to me, lies in rethinking the proposition that if something is not visible, it does not exist or cannot be seen.

The possibility of seeing the invisible calls into question the common phrases "Seeing is believing" and "I'll know it when I see it." The simultaneously optical and invisible experience of *Flicker* shifts one from the sense of sight toward something else, such as "Feeling is believing" or "I'll know it when I experience it." Clearly, something that is not visible *can* be seen, as it is in *Flicker,* even though what is seen is not a physical object. Rather, it is an image produced by optical fatigue—though there are other causes of invisible visions (such as ghosts, dreams, hallucinations of all kinds, images caused by eye malfunctions, mirages, magic, and games of illusion). Experientially, then, *Flicker* initiates a visual impression—the colorless blob registered by the optic nerve—that is radically distinct from what is shown, namely, alternating frames of black and clear celluloid. Viewers ultimately witness the boundary of their visual capacity—their limits as seeing persons—in response to an "outside" stimulus. Put differently, the experience is neither subjective nor objective. The stimulus (film) is not what is seen (the blob), nor is it independent of what is seen. Rather, what is seen combines a world "out there" and a self "in here."

Because it occurs in this interstitial location between objective and subjective, *Flicker* works against the belief that experience is mediated by clearly delineated senders (objects) and receivers (subjects) of information, a duality that lies at the core of the Western philosophical tradition. With few exceptions, in this tradition ideas are located exclusively in the mind. They are therefore distinct from an objective world or, conversely, illustrate the unknowability or lack of existence of that objective world.[2] In contrast, experience of *Flicker* is based within an indivisible object/subject matrix or field. In other words, the most striking effect of *Flicker* is that experience of it is simultaneously self-reflexive—the viewer witnesses the fatigue of his or her own optic nerve—and externally triggered: the eye constitutes the organic boundary of a person watching a movie shown on an external screen. Experience of the film cannot readily be dissected to locate elements exclusively in one or the other domain; it occurs equally within both. Experience of *Flicker* is therefore consistent with John Dewey's conception of aesthetic experience as that which "signifies complete interpenetration of self and the world of objects and events."[3]

Put differently, *Flicker* illustrates the mutual nature of, or correlation between, so-called sense data and stimulus or matter. J. L. Austin describes this correlation: "One of the most important points to grasp is that these two terms, 'sense data' and 'material things,' live by taking in each other's washing—what is spurious is not one term of the pair, but the antithesis itself."[4] Fluxfilms offer rich evidence in Austin's favor.

At the other extreme in pace from *Flicker* is Yoko Ono's film *Eyeblink* (1966), included in the same Fluxfilm program, which consists of a blinking eye filmed at two thousand frames per second on a high-speed camera by the Fluxus photographer Peter Moore. Shown at a regular speed, the film presents an extremely slow motion image of a blink. The slow and partial pulse of muscles in the fatty tissue of the lower lid, the pull of each muscle to move the lid, the tears flowing over and around the eye during the blink, and the partial dilation of the pupil during a fraction of a second only gradually become apparent. The viewer's own blinking action punctuates the pace of the model's (Ono's) blink shown in the film. Significantly, a quick reflex movement—the blink of an eye—has been extended almost unendurably in close proximity and sharp focus.

Since during a blink the eye is never fully open, most of *Eyeblink* shows the eye while it is not seeing—at least while it is not seeing visible things. Rather, the image on the screen shows a prolonged space or interstice between normative visual experiences. From the perspective of the film's viewer, the red curtain of the subject's eyelid closes and opens on the seeing eye of the viewer, who might in turn imagine the fractal patterns seen during the interim by the model. Like *Flicker,* then, *Eyeblink* invokes an invisible visual experience, this time not by way of extreme optical fatigue, but instead through the protracted representation of a space between normative visual experiences. The experiential breadth and limits of the apparatus of perception itself are (once again) the explicit subject matter of the work.

In both films, vision has been placed firmly within the body. The embodiment occurs in *Flicker* through the effect of fatigue on the viewer's optic nerve and eye muscles and in *Eyeblink* through the protracted representation of an interstice of vision. Through this embodiment of nonobjective (yet visible) elements, *Flicker* and *Eyeblink* offer alternatives to the continuous, objective field of vision, or scopic unity, associated with commercial film.[5] They do so by replacing the illusion of a unified field of representation (the perspectivally coherent film space) with primary experience.[6] In contemporary art historical jargon, by forcing the eye to the limits of its visual capacity (*Flicker*) and by accessing the break in visibility characterized by a blink (*Eyeblink*), these films undermine the authority of the disembodied gaze.[7]

The destruction of the disembodied gaze is likewise the subject of Daniel Spoerri and François Dufrêne's *Optique Moderne,* a book displaying altered spectacles. One page shows pins attached to the lenses of a pair of glasses and pointing at the eyes (Fig. 11). One imagines the composed young man (Spoerri) contorting in pain and darkness when the pins pierce his retina. If we understand the pins as single points, this deceptively simple piece seems to reference the destruction of vision as it is subjected (through the trickery of illusion) to the vanishing point of perspective and (through the physiology of glasses) to the focal point of lenses. The problem with such a strict interpretation is that it explains the work only negatively vis-à-vis the lens of the eye. The work thus becomes merely anti-illusionistic and antiretinal—which it is, but only in part. There is another way of looking at it, a positive one: perhaps the artist sees the points coming and, with deliberation and composure, embraces the broader experience of blindness to follow.

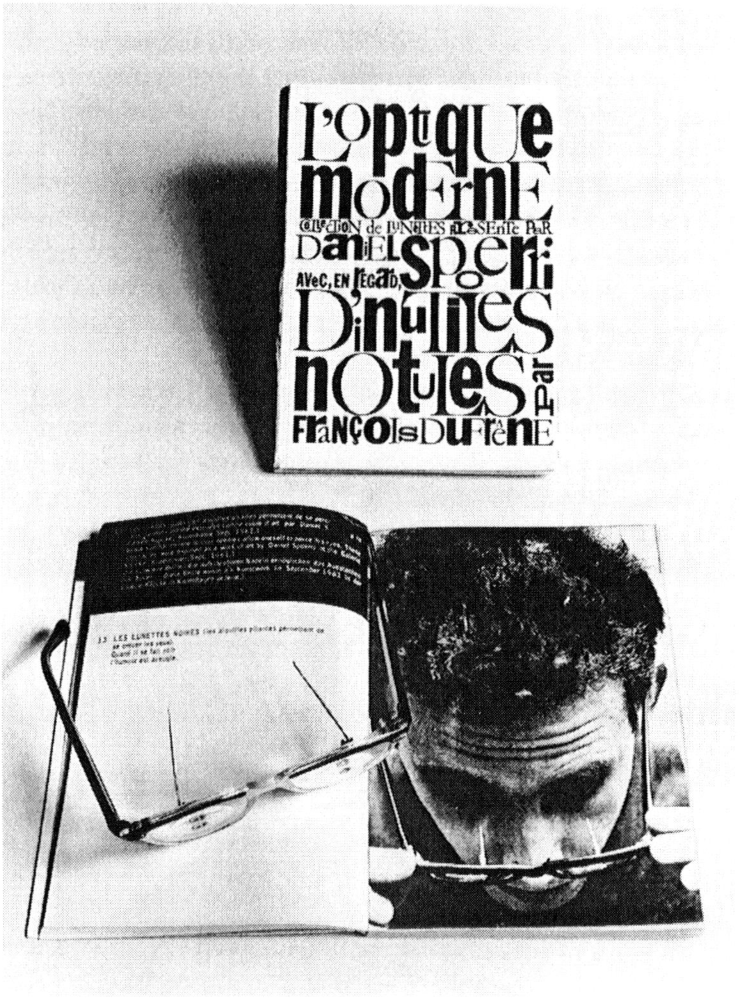

11 Daniel Spoerri and François Dufrêne, *Optique Moderne,* 1963. Photo by Brad Iverson; courtesy of the Gilbert and Lila Silverman Fluxus Collection, Detroit.

Other spectacles were included in *L'Optique Moderne,* among them found prescription and reading glasses with bent earpieces that enabled each to be held at any distance from the eyes.[8] These altered the viewing distance within the normally fixed geometry of the lens/focal length and eye ratios, effectively allowing for increased control of multiple visual experiences by the user. Held at distance *x,* one sees *y,* and at another distance, *z.*

As a whole, then, these glasses do not destroy vision. Rather, they enable new visions of the world by replacing normative vision with various alternatives that are controlled by the viewer. In this manner Spoerri and Dufrêne's *Optique Moderne* provides models for experientially embodied vision similar to those found in *Flicker,* with its exploitation of muscular and optic nerve fatigue, and *Eyeblink,* with its reliance on interstitial visual experience.

In contrast to this experiential modeling of vision, Renaissance perspective, with its disembodied gaze, was, according to the philosophical historian Paul Virilio, "the nodule in which the modeling of vision would develop and, with it, all possible standardization of ways of seeing."[9] This viewpoint makes it very difficult to introduce another visual mode in a post-Renaissance context, for it will inevitably be seen in opposition to perspectivally organized vision. Virilio further suggests that stylistic opposition to the controlling gaze of perspective threatens to destroy all visual connection to the object of scrutiny (i.e., the world): there is no body (social or individual) left viewing when the controlling lens is exposed as a limited means for understanding visual experience. By freeing vision of its definitive and militaristic component, the abandonment of perspective renders order untenable. Without the grid/screen, chaos reigns. "In the West, the death of God and the death of art are indissociable; *the zero degree of representation* merely fulfilled the prophecy voiced a thousand years earlier by Nicephorus, Patriarch of Constantinople, during the quarrel with the iconoclasts: 'If we remove the image, not only Christ but the whole universe disappears.' "[10]

Robert Romanyshyn, in *Technology as Symptom and Dream,* describes vision in terms phenomenologically similar to Virilio's ("When the world is viewed through a window, the world is well on the way to becoming an object of vision") but adds that "a profound difference remains between this objective body of knowledge created in distance from oneself, and one's living body, between the body which one has and the body which one is."[11] In other words, the screen or "devices for seeing" that for Virilio objectify the world in all veristic art by "dispensing" with the body are only one part of visual experience. There are other logics of cohesion. We must not forget the "body which one is."

Both approaches to vision have implications for understanding *L'Optique Moderne, Flicker,* and *Eyeblink.* The Renaissance model expounded by theorists like Virilio finds mere chaos and disintegration beyond the field of scopic unity or spatial illusionism posited by perspectival art and photography. The only alternative to scopic unity is experiential disunity. The embodied vision expounded by Romanyshyn, in contrast, allows for the indomitable "body that is," that lives and takes manifold forms. From Virilio's perspective, the two Fluxfilms and the Spoerri-Dufrêne object would merely resonate negatively with the scopic unity of film and illusionistic images, while from Romanyshyn's perspective the films and the object would affirm the broader physiological basis of vision. By giving the fatigue of the optic nerve or eyelid a physiological framework (*Flicker*) and by representing the eyelid as it blinks (*Eyeblink*), the Fluxfilms locate the eye within the human body, with all its motility and sentience. Together, the three Fluxworks offer an alternative to scopic unity, at the same time rejecting the notion of experiential chaos.

To argue for an embodied eye deep in the core of the viewer seems merely to move the vanishing point into the viewer proper, since it means that the visual logic of the work is oriented to the viewer's world. For the iconoclast, in nonperspectival work the vanishing point of perspective in effect turns in on the viewer, such that the viewer disappears. If we understood the body as a mere extension of passive vision, something simply tacked on behind the eye, this argument might be persuasive. However, the embodied model of vision is dynamic. The experience occurs only if the viewer puts something into it: far from vanishing, the viewer asserts his or her existence in front of the vanishing point.

The effort to make this happen can be described as the performative element of all Fluxus work: the audience has to do something to complete the work. Blink hard. Stare hard. Pick up the glasses. Fluxus artists have consistently described their work, particularly the objects they produce, as performative. The artist and performance scholar Kristine Stiles notes that "Fluxus originated in the context of performance and the nature of its being—the ontology of Fluxus—is performative." She continues in terms that bear directly on this discussion: "The body, in addition to its role as subject, is itself presented as an object. Together, subject and object create a changing and interrelated perceptual field for the investigation between actions, language, objects and sounds."[12]

This "changing and interrelated perceptual field" of performativity is succinctly illustrated in another Fluxus work that invokes the blink. *The Scissors Brothers' Warehouse Sale* graphic, also called *Blink*, was produced in 1963 by George Brecht, Alison Knowles, and Robert Watts (Fig. 12).[13] In addition to being made into a print on canvas, the *Blink* image was printed on bathing suits, pillowcases, matchbooks, and shirts—meaning it could be slept on, worn, and struck. As something used in everyday life, *Blink* suggests that to blink is to inhabit one's body.

The silk-screened image, divided into three horizontal bands, is roughly square and has a brilliant yellow ground. It is thus both fragmented (the bands) and unified (the field of yellow). The top band depicts a wedding ceremony taking place in a thatched room: on the right, a man and woman face the viewer, and on the left, a man stands with his back to the viewer. The bodies of all three are covered with square spirals and vegetal patterns. The bottom band graphically represents three pairs of scissors equally spaced and pointed menacingly upward. Squeezed in a narrower horizontal band between these two registers, in primary red, is the word BLINK.

Because the spaced-out red capital letters appear in the middle register of the image, centered on its width, they word they spell creates an effect something like that of a traffic sign. Instead of commanding me to stop, however, the canvas orders me to blink. I become aware of the act of shutting my eyes: they open on a scissors (blink), then on the woman's face (blink), then on a letter (blink), then on another scissors (blink). They open on another viewer (blink), then on a letter (blink), then on the man's back (blink), and then on another pair of scissors.

Blink plays with one's sense of the visible: like *L'Optique Moderne, Eyeblink,* and *Flicker,* it suggests that some component of the optical experience is predicated on discontinuity in the visual field. Furthermore, even if viewers do not blink themselves, the registers flicker like bands before their eyes, like film frames creeping slowly across the viewer's field of vision. Thus the three-part structure of the image, as the gaze moves across its surface, gives it a serial quality, somewhat like that of *Flicker* and *Eyeblink.* However, unlike the repetitive frames of *Flicker* (black and clear, black and clear) and the continuous image of *Eyeblink,* each band of *Blink* contains a very different image.

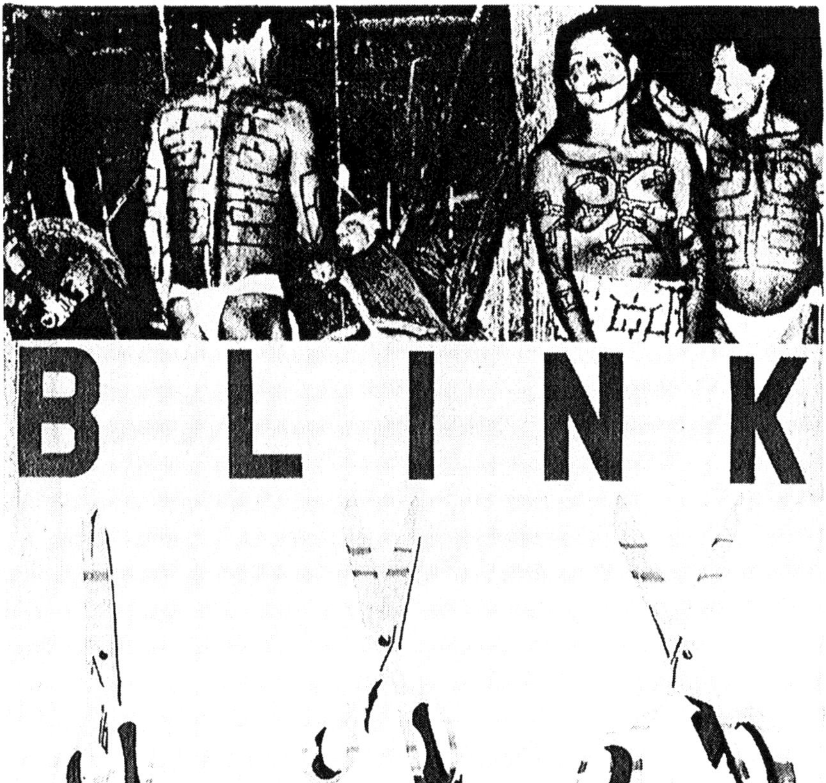

12 George Brecht, Alison Knowles, and Robert Watts, *The Scissors Brothers' Warehouse Sale* (*Blink*), 1963; produced by Alison Knowles. Silk-screen on canvas, 18 × 18 in. Photo by Brad Iverson; courtesy of the Gilbert and Lila Silverman Fluxus Collection, Detroit.

The scissors below the word BLINK invoke the sense of touch. Opening from left to right, it is as if they are moved by an invisible hand. They seem to be printed from the stuff they are made of, their bright silver ink like polished steel. Mundane objects, they nonetheless look interesting to handle, sturdy, useful, and cool to the touch. In these ways they contrast emphatically with their brilliant yellow background. They are not an implicit part of a larger context, a sewing table or factory, for example, that might make them seem real in the faked space of the canvas. Instead they simply hover over the indeterminate yellow field.

This is a haptic image, one that belongs to a "system of perception based on contact values," or touch.[14] Haptic images tend to occur in shallow space and suggest touch by emphasizing the surface textures or outlines of things. Trompe l'oeil images are haptic in this sense.[15] The urge to touch makes an encounter troubling, especially in museums. In the case of *Blink,* the surrogate reality of the represented scissors flickers with an odd sense that they are printed with the stuff from which real scissors are made.[16] By inviting viewers to look closely, to touch, and to imagine the object as actually presented instead of represented, *Blink* offers a multisensory experience.[17]

As a group, *Eyeblink, Flicker, Optique Moderne,* and *Blink* combine visual and visceral elements. This happens phenomenologically in *Flicker,* iconically in *Eyeblink,* through the use of visualizing instruments in *Optique Moderne,* and by way of a haptic presentational framework and verbal content in *Blink.* These Fluxus works expose the distinctions between the optical and the visual by locating vision in a physiological middle ground, by exploring the visual elements in the interstices of normative visual experience, and by explicitly directing the viewer to blink.

The realism of the scissors in *Blink* deflects attention from a negation of standard vision and toward a tactile, empirical, and therefore rich subjective experience (in this it is like *Optique Moderne*). Svetlana Alpers, in her study on seventeenth-century Dutch painting, *The Art of Describing,* depicts the opposition between the empirical quality of the northern tradition and the narrative, spatially contained approach of the Italian Renaissance tradition:

> Attention to many small things versus a few large ones; light reflected off objects versus objects modeled by light and shadow; the surface of objects, their

> colors and textures, dealt with rather than their placement in a single, legible space; an unframed image versus one that is clearly framed; one with no clearly situated viewer compared to one with such a viewer. The distinction follows from a hierarchical model of distinguishing between phenomena commonly referred to as primary and secondary; objects and space versus the surfaces, forms versus the textures of the world.[18]

The discursive framework of Alpers's account helps to explain how vision operates in *Flicker, Eyeblink,* and *Blink*—not merely in the denial of scopic control, but in the affirmation of human experience. The *Blink* graphic is "descriptive" in Alpers's sense in that it provides no clear place for the viewer, who hovers above the scissors but in front of the thatched space while scanning the word as if it were on a page. Instead of "many small things," the viewer is treated to a serial image of an insignificant thing—the pair of scissors that, printed in silver ink, literally reflects light from the viewer's space.

In its disparate sources, as if snatched from various locations; its lack of clear framing; and its emphasis on surface texture, as opposed to location in space, *Blink* seems a direct descendant of seventeenth-century Dutch still lifes and trompe l'oeil images, with their elements of photographic vision: the fragment, the arbitrary frame, and the sense of proximity or tactile immediacy. Equally important for my purposes, descriptive, empirical works offer access to "phenomena commonly referred to as primary," a reference to the sense of immediacy induced by direct physical contact with things. As *Blink* illustrates, in some Fluxus works representation invokes this direct contact with things. Alpers's logic of description, however, occurs even more directly in other Fluxus works that transport the tactile itself into art, effectively bridging vision and the sense of touch. This is true even when a work is only visual, as in the *Blink* graphic, or primarily so, as in George Maciunas's *Fluxpost (Smiles)* stamps (Fig. 13).

These stamps use a dialectical logic to stake part of their claim. In the popular imagination, smiles are pretty (these are not), smiles bespeak happiness and well-being (these do not), and smiles demonstrate wealth in the form of access to good dentistry (these do not). The Fluxsmiles could be construed as an inversion of advertising smiles and family photographs ("cheese"), illustrating poor dentistry in emerging cultures or the inequities of privatized dentistry; by extension,

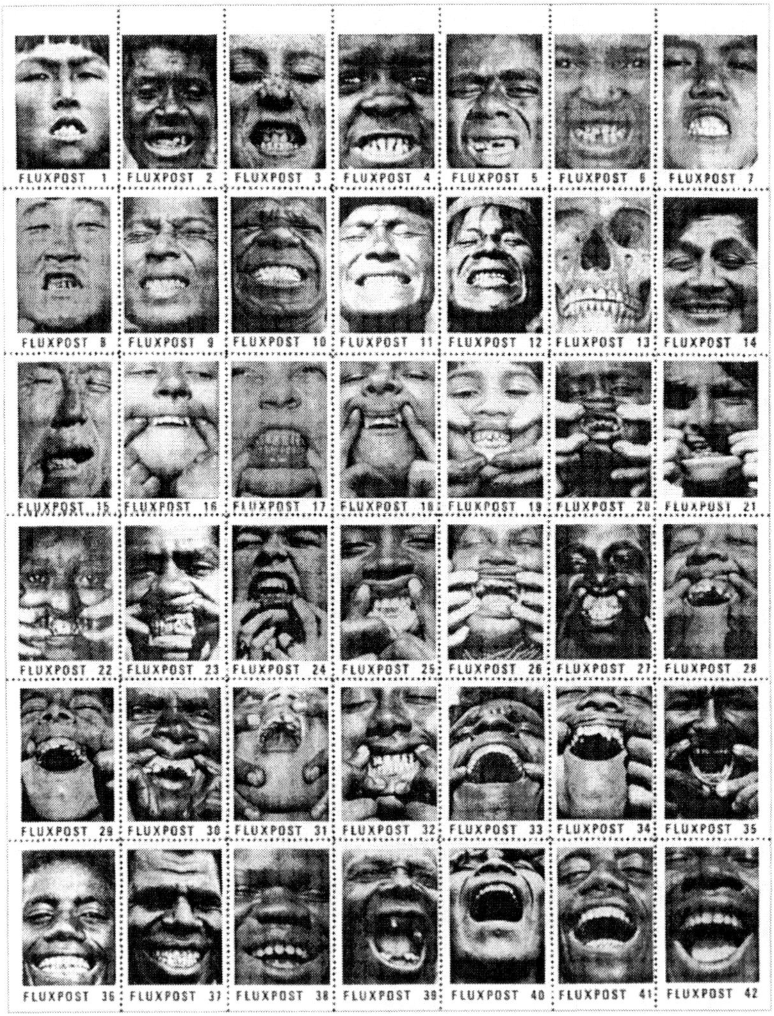

13 George Maciunas, *Fluxpost (Smiles)*, 1977–78. Perforated postage stamp paper, 10⅜ × 8¼ in. Courtesy of the Gilbert and Lila Silverman Fluxus Collection, Detroit.

it might seem that capitalism and its international counterpart, capitalist imperialism, are targeted. Such an interpretation follows a relatively linear path to its logical conclusion.

To understand *Fluxpost (Smiles)* exclusively by such secondary meanings, however, is to miss much of its power, since in this interpretation the experiential element is left out. The chain of signifiers that the image evokes—Western models of beauty, medical access, and health—misses what David Howes calls "the interplay of the senses" in the work.[19] The taste in my mouth as I look at the page of *Fluxpost (Smiles)* is momentarily strange. My teeth feel too smooth, like hardware, as I scan the decayed mouths and teeth depicted on the stamps. The point is not so much that the linear interpretation of the work as cultural criticism is incorrect, as that it misses the experiential dimension of the work.

Fluxpost (Smiles) in fact is linked to the mouth-altering *Flux Smile Machine* of 1970–72 (Fig. 14), an implement of mechanical torture that undoes the normally pleasant association of smiles with physical pleasure or mental happiness.[20] The *Flux Smile Machine* pinches the soft flesh of the inner cheek, gouges the gums, binds the lips, flattens the tongue; it scrapes against the enamel of the users' teeth and sits awkwardly in the mouth, causing excessive salivation or drool. The mixture of blood and metal tastes terrible. Experientially, then, the *Flux Smile Machine* (and therefore *Fluxpost [Smiles]*) belongs as much to the private world of physical discomfort as to the more prosaic world of hardware stores and dentist chairs, not to mention that of high art.

In other words, even where Fluxus works are made to be seen, as in *Fluxpost (Smiles),* they are often also intended to be felt (or, as in the case of *Blink,* worn). This experiential dynamic, characterized by the interpenetration of human consciousness and the world of things, is not unique to the Fluxfilms or objects examined thus far. Far from it. Much of the most evocative work made by Fluxus artists bears this thrust. The art critic and Fluxus scholar Henry Martin links the experiential quality of Fluxus to the "unremitting research" into the relationship between sensing and knowing that "contribute[s] to a sense of integrity and fullness," a quality that is the basis of Fluxus.[21] Martin's phrasing resonates with the words of John Dewey, who described the mechanics of this integrated aesthetic sensibility: "In art as an experience, actuality and possibility or ideality, the new and the old, objective material and personal response, the individual and the universal, surface and depth,

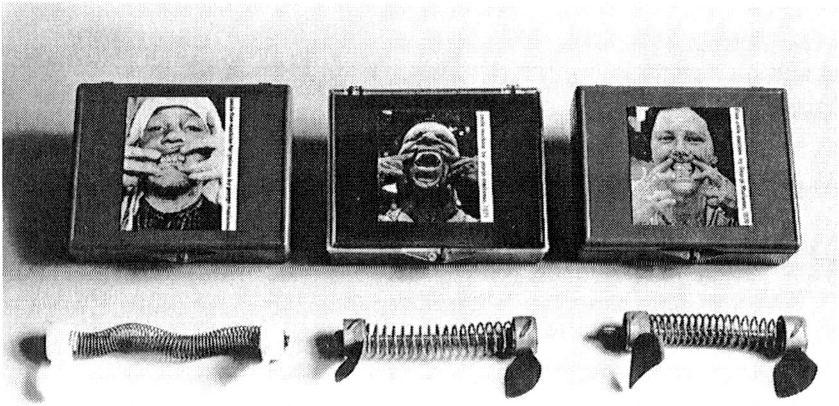

14 George Maciunas, *Flux Smile Machine*, 1970–72. Photo by Brad Iverson; courtesy of the Gilbert and Lila Silverman Fluxus Collection, Detroit.

sense and meaning, are *integrated in an experience* in which they are all transfigured from the significance that belongs to them when isolated in reflection."[22] Aesthetic experience, in short, occurs in an intermediate space between the apparent opposites outlined by Dewey.

To interpret *Fluxpost (Smiles)* only as a form of negative cultural criticism places undue emphasis on Dewey's polarities, and thus necessarily falls short of either integration or transfiguration, terms commonly associated with mysticism that are anathema to the dialectical method. Yet ironically, it is the integration of cultural dualities and personal transformation that characterizes *Fluxpost (Smiles)* and the metal object of the smile machine, whose physical effects resonate with the culture of smiling. Similarly, experience of *Flicker,* whose black and transparent frames are common to all film, but whose blobs are formally unique to each viewer, is at once a shared and transfigured experience. The same is true of *Blink,* which, in its form and seriality, partakes of an ideal or universal geometry, although the objects it comprises are prosaic and have personal associations.

To conceive of Fluxus vision in experiential terms does not mean that any- and everything creates an aesthetic experience. Rather, again in the words of Henry Martin, the experiential basis of Fluxus "can continue to be a motto and a principle no matter how radically [the] gap between art and life may [in theory] reduce and grow slim. . . . When the gap is slim enough, the observance of this principle can itself be seen to be a way of contributing to life's enhancement."[23]

Information and Experience in Fluxkits and Events

Edward S. Reed, in *The Necessity of Experience,* argues for experiential knowledge in terms that bear directly on this discussion:

> As this is written, billions of dollars are being spent to create continent-wide information superhighways along which will flow every conceivable kind of information except one. The information being left out of these developments is, unfortunately, the most important kind: the information—termed ecological—that all human beings acquire from their environment by *looking, listening, feeling, sniffing, and tasting*—the information, in other words, that allows us to

experience things for ourselves. . . . For understanding our place in the world, ecological information is thus primary, processed information secondary.[24]

Fluxfilms, like the *Blink* objects and the *Flux Smile Machine,* offer the ecological form of experiential knowledge that Reed says allows us to understand "our place in the world." In particular, the *Flux Smile Machine* uses three of the senses he lists: it is felt, seen, and tasted when in use. It is also a Fluxkit—one of the many small boxes of inexpensive materials assembled for personal use that Maciunas invented in 1962.

The first Fluxkit, *Fluxus 1* (see Fig. 4), was designed by Maciunas and contains objects, visual work, and essays by thirty-nine artists, not all of whom were Fluxus artists as defined by social integration or friendships with the group. The various items in *Fluxus 1* yield multisensory, primary information. These include a song, with words and melody (therefore involving sight, motility, and hearing); a napkin, meant to touch hand and mouth (therefore involving tactility and perhaps taste); a medical examination glove, with the look and smell of latex (therefore involving touch—both in and through the glove—sight, and smell); photo portraits, which appeal to the eye; performance and music scores, which involve all senses (and are thus synaesthetic); and visual and sound poems, meant to be read, heard, and performed (which therefore involve the eye, the ear, and the body of the performer).[25]

Some of the Fluxkits subsequently made by individual artists are full of boxes with finger holes and mysterious contents for touching, instructional performance cards, Event scores, balls, real food (beans), plastic food, blow horns, a chess set with pieces identifiable only by smell, and prophylactics, to name but a few.[26] *Orifice Flux Plugs* by the American Fluxus artist Larry Miller typifies the primary experience offered by the Fluxkit and theorized by Reed (Fig. 15). The scale of the individual plugs invites the user to hold and finger them: to unroll condoms; to consider soft, small plugs for insertion into the nose, ear, vagina, or anus; to examine statuettes that might enter any orifice of the user. Where would this fit? Could I really use this? How blunt is this tip? How sharp is this edge? Will the fuzz shed all over the inside of my nose or ear? It is difficult to reroll a condom. Who else hates the smell and feel of latex? Will I break out in a rash? What if this is used?

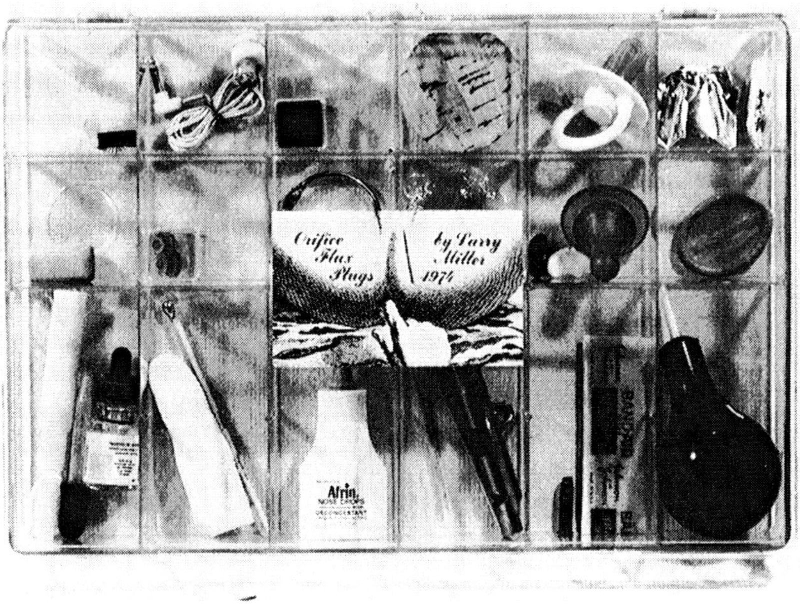

15 Larry Miller, *Orifice Flux Plugs*, 1974. 9 × 13 × 2¼ in. Photo by Buzz Silverman; courtesy of the Gilbert and Lila Silverman Fluxus Collection, Detroit.

The tactility of these orifice plugs suggests how the users of Fluxkits are linked to their physical environment through a sensory encounter with it. An analysis of the history of prophylactics would miss the point of the work, since "The fact that I can touch an object, hold it, push it, gives me a sense that there is really something there, that I am not the sport of a trick or an illusion."[27]

In the *Flux Smile Machine, Fluxus 1,* and *Orifice Flux Plugs* the stuff in the Fluxkit makes an experience for the handler that *is* the sensation contained in it; the Fluxkit is not *about* the sensation. The operative word *about,* like the word *of,* insists on the distance between object and user: "That is a painting about pain" or "of a pipe." In the Fluxkits, actual stuff is present—"That is a pom-pom"; it is not *about* a pom-pom unless a particular user proceeds down that path of association. Removing *of* and *about* represents two challenges to entrenched patterns of thought: first, if a piece is not *about* things but actually *is* them, then the signifying chain often applied to visual art in semiotic analyses needs to be modified to make physical or actual experiences central to the process of signification; second, and more important for my purposes, these works problematize the Western metaphysics since Plato and Aristotle, which insists on dividing primary experience (the feel or scent of the pom-pom) from secondary experience (mental concepts about it).

In the early twentieth century, William James and John Dewey effectively argued this connective philosophical tradition; Dewey produced a theory of democratic culture based on the importance of experience, a mode with profoundly ecological implications.[28] The tactile tools he used in his educational experiment at the Lab School in Chicago, often containers holding objects destined for a range of multisensory explorations, function strikingly like Fluxkits. In *Art as Experience* Dewey writes, "The senses are organs through which the live creature participates directly in the world about him."[29] The Lab School kit, like the Fluxkit, thus has the effect of stimulating the individual's sense of participation. It follows that both kits have a social dimension, which I will address momentarily.

Recently, Hilary Putnam and John McDowell have advocated for a reconstruction of philosophy that favors linking experience with secondary knowledge.[30] Put another way, embodied knowledge produces abstract knowledge, and not the other way around. Putnam's terms in particular have implications for understanding the Fluxkit (and the Event) as examples of cognitive powers reaching all the way to objects so that subjectivity is not merely a projection of external ideas, as in the notion of constructed identities: "The natural realist holds that successful perception is just a seeing, or hearing, or feeling, etc., of things out there; and not a mere affectation of a person's subjectivity by those things."[31] Whereas in the idealist and structuralist philosophical traditions "our cognitive powers cannot reach all the way to objects themselves," Putnam argues to the contrary that our direct sensation of things forms the basis for cognition itself.[32]

By criticizing the principle of an affective relationship that separates things "out there" from human subjectivity, Putnam's account erodes the apparent division between object and subject in perceptual experience. Significantly, since primary experience and perception occur across all senses (sight, sound, scent, taste, and touch), a wide variety of sensation is necessary to the "natural realist" encounter. In this sense, the Fluxkit produces sensate forms of knowledge. Texts and objects are unrolled and unfolded to be heard, seen, and read; plugs are examined. Similarly, in Events water is heard, seen, and felt dripping; the hand feels the wood of the violin through an old cloth, the polish smelling vaguely toxic; a scene is witnessed through a keyhole. As generators of primary experiences, Fluxkits and Events "allow us to experience things for ourselves," thereby generating a mechanism for our "understanding [of] our place in the world," in Reed's terms, and thinking "all the way to objects themselves," in Putnam's.

From person to person, these understandings, however similar, also differ in significant ways. Put differently, in offering a primary experience of matter as art, Fluxkits and Events have ramifications that both do and do not necessarily include the normative context called fine art. The multiple experiences of Fluxkits and Events suggest ways of understanding the contested relation many Fluxus artists have to the term *art* and its association with such features as name, date, style, psychology, context, and fixed meaning.

Insofar as the Fluxkit is multisensory, it exemplifies the modality of knowledge that the philosopher David Michael Levin has called "ontological thinking." For Levin, that term implies a directive to incorporate into one's sense of self a greater sense of being than is produced by the visual paradigm of truth that originates with the Italian Renaissance, or by scientific rationalism for that matter:

> "Overcoming" metaphysics means overcoming the metaphysical misunderstanding of the being of the human body. It means overcoming our deep-seated

> guilt and shame, flaming into a terrible *hatred* of the body. The history of mind/body dualism and the history of the subject/object dualism are two symptomatic manifestations of a violent, nihilistic rage at the very heart of our metaphysics. . . . Ontological thinking is radically different: it engages us in the opening wholeness of our being, and "takes place" as much in the life of our feet and hands and eyes as it does in our head, our brains, or our "mind."[33]

Ontological thought, then, encompasses multisensory experiences in ways that reinforce our connectedness to the world. This occurs through the specific sensations experienced in the body of the perceiver. Levin quotes from Maurice Merleau-Ponty's *Phenomenology of Perception:*

> To have senses, sight for example, is to possess that general setting, that framework of potential, visual-type relations with the help of which we are able to take up any visual grouping. To have a body is to possess a universal setting, a schema of all types of perceptual unfolding and of all those inter-sensory correspondences which lie beyond the segment of the world which we are actually perceiving.[34]

Our bodies, far from limiting us in our encounter with the world, simultaneously give us access to what our senses perceive and link us to the whole universe of human perceptions.

I believe that the ultimate goal of Fluxus lies precisely in this task: to form multiple pathways toward "ontological knowledge" and the expansion of the "setting of human experience." Levin describes this expansion as becoming "more fully human," which, far from being predicated on any notion of universal human knowledge, is richly determined by a belief in the unique significance of particular experiences.

Similarly, the primary experiences that Fluxkits generate, which make ontological knowledge possible in Levin's sense, also generate an unmediated truth, even though that truth, by definition, cannot be universal (in the Idealist sense). Other Fluxkits demonstrate the same pattern of leading to experientially based truth.

For example, the most tactile pieces in Fluxus are undoubtedly *Finger Boxes,* by the Japanese Fluxus artist Ay-O. First produced in 1964, these works have subsequently been sold singly and in Fluxkits (Fig. 16). The boxes contain various

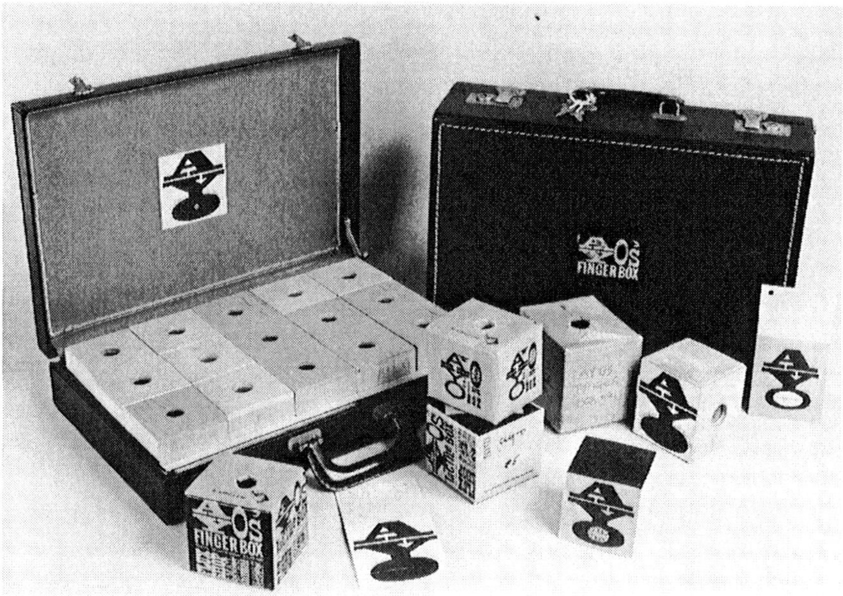

16 Ay-O, *Finger Box* (valise edition), 1964; designed by George Maciunas based on prototype (rear right) by the artist. Mixed media in wooden boxes in vinyl briefcase, 12½ × 17 × 3¾ in. Sizes of individual boxes (mixed media in cardboard) vary. Photo by Brad Iverson; courtesy of the Gilbert and Lila Silverman Fluxus Collection, Detroit.

tactile elements ranging from nails to sponges, beads to cotton balls, and bristle brushes to hair. (An envelope version of this idea, consisting of a slit envelope and—sometimes—a nylon inside, was included in *Fluxus 1.*) For all practical purposes the boxes look identical from the outside, which means that the experience of these works occurs only when the user probes within: the realm of touch is supreme as, handled, they prick, cushion, roll against, squeeze, and wrap around an inserted finger. Merely to look at them is to experience them only partially. George Brecht's *Valoche/A Flux Travel Aid* similarly consists of a box filled with things: twenty-six balls, toys such as badminton birdies, rubber bands, bowling pins (Fig. 17). The balls have different textures and weights. The birdie might be tossed in the air, rolled between the user's fingertips, or used to fire down a bowling pin. A rubber band could be snapped or used to bundle other things together. Ay-O's *Finger Boxes* and the items in Brecht's travel aid kit require careful handling and manual exploration. They give us tactile, cutaneous information, creating an interpenetrative experience.

Cutaneous information is gained by direct contact with materials. Apart from the lips and tongue, the index fingertip is the most sensitive cutaneous organ and is therefore particularly well suited to use with the *Finger Box.* When users plunge a finger into the box, their curiosity has overcome the sense of fear inherent in exploring the unknown. That several *Finger Boxes* contained nails indicates Ay-O's determination not to sidestep the challenge the work could issue: the danger to the instinctively apprehensive, hesitant user, who must touch the box, but carefully, with an "enquiring, learning gesture."[35]

By requiring users to handle them gently, the boxes set up the potential for nondestructive knowing. Heidegger distinguishes use from using up in terms that are useful here, and which in turn differentiate the information gained through the enquiring gesture from that gained through a "grasping" for truth: "When we handle a thing, for example, our hand must fit itself to the thing... use itself is the summons which determines that a thing be admitted to its own essence and nature, and that the use keep to it. To use something is to let it enter into its essential nature, to keep it safe in its essence."[36]

David Michael Levin also discusses this access to the essential characteristic of a thing—or for our purposes, the substance inside a *Finger Box*—in terms of a "careful touch, which is open to feeling what it touches and uses, gets in touch more

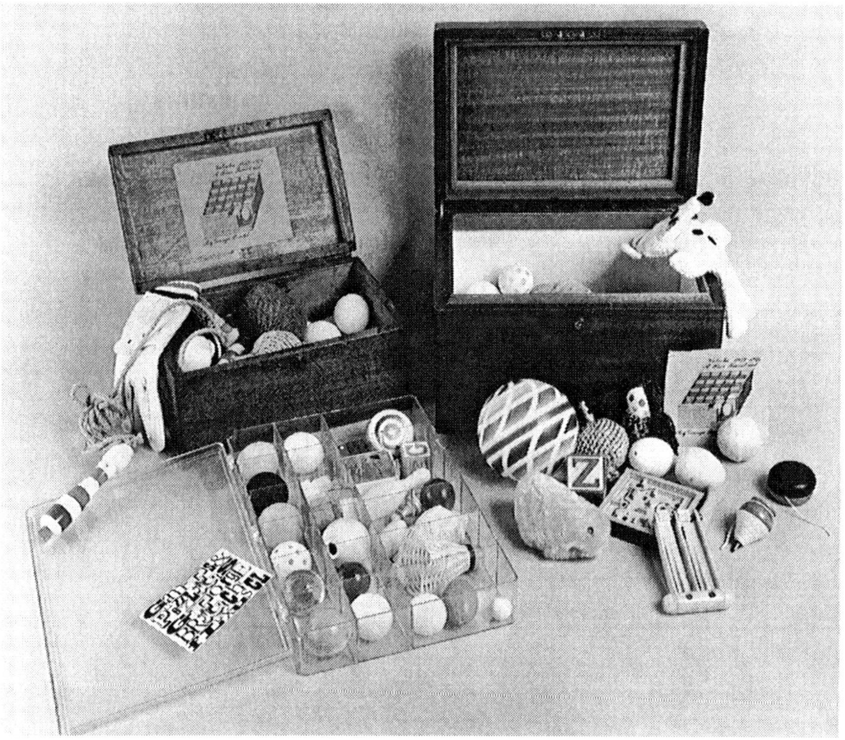

17 George Brecht, *Valoche/A Flux Travel Aid*, various examples, late 1960s–1975; designed by George Maciunas. Wooden and plastic boxes with mixed-media contents. Photo by Brad Iverson; courtesy of the Gilbert and Lila Silverman Fluxus Collection, Detroit.

deeply and closely than the hand which willfully grasps and clings." Not knowing what is inside a *Finger Box,* the user must be careful, willing to let the object yield information about itself, instead of "grasping and clinging" to get it. The information gained, however, is not meant to be enjoyed entirely in solitude. Solid little constructions, the *Finger Boxes* are intended for multiple users, so that the experience they offer is potentially social—as is appropriate to the tactile sense they employ. Touch is particularly intimate, not only because of its associations with the sensual, but also because, of all the senses, it can be the most directly social and socially motivated. What is touched touches back. "Touching," writes Levin, "presupposes our capacity to be correspondingly touched, and this primordial reciprocity calls into question our inveterate tendency to polarize the tactile field into a subject and object."[37] Cutaneous information thus works to eradicate the distinction between subject and object in Western metaphysics: "The skin serves both as receptor and transmitter of messages, some of which are culturally defined. Its acute sensitivity allows the development of such an elaborate system as Braille, but tactilism is more basic than such oddities imply and constitutes a fundamental communication form."[38]

Because they are premised on the shared experience of unseen materials, Fluxkits in general and the *Finger Boxes* in particular have a communicative dimension that is distinctly community-building, in Levin's sense. Fluxkits offer, not the perspectivally controlled and controlling visual model of veristic art, which the Fluxus films and images discussed above already complicated considerably, but sensory information for a radically empowered experience of art that connects the individual to a greater social or environmental context. It should come as no surprise that other Fluxus artists have invoked the senses—especially smell and taste—to similar ends.

Constance Classen, David Howes, and Anthony Synnott, exploring the social dimension of olfaction, link odor to ontological thought and social communion and division in their book *Aroma: The Cultural History of Smell.* Their account contrasts sight, which has direction, with odors, which are amorphous, and explains the ignominy of scent as historically determined by mainstream Western values.

> Odours cannot be readily contained, they escape and cross boundaries, blending different entities into olfactory wholes. Such a sensory model can be op-

posed to our modern, linear world view, with its emphasis on privacy, discrete divisions, and superficial interactions.

This is not to suggest that an olfactory-minded society would be an egalitarian utopia with all members harmoniously combining into a cultural perfume. As we shall see, olfactory codes can and often do serve to divide and oppress human beings, rather than unite them. The suggestion is rather that smell has been marginalized because it is felt to threaten the abstract and impersonal regime of modernity by virtue of its radical interiority, its boundary transgressing propensities and its emotional potency. Contemporary society demands that we distance ourselves from the emotions, that social structures and divisions be seen to be objective or rational and not emotional, and that personal boundaries be respected.[39]

The radical interiority, emotional potency, and physical amorphousness of scent render its relation to the social and philosophical systems of the modern Western world deeply ambiguous.

The *Smell Chess* works created by the Fluxus artist Takako Saito experiment with how scent functions both subjectively and more universally, in mainstream Western culture (Fig. 18).[40] By assigning specific scents (those of spices, in one work) to chess pieces, she demonstrates how "olfactory codes ... serve to divide and oppress human beings," with the "boundary transgressing propensities and ... emotional potency" of scent creating an ironic counterpoint to the highly choreographed, ritualized moves of the game of chess. Each player holds the scent-bottle pieces carefully, even intimately, sniffing them to determine their identity and then to move them accordingly. Saito's *Smell Chess* therefore links odors to the status and movement of individuals in society generally, and also proposes them as a sensory counterpoint to social boundaries and mobility.

In 1976 a room-size variation on *Smell Chess* was projected (though never realized) for a Fluxlabyrinth built in Berlin. Bodily associations abound in a letter the artist Larry Miller wrote to George Maciunas, his collaborator on the project: "Smell room needed: smells[.] Perhaps the entry door could be whoopee cushion or whoopie cushions somewhere on floor to make a fart sound. Then we could have sulphur smell." Besides the whoopee cushion and sulphur smell, which refer to flatulence, the unrealized smell room was to have included the smell of tar, hashish, and aerosols.[41] The visitor entering the room, assailed by a noisome body

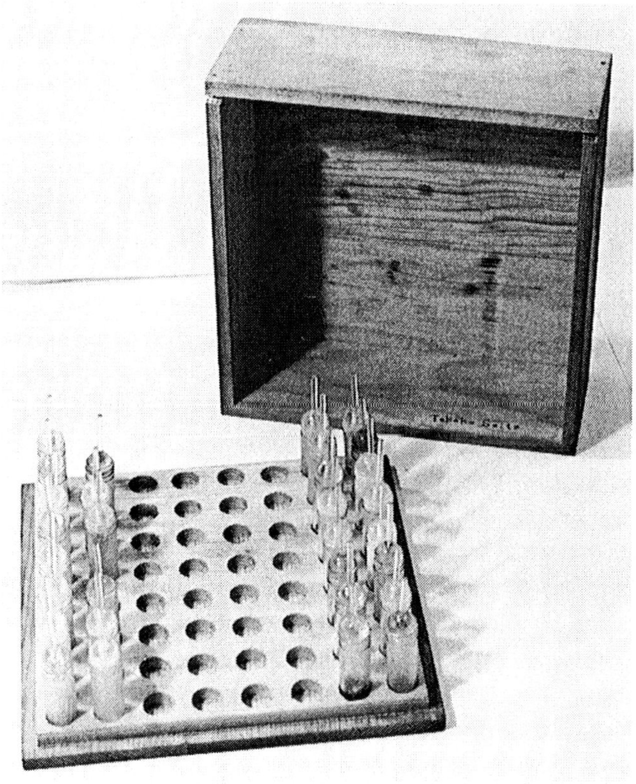

18 Takako Saito, *Smell Chess*, 1964–65. Wooden box with glass bottles, 8 × 8 × 3⅜ in. Photo by Lori Tucci; courtesy of the Gilbert and Lila Silverman Fluxus Collection, Detroit.

odor, might wonder momentarily if another visitor had produced it, and then realize that other smells—the sticky odor of hot tar, the pungent scent of hashish, or the sweet aromas of spices or flowers—were mingling with it. In each case the odors, alone or combined, would elicit very different responses from visitors, as well as varying emotional associations.

In neither *Smell Chess* nor the *Smell Room* is odor meant to be isolated from other sensations. Small, appealing bottles, which must be opened carefully, are then moved around by hand on a chessboard; a doorway is opened and a room circumnavigated. In both cases scent is linked to movement. The handheld pieces or the human body moves through space and time in reference to other pieces on the board or other visitors to the room. The works assert that scent, despite its radical interiority, is a profoundly social sense: odors in Fluxus constitute community phenomenologically by making the "radically interior" sense of smell a shared sense.

Odors, of course, have no clear, material identity, since, as Classen, Howes, and Synnott point out, they "cannot be readily contained, they escape and cross boundaries, blending different entities into olfactory wholes." They continue: "Olfactory signals are transmitted directly via the tiny hairlike cilia at the ends of the olfactory neurons into the limbic region of the brain, the core of emotions and memory."[42] Thus, the evocative effects of *Smell Chess* and *Smell Room* have a physiological basis. The radical interiority of smell enables scent-based work to reach the human brain directly, precisely illustrating that our cognitive powers do indeed reach all the way to objects themselves and that perception, as Putnam says, is "not a mere affectation of a person's subjectivity by those things."[43]

The fact that smell is experienced both communally and individually does not mean, however, that odor can be analyzed as a communications system, like language. For unlike words, smells offer a primary form of experience; they occur "in between the stimulus and the sign, the substance and the idea."[44] The emotional and memory-based associations of smell arise from direct contact with matter itself—and not from its representation or reproduction. "It is for this reason," note Classen, Howes, and Synnott, "that matter and meaning become, in a sense, 'miscible fluids' insofar as smells are concerned, which is an abomination from the perspective of the (always detached) semiotician. This establishes precisely the irrelevance (or whatever other) dichotomy the semiotician might seek to impose."[45] Since smell is not semiologically detached—there is no semiotic divide between the signifier and the signified—smell is ill suited at best to the mediated format of language, despite the vividness with which smell can be experienced and remembered.[46]

This may explain why several prominent epistemologists qualify the usefulness of smell as well as the related sense of taste in certain contexts. For example, in *Frames of Mind: The Theory of Multiple Intelligences,* Howard Gardner writes that although "acute use of sensory systems is [an] obvious candidate for a human intelligence . . . when it comes to keen gustatory or olfactory senses, these abilities have little special value across cultures."[47] And Rudolf Arnheim, arguing for the equation of sight with mind, asserts that "one can indulge in smells and tastes, but one can hardly think in them."[48]

Many Fluxus works, however little known to a wider public, function through taste and smell. Alison Knowles, for example, produced three food Events: *Make a Salad* (1962), *Make a Soup* (1962), and *The Identical Lunch* (1967–73). The olfactory and gustatory elements of such work, however, tend to be relegated to the margins. This is certainly true of the series of meals called Fluxbanquets (featuring, for example, an array of clear foods, or of rainbow foods), which are routinely described as attempts to revive the movement after the "heroic" period of the early 1960s. These banquets took place on Christmas Day 1967 and New Year's Day 1968 and 1969 and intermittently until Maciunas's death in 1978. (Since then, individual Fluxus artists have continued to work with food.) Food at these banquets ranged from distilled coffee, tea, and tomato and prune juices ("all clear like water but retaining the taste") at one meal,[49] to eggshells filled with cheese, brewed coffee, or noodles at another, two of rainbow foods at a third.[50] Maciunas also imagined a related series of monomeals, in which all foods would have the same basis, such as fish (candy, drink, ice cream, aspic, pastry, pudding, salad, and tea) or milk. Imagine a roomful of artists discussing eggs—how does a cheese egg thump, or a noodle egg spin?—or deciding the substance of a beverage or the sequence of dishes in an all-fish meal. At once highly subjective and broadly social, humorous and earnest, the monomeals were definitely about gustatory perception and knowledge. "Here, try this coffee egg, it's got a noggy flavor." "How's the fish jello?—I'll bet it's better with salt." "How about some black whipped cream with that noodle egg?"[51]

In "Matters of Taste in Weyéwa," Joel C. Kuipers describes how "taste substances are systematically ordered by a given culture, sometimes in ways that actually transmit messages."[52] Six basic descriptive terms—*sweet, savory, bitter, spicy, sour,* and *bland*—are transcultural, but the meaning of each in a given society and their combination in particular cuisines are not. Kuipers analyzes the situational, ritual, and morphological marking of taste, its patterns of evolution and sequencing, in the Weyéwa culture. Certainly in American culture, taste terminology and experience are marked as well, and this is precisely what the distilled beverages and fun-filled eggs of Maciunas's banquets play with. Sometimes expectations would be slyly reversed: looking identical, a cup of distilled coffee might start a meal, while a clear, savory tomato juice cocktail might end it. The notion of a sweet made out of fish—savory fish ice cream, for example—may sound repulsive, but merely for reasons of convention. In the case of an all-fish meal, the diner's expectations would be compressed into a narrower-margin "fish": fish aperitifs, fish food, fish beverages, fish desserts. Once the standard is established, even these bizarre food items would be worth trying, just for the experience.

Other examples of Fluxus gustatory work feature a certain randomness that similarly disrupts the traditional sequence of flavors in a meal. Beginning with the Fluxus Festival in Nice in 1963, Ben Vautier, in his *Flux Mystery Food,* purchased unlabeled cans of identical size in the grocery store and ate whatever was inside them—whether lychee nuts (as at the first performance) or salmon, canned sausages or sauerkraut; in 1966–67 he launched a variation on this theme, having Maciunas relabel each can as "Flux Mystery Food." In these Fluxus food works the food appears the same or very similar, thus relegating differentiation by sight to the periphery of the eating experience. Habitual flavor markers (such as sweet for ice cream or candy) are altered, or foods are left unidentified until ready to be consumed, to challenge culture-wide gustatory expectations and expand personal experience. Other Fluxus food work has emphasized the ritual of eating, associations between food and nonfood, and the obsessive measuring and counting of foods characteristic of a society preoccupied with personal hygiene and self-control.

Beginning in 1967, Alison Knowles began each day to eat the same lunch—a tuna fish sandwich on whole wheat toast with butter, no mayo, and a cup of buttermilk or the soup of the day—at the same time and location, Riss Foods Diner in Chelsea. With Philip Corner, this became an extended meditation, score, and journal.[53] Repeating the gesture made the meal a self-conscious reflection on an everyday activity. Friends and interested artists joined in. Receipts were kept, and slight differences in the meal noted. The *Identical Lunch* thus became a carefully documented experience of both the taste and habits of a particular diner. In 1971 Maciunas suggested an adaptation: put it "all into a blender."[54]

Other Fluxus food works aim to create associations between food and nonfood items. In 1969 Knowles cooked a mashed bean dish that Maciunas subsequently misidentified as "Shit Porridge" for the New Year's banquet. That same year he proposed a series of nonedible eggs filled with whites (paint, shaving cream, and so forth). More recently, in 1992 Ben Patterson grilled several dozen ducks under a Citroën 2CV automobile for the opening of "Fluxus Virus" in Cologne. All these works associate something edible with something inedible through resemblance. The Citroën, which is virtually unknown in the United States, actually resembles a duck, while "Shit Porridge," well...

A last category of food-based Fluxus work involves measuring and counting. Over the course of 1972–73, for example, Maciunas carefully collected all the food containers he used. Because his diet was famously monotonous, the collection included staggering quantities of similar containers such as those for frozen orange juice. Maciunas assembled all the containers as a wall object, calling it *One Year.*[55] Obsessive accumulation has a logical counterpart in obsessive division or measuring, which many other Fluxus works focus on as well.[56] Of particular note for this discussion is Eric Andersen's invitation to an audience in 1993 to eat a brick of cheese by dividing it in half repeatedly. He provided microscopes so that divisions could be precise.[57]

Although there are many other Fluxus food works, those I have described suggest a strong inclination on the part of Fluxus artists to work with food and taste. The problems of analyzing the works are significant, however. Few epistemologists have theorized on taste and smell, nor have art historians considered these elements in art. Fluxus food works are effectively marginalized, therefore, both because they fail to conform to a visual model of artistic practice and because few practical texts exist on which to base an analysis.

We can look for guidance, however, to two literary figures, Walter J. Ong and Marshall McLuhan, who theorized multisensory thinking in the 1960s. After seeing his magnum opus, *The Gutenberg Galaxy,* to publication in 1962, McLuhan collected his and others' attacks on literary modes of thought, which were seen as based too much in the head or mind, publishing the anthology *Verbi-Voco-Visual Explorations* with Fluxus's Something Else Press.[58] In his essay "The Shifting Sensorium," meanwhile, Ong, insisting "that man communicates with his whole body through all his senses,"[59] discussed how the "ratio or balance of the senses" varies from culture to culture. The implication for my argument is that the strong basis of smell and taste in Fluxus work stands apart from the standard hierarchy of senses in the West, where vision is followed by sound, then touch, and, at a distance, smell and taste. It does not follow, however, that these last two are capable of triggering only minor art forms. Elsewhere, they reign supreme (as in the Weyéwa mentioned above).

The meals, like the films and Fluxkits—whether they present users with art based on sound, touch, smell, or taste—frame art as experience in Putnam's natural realist sense. Much Fluxus work rejects the representational approach to art. Instead it is generally presentational or reality based. Even a Fluxus artist choosing a representational mode, as in the *Blink* image or Fluxfilms, uses it at cross-purposes to conventional representation, to undermine the tenets of Western illusionism and push representation itself toward the primary mode of experience discussed here.

Like Fluxus films, Fluxkits, and Fluxus meals, which yield primary information to the senses—taste, smell, and touch—the Fluxus Event also has a sensory basis. A typical Event like George Brecht's *Drip Music* (see Fig. 2) may occur by chance or by choice and in accordance with almost any circumstances, being neither site specific, performer specific, nor specific to a performance situation. Brecht's scores for various works, handwritten and mimeographed in about 1962, suggest similarly aleatory and nonspecific formats for Events (Fig. 19). A string quartet shakes hands; a vase of flowers is placed on a piano; a flute is assembled and disassembled. Each Event, in other words, comprises a wide range of possible experiences.

These can take a caring, exploratory form or a destructive one. (Many accounts of Fluxus are flawed in their overemphasis on the iconoclasm or destructiveness of the Events, which are then simply dismissed or heralded as mere anti-painting.)[60] Two Events are particularly useful for establishing the range of Fluxus in general from destructive to nondestructive, and of Events in particular: Brecht's

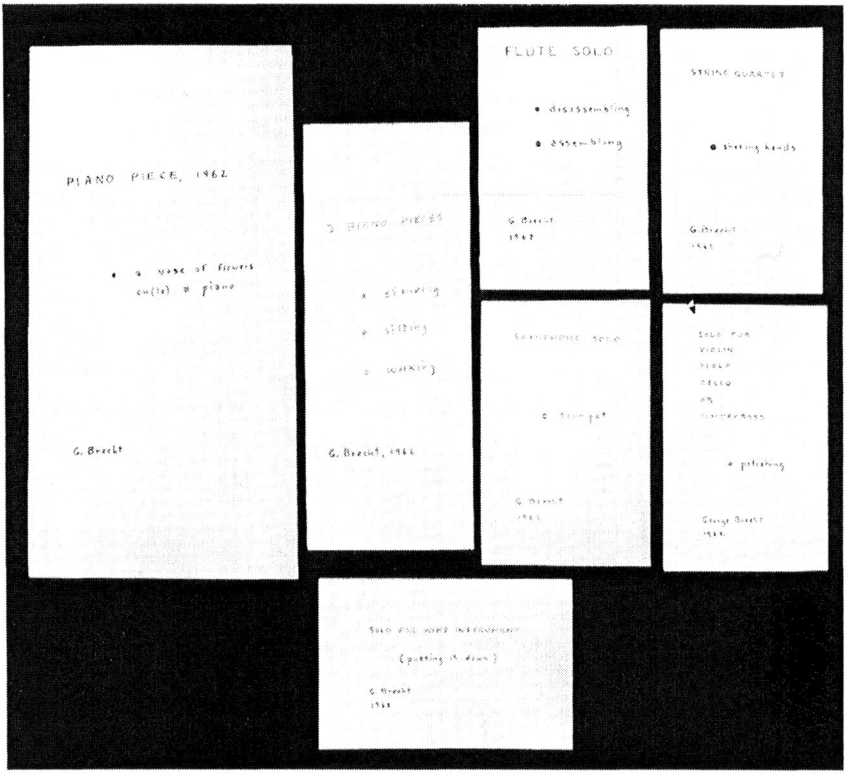

19 George Brecht, *Event Cards,* ca. 1960. Handwritten, then mimeographed; sizes vary. Courtesy of the Library, Getty Research Institute, Los Angeles.

Solo for Violin, Viola, Cello, or Contrabass (1962; Fig. 20) and Nam June Paik's *One for Violin* (1961; Fig. 21). The dichotomy is explicit. Brecht's score reads simply "polishing," whereas in Paik's piece, "the performer raises a violin overhead at a nearly imperceptible rate until it is released full-force downward, smashing it to pieces."[61] These Events might be performed in the same evening, thereby demonstrating both the caring and destructive aspects of Fluxus and offering a range of experiential options, from the protective to the nihilistic.

Another example. In Philip Corner's *Piano Activities,* performed in 1962 at the first Fluxus-titled festival in Wiesbaden, Germany, Dick Higgins, George Maciunas, Alison Knowles, and Emmett Williams engaged in the apparent destruction of an old, unplayable piano belonging to the Kunstverein. They did destroy the instrument, but not haphazardly. Figure 22 shows fine gestures: the careful rubbing of a brick over the strings, patient waiting for the right moment to use a hammer.

According to David Michael Levin, "The things we handle will always reciprocate the treatment they receive in our hands. Thus, when our gestures become very caring, they receive back from the things we have handled with care a much deeper disclosure of their ontological truth."[62] This concept of the reciprocal relationship between things and their handling is relevant. Levin postulates the possibility of radically multiplied experiences if we focus on simple gestures at least temporarily, thereby effectively divesting them of their secondary associations. Caring takes many forms: Levin's point is that meaning has a visceral basis. In the three Events I have described, the artists get to know their instruments on many levels, by polishing, smashing, or altering them. Subsequent meaning appends to the physical action.

But the visceral basis of meaning only partly explains the internal logic of the Event. As the scores discussed thus far imply, the Event originated, both practically and conceptually, in Cage's 1958–59 music composition class at the New School. The Event must therefore be understood as relating somehow to Cage's musical idiom, wherein time (rhythm in a broad sense) is the determining standard for musicality. Cage accepted whatever sounds occurred within a specific period of time. Those sounds determined the music—but not in the prosaic sense. Attentiveness and concentration (the listeners' intentionality) are required, or the sound is mere noise. Similarly, in Brecht's Events, the minimalist structure and

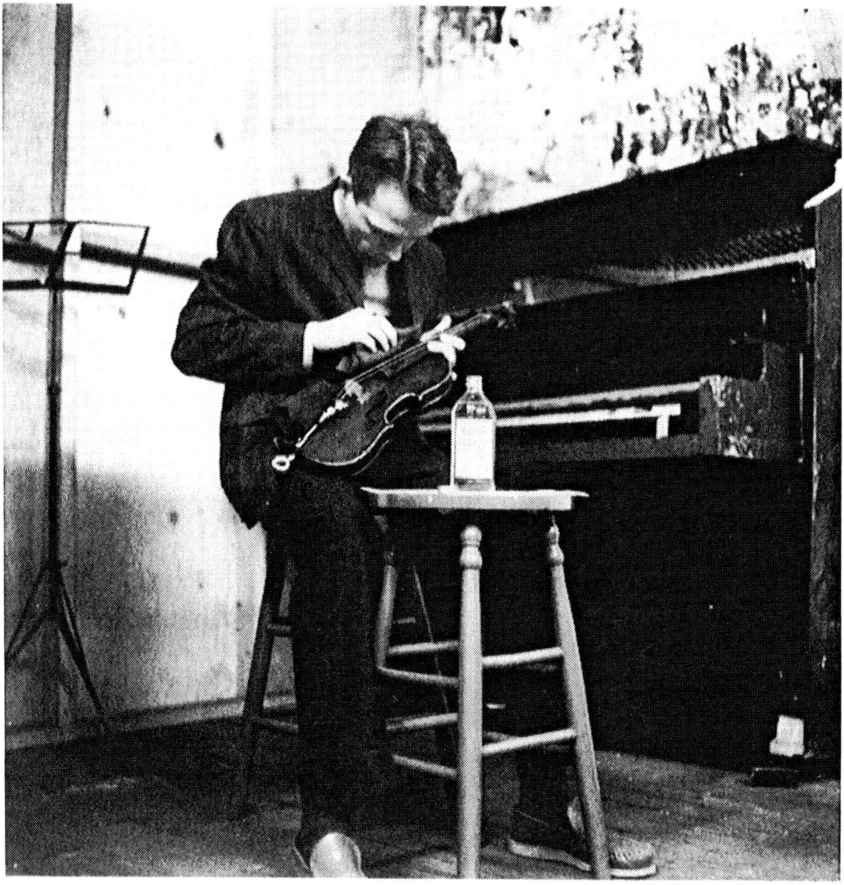

20 George Brecht, *Solo for Violin, Viola, Cello, or Contrabass,* 1962. Performed at the Fluxhall, New York City. Photo by George Maciunas; courtesy of the Gilbert and Lila Silverman Fluxus Collection, Detroit.

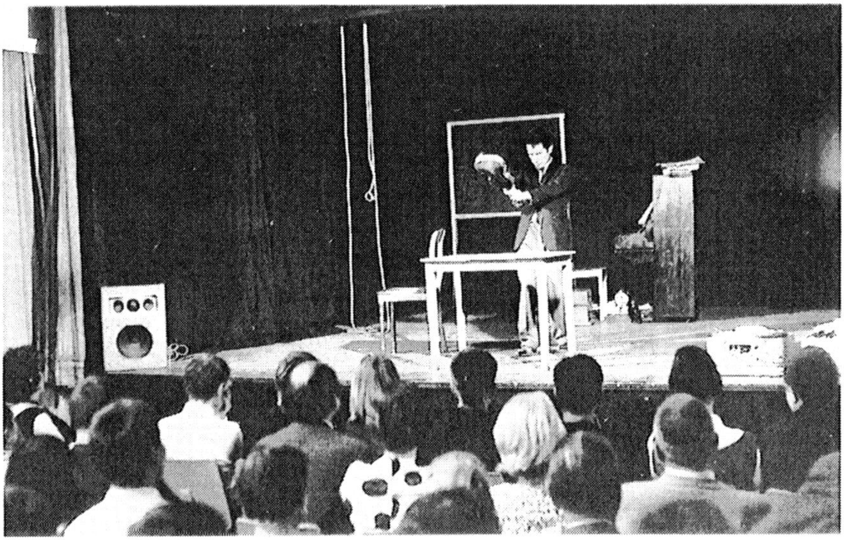

21 Nam June Paik, *One for Violin,* 1961. Performed here in 1962 by Nam June Paik in Düsseldorf. Photo by George Maciunas; courtesy of the Gilbert and Lila Silverman Fluxus Collection, Detroit.

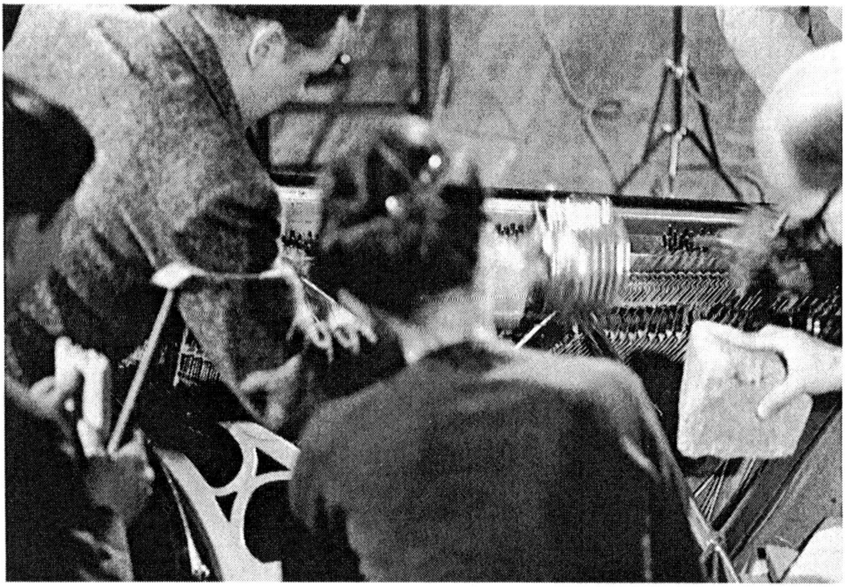

22 Philip Corner, *Piano Activities,* 1962. Shown here at the Wiesbaden Kunstverein. Photographer unidentified; courtesy of the Gilbert and Lila Silverman Fluxus Collection, Detroit.

reduced format elicit the participants' focus on the activity at hand. In Figure 23, depicting an unidentified Event, the performers' level of concentration is striking. Because of the focus on the action at hand, the Event format is not well suited to political activism or to the service of artists' individual egos, which require clarifying exchanges with an audience on the one hand, and self-expression on the other. Is it confusing matters, then, to suggest that the musical basis of the Event means that it is a fundamentally abstract, even aesthetic, art form?

Heidegger's description of music as radically visceral confirms the positive effects of musical thinking in Events. Music, he says, "stands for and encourages resistance to all forms of reification, totalization and reductionism [and] encourages *epistemological humility*, a rigorously experimental attitude, always provisional, always questioning, always alert to the fact that the being of beings is such that beings continually offer themselves to a multiplicity of interpretations."[63] Heidegger's state of "being" here fits the open-ended musical nature of the Event. The "epistemological humility" that music in general and Events in particular foster is intimately bound up with its everyday aspect, its directness, its experimental quality, its provisionality, its availability to multiple realizations, and its rigorous placement in time.[64] The violin may be polished or destroyed, the piano adorned with a vase or eviscerated, a piece of paper carefully inscribed or rolled up, torn to bits, and thrown at the audience, as in Ben Patterson's Event classic, *Paper Music* (Fig. 24).

The musicality inherent in the Event, then, while critiquing mainstream Western epistemology, also deconstructs the "reification, totalization and reductionism" of structured secondary knowledge formations (the disciplines of art history, musicology, philosophy, and literature, for example). The musicality of the Event enables a certain "openness to Being" (Heidegger's term), a characteristic strong in the compositions of Cage. The process of deconstruction thus occurs only when the artists and audience members seek out a multiplicity of exploratory, constructive, and destructive experiences.

Levin, commenting on Heidegger, distinguishes between knowledge acquired visually and that gained by listening, in terms of experience as well as philosophical attitudes about vision that originate in the Enlightenment. "The 'metaphysics of presence,'" which is rooted in vision, results in "an observation or contemplation that is immobile and impassive, *untouched* and unmoved by what it sees ... the visual Gestalt, reduced to the subject-object relationship, tends to be and often is,

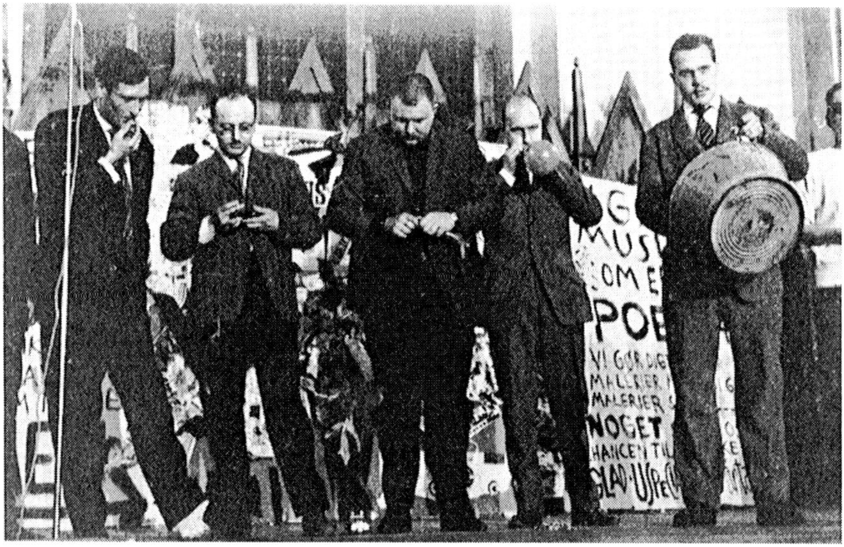

23 Unknown piece performed at Fluxus Festival, Nikolai Church, Copenhagen, 1962. *From left:* Arthur Køpke, [unknown], Wolf Vostell, Emmett Williams, Dick Higgins. Photo by Eric Andersen; courtesy of the photographer.

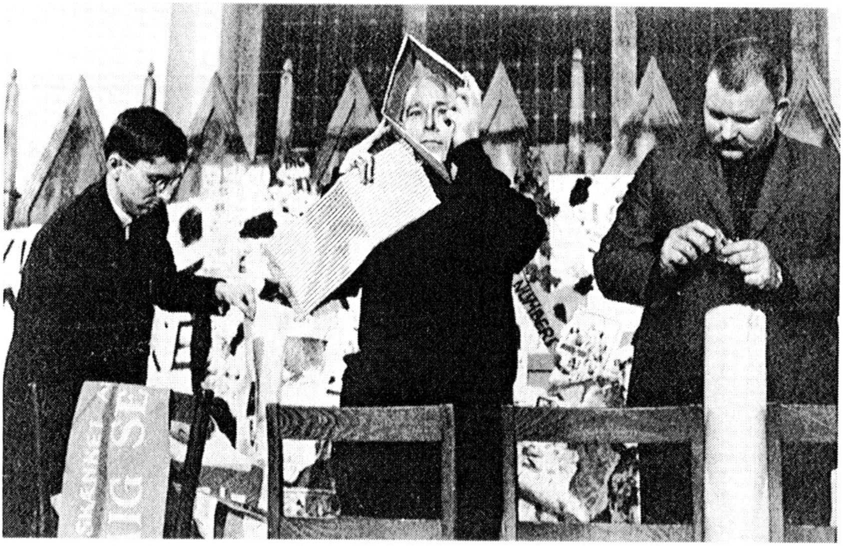

24 Ben Patterson, *Paper Music,* 1962. Fluxus Festival, Nikolai Church, Copenhagen, 1962. *From left:* George Maciunas, Emmett Williams, Wolf Vostell. Photo by Sisse Jarner; courtesy of Eric Andersen.

driven by the will to power."[65] The act of listening, however, is relatively interactive and communicative; indeed, for Heidegger as for Levin, the ideal sensory organ for "openness of Being" is the ear—identified with speech, listening, and music. "Informed by an interactive and receptive normativity," Levin writes, "listening generates a very different episteme and ontology—a very different metaphysics," one based in "communicative rationality" and allowing for "progressive, emancipatory development of our historical potential."[66]

Fluxus materials are useful in precisely such an emancipatory sense—not because they construct political ideologies but rather because they provide contexts (the Fluxkit and the Event) for primary experiences. In offering opportunities to gain knowledge by multisensory and performative means, Fluxus has political implications in the unfixed, unassigned, perhaps anarchic sense. (Sometimes the compression of shared experience, form, and content is called concretism, but to avoid confusion with concrete poetry, I will call it "mattering" henceforth.)

On the Problem of Authenticity

Direct perception, primary information, material knowledge, and experience itself are difficult values to sustain in the current art-philosophical climate, and particularly in a movement like Fluxus that is typically described as politically motivated and broadly deconstructive. In *Of Grammatology*, for example, Jacques Derrida criticizes Heidegger's experience, "openness to Being," as evidence of the transcendental signified of Western philosophy: "As for the concept of experience... it belongs to the history of metaphysics and we can only use it under erasure. 'Experience' has always designated the relationship with a presence, whether that relationship had the form of consciousness or not."[67]

Like Derrida, who warns that we must "escape 'empiricism' and the 'naive' critiques of experience at the same time,"[68] W. J. T. Mitchell rightly notes the dangers of an unexamined empiricism: "There would be nothing wrong with this sort of redescription [of empiricism into aesthetic experience] if it were not advertised as a liberation from metaphysics into a new science.... How riddled with notions of indirect, symbolic mediation are the supposedly 'direct' perceptual mechanisms of the empirical tradition."[69] If, as I contend, Fluxkits and Events produce primary experience, my redescription of Fluxus as aesthetic runs the risk of becoming a merely mystifying incoherent religion of Fluxus Experience. However, Mitchell continues, "the sort of contortion and contention that discourse is obliged to undergo, exhaust the resources of the concept of experience before attaining and in order to attain, by deconstruction, its ultimate foundation."[70]

In other words, even if experience should be deconstructed as Derrida suggests, and even if it is a product of discourse, as Mitchell maintains, the experiential dimension of Fluxus work nonetheless has the capacity (real or by way of a discourse on the empirical basis of experience) to offer ontological knowledge that connects people to a real world and to each other, expanding the individual's sense of belonging to a place and a group. Although, following Mitchell, it may be inaccurate to posit authentic experience as the ontological core of Fluxus objects and performances, the aesthetic emotion aroused by Fluxus works is certainly experienced *as* real. This is, of course, the lure of metaphysics. In other words, the empirical and experiential basis of Fluxkits and Events, graphics and objects, means something *as art.* The primary information itself is highly temporary, becoming secondary as soon as the experience is set into a framework that makes it matter to a person or a group; it is impossible to devise a system able to account for the vast range of meanings and associations Fluxus evokes for the audience. Instead, Fluxus is better understood on its own terms: as producing diverse primary experiences and interactions with reality, plain and simple. This is not to deny that much can be learned from interpretively studying how, for example, the cheap stuff in the Fluxkits came from seconds bins on New York's Canal Street, or how the Fluxplugs could have been conceived only during the sexual revolution of the 1960s and 1970s, or how Joe Jones deconstructed musical virtuosity by replacing the human performer with a mechanical device (Fig. 25); these observations, however, illuminate only single facets of the complex experiential surfaces created by Fluxus works.

The Event and the Fluxkit argue ontologically for the value of primary experiences over secondary experiences—that is, interpretations or associations. Though present, secondary experience is not the point of the work: Fluxus is not a metadiscourse in the postmodern sense. To account for Fluxus as experience, moreover, does not preclude making other claims for its importance. Rather, to insist that primary experience is paramount in Fluxus counters any move to assign specific and permanent meanings to the work. This discussion thus arrives at an impasse

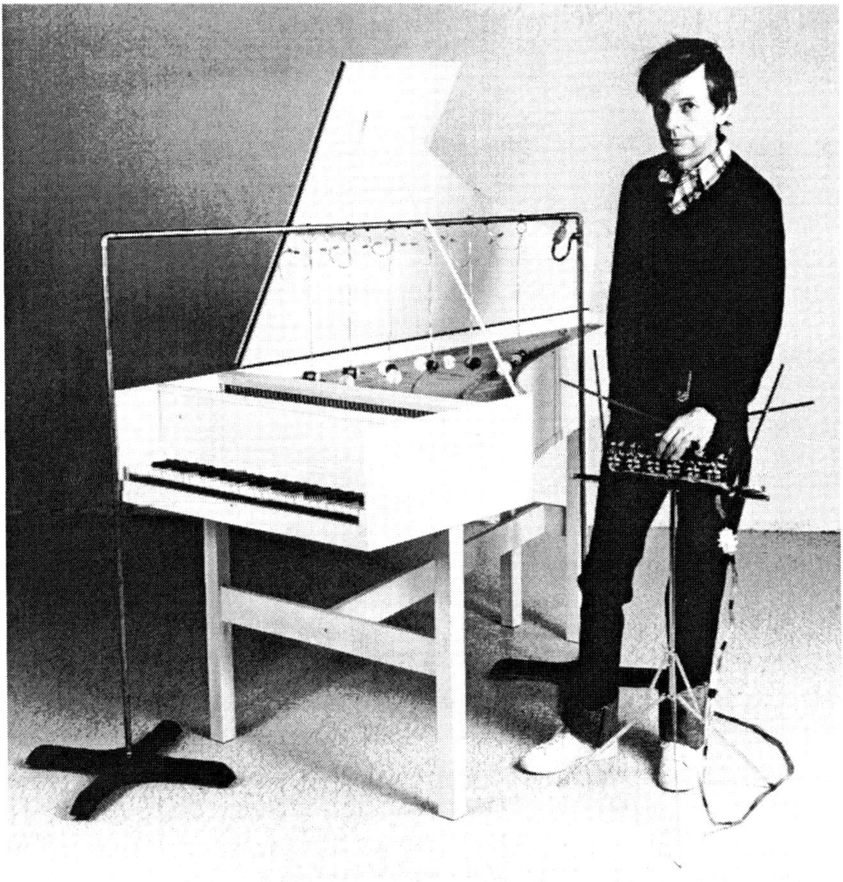

25 Joe Jones, *Fluxharpsichord*, ca. 1980. Photo by Brad Iverson; courtesy of the Gilbert and Lila Silverman Fluxus Collection, Detroit.

of sorts: we have liberated the work from the functionalist idealism of a single agenda, only to banish it to the apparent black hole of experience, beyond the realm of language, that seems to "indefinitely and irretrievably distance the world through a system of intermediate signs," to borrow Mitchell's apt terms.

The remainder of this chapter presents an attempt to negotiate the impasse, to locate Fluxus in a world of authentic experiences yet at the same time create a discursive context for understanding Fluxus objects. The empiricism of Fluxus objects, after all, was not conceived in a vacuum. With Fluxkits and Events artists were getting at something that either was, or seemed, "real" in an art world that values work according to prevailing aesthetic conventions. Interpretation of the experiential dynamic must therefore be both culturally specific and, however radical vis-à-vis normative artistic practice, arguably conventional vis-à-vis the avant-garde. Think Duchamp. I will return to this point in Chapter 2.

Almost all Fluxus artists, however, far from retreating into a world of artistic habit and forever producing minimal Fluxkits and Events, also work in traditional artistic media, as the *Blink* graphic demonstrates. Fluxus is definitely not a practice that is *exclusively* empirical, pretending "to guarantee veridical access to the world"; it originally staked its claim to empiricism in a context of art where personal expression (as in expressionism) was the order of the day. As a project, rather, Fluxus modestly proposed the real value of real things and the possibility of deriving knowledge and experience from these things, in the belief that these proposals had implications for art and for culture generally.

In *What Is Art For?* the Darwinian art historian Ellen Dissanayake asserts that the production of art is a universal biological imperative, like language, though it differs from language in both form and function. Art produced by all peoples is "special," she argues, even if these peoples have no notion of high art (as made by fine artists). Dissanayake explores three characteristics of art that transcend both individual practice and cultural norms: all societies produce art; art institutions are integral to social order; and art is a psychologically, psychically, and intellectually pleasurable form of engagement between people.[71] Her findings help explain Fluxus experiences *as art.*

In the chapter titled " 'Making Special': Toward a Behavior of Art," Dissanayake defines the pleasure in art as a bio-behavioral necessity because it marks reality according to belief systems and therefore promotes human sociality. After describing the importance of play and ritual and their interaction, Dissanayake states:

> Art makes use of out-of-context elements, redirecting the ordinary elements (e.g., colors, sounds, words) into a configuration in which they become more than ordinary. . . . Reality is converted from its usual unremarkable state—in which we take it or its components for granted—to a significant or specially experienced reality in which the components, by their emphasis or combination, or juxtaposition, acquire a metareality.[72]

Art gives things this metareality (that is, transcendent reality) by "redirecting the ordinary" toward significance. The fact that "something, and indeed a very great deal, is always lost when we try to think about art in terms of pre-existent systems" only underscores the notion that Fluxkits and Events, in their intensive studies of things or actions, are not structured according to any one model of describing experience.[73] Rather, the Event or Fluxkit is a metarealistic trigger: it makes the viewer's or user's experience special.

Dissanayake's anthropological framework, though it has no program for evaluating art, nevertheless allows for aesthetics: "Acts of masturbating or carving oneself up in themselves are not artistic activities; performed deliberately for aesthetic reasons, out of context, 'made special' by the occasion and making the occasion special and extraordinary, they are."[74] Fluxkits and Events make ordinary reality special as occasions and as objects both in- and outside the aesthetic situations called art. Even though these works occasionally function as art in a relatively traditional sense (they are shown in museums and performed in concert halls), Fluxus artists in New York, working in an art context that privileged painterly abstraction, clearly yearned for something else. Rather than convey their own emotional world abstractly, Fluxus artists directed their audiences' attention to concrete everyday stuff—addressing aesthetic metareality in the broadest sense. As Henry Martin puts it, "We . . . learn to make a space in our lives for Events, experiences, emotions and sensibilities that can contribute to a sense of integrity and fullness and that otherwise, and mistakenly, we might consider to be gratuitous."[75]

The pattern of the public's interacting with Fluxus materials and adapting them to their own circumstances suggests the essential fluidity of Fluxus. And my own experience confirms it. In 1966 the Japanese Fluxus artist Hi Red Center performed *Street Cleaning Event,* meticulously cleaning a patch of sidewalk in New York City with solvents (Fig. 26). I grew up knowing this work. When I took on a job in college as a cleaning woman, I recalled it, and it became for me a means of connecting profoundly with my environment.

The installations of the Danish Fluxus artist Eric Andersen—which extend into the environment, and everyday lives, of audience members—demand a continuous interaction with materials. A particularly successful work, Andersen's *Travelling Wall* (1985), instructed passersby to move bricks forward from a source pile. The normally staid plaza of Roskilde, Denmark, was thus transformed into a maze of brick towers, pathways, and domino-falls at the hands of a spontaneous crew of brickworkers.

Fluxus often leaks from art into life. For example, my mother-in-law, Laurie Reinstein, who is on the Women's Board of the Chicago Museum of Contemporary Art, is knowledgeable about contemporary art. After the "In the Spirit of Fluxus" show arrived in Chicago (from Minneapolis's Walker Art Center) in 1993, I entered her living room one day and found a clear plastic rectangular box; it was divided into sections, into each of which she had placed a small, favorite thing—tickets, balls, pins, and other knickknacks. She has never called this an art object or a Fluxkit, and indeed in one conversation, she seemed embarrassed by the suggestion. For to call what she had done "art" would imply hubris: art, after all, is in museums and made by professionals. Her sort-of Fluxkit was, instead, a box of little things special to her but undistinguished by monetary value, rarity, or artisanal skill. By putting these items in a special place all together, she nonetheless claimed, to anyone who looked into her box, that they were significant. That claim makes possible certain conversations about her life and interests. In Dissanayake's terms, she redirected the ordinary toward a metareality, effectively making art in the affirmative, anthropological sense. In Martin's terminology, she made a space for events, experiences, emotions, and sensibilities that those around her might otherwise have ignored as meaningless.

To value prosaic materials and experiences seems to me to go some way toward an appreciative (as opposed to cynical) and empathetic (as opposed to alienated) cognitive model that maintains a critical relationship to the subject while remaining open to it as well. Fluxus in these terms offers tools with which to create a sense of belonging in the world. Dissanayake makes a similar point in a chapter that links cultural survival to the practice of "making special."

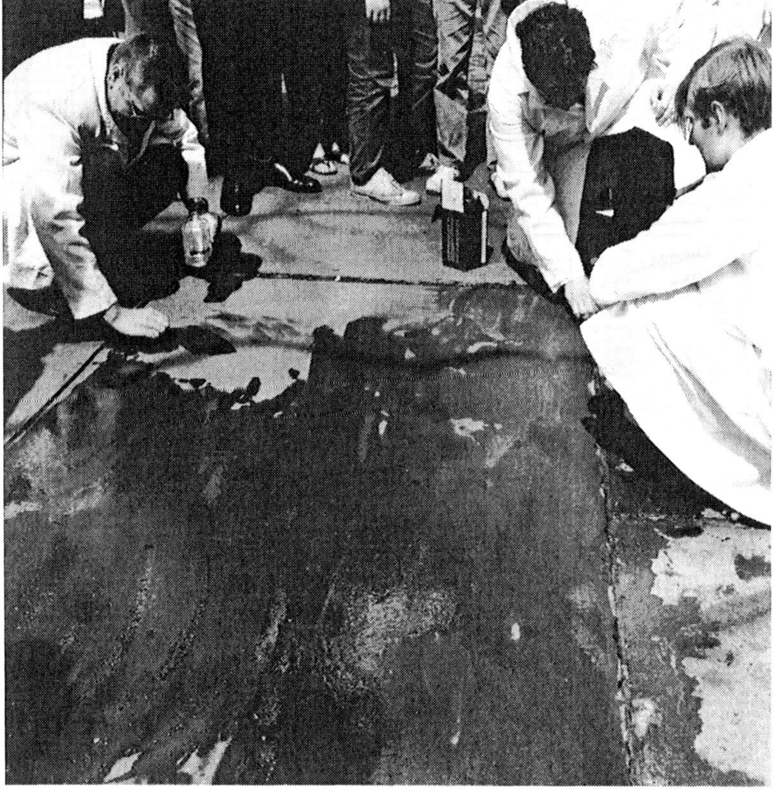

26 Hi Red Center, *Street Cleaning Event,* New York City, 1966. Photo by George Maciunas; courtesy of the Gilbert and Lila Silverman Fluxus Collection, Detroit.

Dissanayake's next book, *Homo Aestheticus,* expands on this crucial function of art. Her thesis is that art is "an inherited behavioral tendency to act in a certain way in certain circumstances, which during the evolution of our species helped us to survive." Although she has stated repeatedly that her work is not prescriptive, it is possible to extrapolate from it a sense of Fluxus as a model—Fluxus offers to replace elements of our Euro-American high culture that may not be helping our survival. Dissanayake notes again in this book how things are recognized as special and selected for a realm called art:

> While "special" might seem too imprecise and naively simple, or suggest mere decoration, it easily encompassed an array of what is done in making the arts that is generally different from making nonarts: embellishing, exaggerating, patterning, juxtaposing, shaping and transforming.... Special also denotes a positive factor of care and concern that is absent from the other words. It thus suggests that the special object or activity appeals to emotional as well as perceptual and cognitive factors—that is, to all aspects of our mental functioning.

Making special is thus a function of the rich interplay of mental functions that include human emotion, perception, and cognition. And the aesthetic pleasure of art (in this case, Fluxus art) gives us insight into these interactions, which supports our survival. By this theory—a radical departure from most psychologizing accounts of art in culture—art is not necessarily a by-product of psychological trauma, though it may be precisely that for an individual or even a culture. Instead, art connects individuals to the culture. Dissanayake, critical of contemporary Western culture, states:

> Caring deeply about vital things is out of fashion, and, in any case, who has the time (or allows the time) to care and to mark one's caring?... Human history has demonstrated that people can endure surprising amounts of hardship and suffering—conditions that usually elicit a serious and religious attitude toward life. Whether people are as well equipped to thrive under conditions of unprecedented leisure, comfort, and plenty is a question that is being tested on a large scale in our present circumstances: the answer does not appear to be promising.[76]

The psychotherapist James Hillman has described the objet trouvé (as in Duchamp's readymades) as art, in terms that resonate both with Dissanayake's conception of the special and with the ordinariness of the Fluxus Event and the prosaic Fluxkit. Significantly, the objet trouvé does not signify an end of art (as it may have for Duchamp, initially), but rather the beginning of a transcendent metareality that for Hillman is alive:

> Ordinary things come alive, become metaphors, have humor. No longer just Kmart and throwaway.... Rusty girders, or the ruins of an old car, that's right. It makes me see things that are animated. So I don't think art is guilty for the neglect of anima mundi. With the objet trouvé, it rescued and made use of discarded materials.[77]

For "things to come alive," a certain unpredictability must be admitted into their status as living. This unpredictability does not mean that one should not try to understand things, explore them, consider them deeply. It does mean that the objet trouvé—which for my purposes constitutes the substance of Fluxkits, the dynamic logic of Events, and the many acts of production in Fluxus that evoke tactility and bodily presence—extends toward a vital sense of contextual interplay.[78] The interplay of the senses in Fluxkits and Events, along with the interplay of history models and of art movements and discourses that is typical of Fluxus, should be seen, then, not as a mere negation of the Western Idealists' episteme. Rather, in its materialism Fluxus radically intervenes in human survival, its resistance to rationalizing schemes of all kinds a testament to its experiential breadth.

In *The Case against the Global Economy,* Jerry Mander argues for deep democracy, tolerance, and attentiveness to all the voices of experience—elements necessary for the survival of all humans.[79] The breadth of Fluxus works and the persistence of multiple perspectives on Fluxus in the group make Fluxus a model for deep democracy—despite the anxieties, feuds, and tensions attendant on the consideration of others' perspectives. Not a happy pluralism that negates action by absorbing it into a to-each-his-own passivity, Fluxus is rather a democracy that, though perhaps fractured at the root, is held together by a common respect for differences.

The most fragile moments in the history of Fluxus, when it seemed most vulnerable to breakdown, have been those moments when zealous members tried to pin it down. Still a living creature, it resists being impaled. Culturally, there is much food for thought in that writhing resistance. As co-performers in a Fluxus artist's Fluxkit or Event, we need only touch, listen, taste, feel, and look to gain the sense of place that makes life rich in terms not only of art but also of life. It is a richness that belies convention.

The exploration of prosaic things and activities in Fluxkits and Events generates primary knowledge and multisensory experience. That is the point of Fluxus, even though to discuss this experience necessarily renders it in part secondary or discursive. Far from being cynical and alienating, the Fluxus experience, in its matter-of-factness, situates people radically within their corporeal, sensory worlds. Such materiality is fundamentally incompatible with a radical division of object and subject, of perceiving and knowing.

The substance chosen for exploration—the content of the Fluxkit or Event—is significant, for it is attributed with "specialness" not only by the artist but also by the user of the Fluxkit or the performer of the Event. The materials of Fluxus thus matter profoundly both personally and socially, in part because they gain meaning as art, but also (and more important) because, despite their otherwise unremarkable status in everyday life, they enable transcendent aesthetic experience.

CHARTING FLUXUS

Picturing History

2

"From my point of view," wrote George Brecht in a June 1964 *Fluxus* newspaper article titled "Something about Fluxus,"

> the individual understandings of Fluxus have come from placing hands in Ay-o's *Tactile Boxes,* from making a poem with Dieter Roth's *Poem Machine* published in the Fluxus newspaper, from watching Ben Vautier string Alison Knowles–on-the-blue-stool to objects in the room and to the audience in Kosugi's *Anima I.* . . . The misunderstandings have seemed to come from comparing Fluxus with movements or groups whose individuals seem to have some principle in common, or an agreed upon program.

If the experience generated by the Fluxkit and Event pose problems for philosophical idealism in general and for mainstream art history in particular, Fluxus artists might be expected to have difficulty describing the bonds that link them to one another and to the contexts designated by the term *art.* George Brecht suggests that is indeed the case:

> In Fluxus there has never been any attempt to agree on aims or methods; individuals with something unnameable in common have simply naturally coalesced to publish and perform their work. Perhaps this common something is a feeling that the bounds of art are much wider than they have conventionally seemed, or that art and certain long established bounds are no longer very useful.[1]

Attempts to conventionalize or "agree on aims or methods" for Fluxus that embed individual experiences in a common structure merely generate "misunderstandings." Nevertheless, some members of Fluxus continue to be motivated by the "long established" institutional and disciplinary boundaries that Brecht describes as "no longer very useful."

The distance between these perspectives has implications for describing Fluxus experiences in the sense described in Chapter 1. One point of view privileges primary experience, the other secondary, since one is predominantly experiential and the other largely interpretive. From these two opposing positions emerge different ideas about how Fluxus is organized, why it matters, and what its social structure and historic function might be.

Of the two points of view, one describes Fluxus as discontinuous and in essence experiential, the other as continuous with the historical avant-garde, which issued political manifestos based on "agreed on aims or methods" that set out a comparatively narrow menu of stylistic possibilities. From the latter perspective, the work of Fluxus conforms to an argumentative logic: that is, it demonstrates a particular (il-logical) point of view. If we cannot say that Fluxus means nothing, it is nonetheless accurate to say that its experiential nature makes it unlikely to mean any one thing.

These two perspectives on Fluxus—as experiential and as avant-garde—have been diagrammed many times. I have selected three representative diagrams for analysis and will emphasize the two that are most polarized (the third falls halfway between) (see Figs. 29, 33, and 36). They can be evaluated in relation to specific events in and attitudes about Fluxus throughout its history, which in turn can help us analyze the usefulness of each perspective on Fluxus. With adherents of both perspectives in Fluxus, neither, strictly speaking, can be considered right or wrong. They differ, however, in their inclusiveness of the work produced by Fluxus artists, both individually and as a group, as well as by how the boundaries of Fluxus are applied within each artist's oeuvre.

A Common Front

Several incidents in early Fluxus history illustrate its diversity. The first occurred on 30 August 1964, when an experimental opera by the German composer Karlheinz Stockhausen had its American premiere at the annual New York Festival of the Avant-Garde in New York City. Stockhausen is best known as a composer of serialist music, in which modules are played in various sequences according to the performers' choice. In the early 1960s Stockhausen was also experimenting with verbal scores, which, like Fluxus Events, "constitute... different incitements to produce a musical action, generally in a group."[2] The resulting opera overlaid multiple performance activities in various forms: simple gestures, theatrical movements, instrumental music, noise, and so forth. The piece was enthusiastically attended by almost all sectors of the New York avant-garde art scene, including Stockhausen's former student Nam June Paik, who was associated with Fluxus. In addition to Paik, several Fluxus artists were by then in contact with Stockhausen as well, their associations dating back four to six years.

In 1962, when George Maciunas was organizing a series of fund-raisers for a projected *Fluxus* magazine (actually the first Fluxus-titled concerts, consisting of Events that Fluxus artists had been performing since the late 1950s), he contacted Stockhausen's wife, Mary Bauermeister, to see if she might be willing to participate: "Could we hold a festival in your studio in June or July? It would be a good beginning for fluxus series."[3] The collegial relationship of Bauermeister, Stockhausen, and Maciunas seemed secure: Maciunas listed Stockhausen as a contributor of musical works to the first four concerts raising funds for his new magazine.[4]

The inclusion of Stockhausen in these concerts, however, represented a diplomatic concession on Maciunas's part. Paik, who aided Maciunas in organizing the fund-raisers, had lobbied for Stockhausen's inclusion.[5] Correspondence between the two men in 1962 reveals that Paik supported Stockhausen's inclusion because he had been his teacher and Paik appreciated his work, whereas Maciunas criticized Stockhausen as elitist, a prima donna.[6] Some basic differences already separated Maciunas and Stockhausen.

The conflict that arose is not entirely surprising: with the exception of verbal scores like that for *Originale,* which could be performed by nonmusicians, Stockhausen's serialist compositions retained many elements of traditional music. While a Fluxus Event could be performed by almost anyone and could involve almost any of the senses, Stockhausen's formal compositions retained, in the words of John Cage,

> the two most essentially conventional aspects of European music—that is to say, the twelve tones of the octave (the frequency characteristic of the material) and regularity of beat (affecting the element of method in the composing means)[. As a consequence], the performer—in those instances where his procedure follows any dictates at all (his feelings, his automatism, his sense of universality, his taste)—will be led to give the form aspects essentially conventional to European music.[7]

There are, then, significant differences between the unconventional Event and Stockhausen's "essentially conventional" musical form. The early disagreement between Paik and Maciunas over Stockhausen's inclusion, combined with the ontological difference between the Event and Stockhausen's serialism, suggests why there might subsequently have been conflict in Fluxus with regard to Stockhausen.

And so there was.

Originale's U.S. premiere took place at Judson Hall, a venue for experimental theater. The concert program lists as performers and/or exhibitors the Fluxus members Nam June Paik (not surprisingly), Dick Higgins, Jackson Mac Low, Joe Jones, and George Brecht, along with Charlotte Moorman, Mary Bauermeister, Lette Lou Eisenhauer, Allan Kaprow, and Michael Kirby, who sometimes performed with Fluxus.[8] Meanwhile, other Fluxus artists—Ben Vautier, Takako Saito, George Maciunas, and Henry Flynt—distributed a flyer at the concert protesting it (Fig. 27). Contributing to the confusion, at least three artists (Dick Higgins, Allan Kaprow, and Alison Knowles) both performed in and demonstrated against the concert.[9] Kaprow wrote years later that "there is no essential difference between the music of Mozart in a concert hall and the music of Karlheinz Stockhausen in a concert hall. Museum and concert hall embed the works equally in late Western cultural history."[10] By both performing and demonstrating, Kaprow and the others took a position for as well as against this history, attempting to step inside and remain outside the "museum and concert hall."

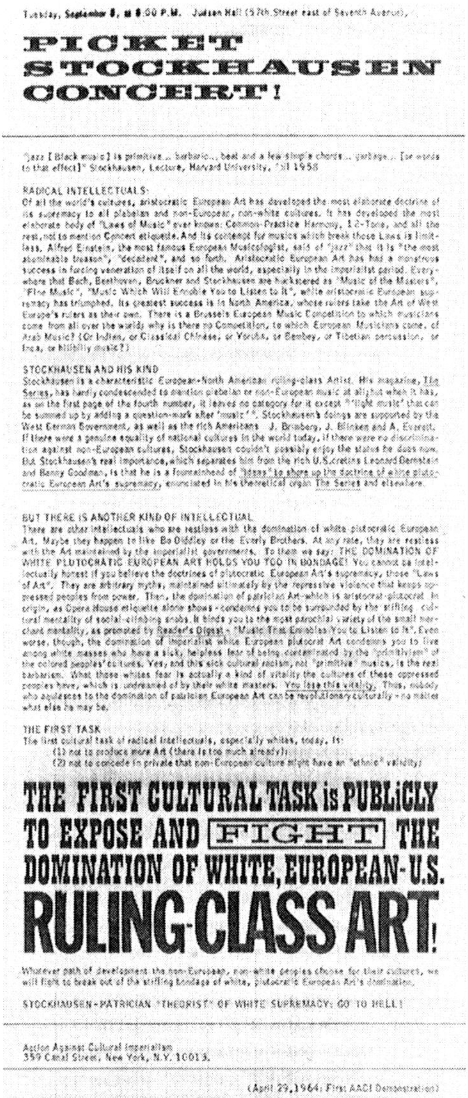

Tuesday, September 8, at 8:00 P.M. Judson Hall (57th Street east of Seventh Avenue),

PICKET STOCKHAUSEN CONCERT!

"jazz [Black music] is primitive... barbaric... beat and a few simple chords... garbage... [or words to that effect]" Stockhausen, Lecture, Harvard University, Fall 1958

RADICAL INTELLECTUALS:
Of all the world's cultures, aristocratic European Art has developed the most elaborate doctrine of its supremacy to all plebeian and non-European, non-white cultures. It has developed the most elaborate body of "Laws of Music" ever known: Common-Practice Harmony, 12-Tone, and all the rest, not to mention Concert etiquette. And its contempt for musics which break those Laws is limitless. Alfred Einstein, the most famous European Musicologist, said of "jazz" that it is "the most abominable treason", "decadent", and so forth. Aristocratic European Art has had a monstrous success in forcing veneration of itself on all the world, especially in the imperialist period. Everywhere that Bach, Beethoven, Bruckner and Stockhausen are huckstered as "Music of the Masters", "Fine Music", "Music Which Will Ennoble You to Listen to It", white aristocratic European supremacy has triumphed. Its greatest success is in North America, whose rulers take the Art of West Europe's rulers as their own. There is a Brussels European Music Competition to which musicians come from all over the world; why is there no Competition, to which European Musicians come, of Arab Music? (Or Indian, or Classical Chinese, or Yoruba, or Sembey, or Tibetian percussion, or Inca, or hillbilly music?)

STOCKHAUSEN AND HIS KIND
Stockhausen is a characteristic European-North American ruling-class Artist. His magazine, The Series, has hardly condescended to mention plebeian or non-European music at all; but when it has, as on the first page of the fourth number, it leaves no category for it except "'light music' that can be summed up by adding a question-mark after 'music'". Stockhausen's doings are supported by the West German Government, as well as the rich Americans J. Bromberg, J. Blinken and A. Everett. If there were a genuine equality of national cultures in the world today, if there were no discrimination against non-European cultures, Stockhausen couldn't possibly enjoy the status he does now. But Stockhausen's real importance, which separates him from the rich U.S. cretins Leonard Bernstein and Benny Goodman, is that he is a fountainhead of "ideas" to shore up the doctrine of white plutocratic European Art's supremacy, enunciated in his theoretical organ The Series and elsewhere.

BUT THERE IS ANOTHER KIND OF INTELLECTUAL
There are other intellectuals who are restless with the domination of white plutocratic European Art. Maybe they happen to like Bo Diddley or the Everly Brothers. At any rate, they are restless with the Art maintained by the imperialist governments. To them we say: THE DOMINATION OF WHITE PLUTOCRATIC EUROPEAN ART HOLDS YOU TOO IN BONDAGE! You cannot be intellectually honest if you believe the doctrines of plutocratic European Art's supremacy, those "Laws of Art". They are arbitrary myths, maintained ultimately by the repressive violence that keeps oppressed peoples from power. Then, the domination of patrician Art—which is aristocrat-plutocrat in origin, as Opera House etiquette alone shows—condemns you to be surrounded by the stifling cultural mentality of social-climbing snobs. It binds you to the most parochial variety of the small merchant mentality, as promoted by Reader's Digest—"Music That Ennobles You to Listen to It". Even worse, though, the domination of imperialist white European plutocrat Art condemns you to live among white masses who have a sick, helpless fear of being contaminated by the "primitivism" of the colored peoples' cultures. Yes, and this sick cultural racism, not "primitive" musics, is the real barbarism. What these whites fear is actually a kind of vitality the cultures of these oppressed peoples have, which is undreamed of by their white masters. You lose this vitality. Thus, nobody who acquiesces to the domination of patrician European Art can be revolutionary culturally—no matter what else he may be.

THE FIRST TASK
The first cultural task of radical intellectuals, especially whites, today, is:
(1) not to produce more Art (there is too much already);
(2) not to concede in private that non-European culture might have an "ethnic" validity;

THE FIRST CULTURAL TASK is PUBLICLY TO EXPOSE AND FIGHT THE DOMINATION OF WHITE, EUROPEAN-U.S. RULING-CLASS ART!

Whatever path of development the non-European, non-white peoples choose for their cultures, we will fight to break out of the stifling bondage of white, plutocratic European Art's domination.

STOCKHAUSEN—PATRICIAN "THEORIST" OF WHITE SUPREMACY: GO TO HELL!

Action Against Cultural Imperialism
359 Canal Street, New York, N.Y. 10013.

(April 29, 1964: First AACI Demonstration)

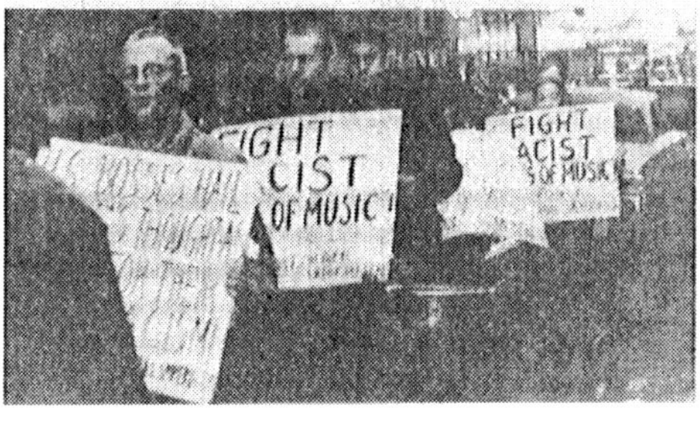

27 Flyer, "Action against Cultural Imperialism, 'Picket Stockhausen Concert!'" 1964; text by Henry Flynt, designed by George Maciunas. Offset on paper, 17⅜ × 6 in. Photo by the Walker Art Center; courtesy of the Gilbert and Lila Silverman Fluxus Collection, Detroit.

George Brecht, in "Something about Fluxus," suggests the diversity (or fluidity) of positions available to Fluxus members: "Whether you think that concert halls, theaters, and art galleries are the natural places to present music, performances, and objects, or find these places mummifying, preferring streets, homes, and railway stations, or do not find it useful to distinguish between these two aspects of the world theater, there is someone associated with Fluxus who agrees with you."[11] These three positions, though indisputably taken by Fluxus members, were not reported to the public by the press. Instead the media presented only one view of Fluxus, a uniformly activist one that associated the name Fluxus exclusively with the demonstrators. *Time* magazine reported that "the opening at Judson Hall could not have been more auspicious; it was picketed by a rival group calling itself 'Fluxus,' bearing signs: 'Fight the rich man's snob art.' "[12] The *Nation* presented a similar description of the protestors, who "are also against 'the rich U.S. cretins [Leonard] Bernstein and [Benny] Goodman.' Their aim is to promote jazz ('black music') and not to promote more art ('there is too much already')."[13]

The public face of Fluxus, in both the mainstream and the alternative press, was thus that of the demonstrators, led by Maciunas. This version suggests that Fluxus is a politically motivated, centrally organized, anti-art group—what Maciunas called a "common front" against dominant culture—one fundamentally at odds with the experiential viewpoint. Although the reporters' version has a basis in Fluxus, it is a minority viewpoint among Fluxus members themselves.

Even within the "common front," however, ideological complications arise. The demonstrators called their anti-Stockhausen initiative an "Action against Cultural Imperialism"—a title for several similar actions invented by artist Henry Flynt[14]—not a "*Fluxus* Action against Cultural Imperialism." The adoption of Flynt's unelaborated title suggests the existence of multiple viewpoints even among the organizers themselves.

After the demonstration (and the windfall of publicity), Maciunas—the group's self-proclaimed leader, impresario, and (not insignificantly) most gifted designer and inventor of the Fluxkit—ordered the expulsion from Fluxus of all who had participated in the concert. The demonstrators did not face that threat. This act underscores the tension within the movement, created by conflicting alliances that range from ideological agreement (the "common front") to an unprogrammatically aligned constellation of artists "with something unnameable in common."

The Stockhausen incident simultaneously supports two views of Fluxus: as political and programmatically narrow, on the one hand, and experientially broad and socially elastic, on the other. Each artist had three options: to demonstrate against Stockhausen and maintain ties to Maciunas and his common front principle (though to demonstrate would not necessarily mean endorsing that principle); to participate in the concert and thus identify with fellow Fluxus artists; or to do both, thereby occupying a dynamic middle ground that "did not find it useful to distinguish between" street demonstrations and attendance at or participation in concert performances.

The Stockhausen concert incident was not an isolated one. Most of those participating in or attending it—the nondemonstrators—had been involved in an earlier dispute within Fluxus. The controversy around *Fluxus News-Policy Letter* number 6, dated 6 April 1963, sparked a legendary Fluxbattle.[15] Where earlier letters referred to organizational details of specific concerts or projects, this one detailed an ideologically determined series of propaganda actions—for example, sabotaging museums by flooding them with C.O.D. packages filled with bricks and creating mayhem during rush hour by abandoning cars at major intersections. This was also the first newsletter to combine the terms *Fluxus* and *policy* in the title, so it seemed to establish a precise political agenda for the group in a "Proposed Propaganda Action for November Fluxus in N.Y.C." This proposed action would have linked a dadaesque act of overt iconoclasm with the name Fluxus, an association Maciunas himself had suggested in the 1962 so-called Fluxus (or Purge) Manifesto, published and distributed but never signed or agreed to by Fluxus artists (Fig. 28).[16]

In newsletter number 7 Maciunas retreated from the confrontational position: "This Newsletter 6 was not intended as a decision, settled plan or dictate, but rather as a synthetic proposal or rather a signal, stimulus to start a discussion among, and an invitation for proposals from—the recipients."[17] The apparent aim of *Fluxus News-Policy Letter* number 6 was merely to instigate debate among Fluxus members, and it might therefore be seen as a sign of variability within the group. However, this openness constitutes a retraction of sorts. In *Fluxus News Letter* number 5, published on 1 January 1963, a statement was made that all Fluxus authors should give exclusive rights for their past, present, and future material to Fluxus: "It is believed that such a common front would facilitate establishment of

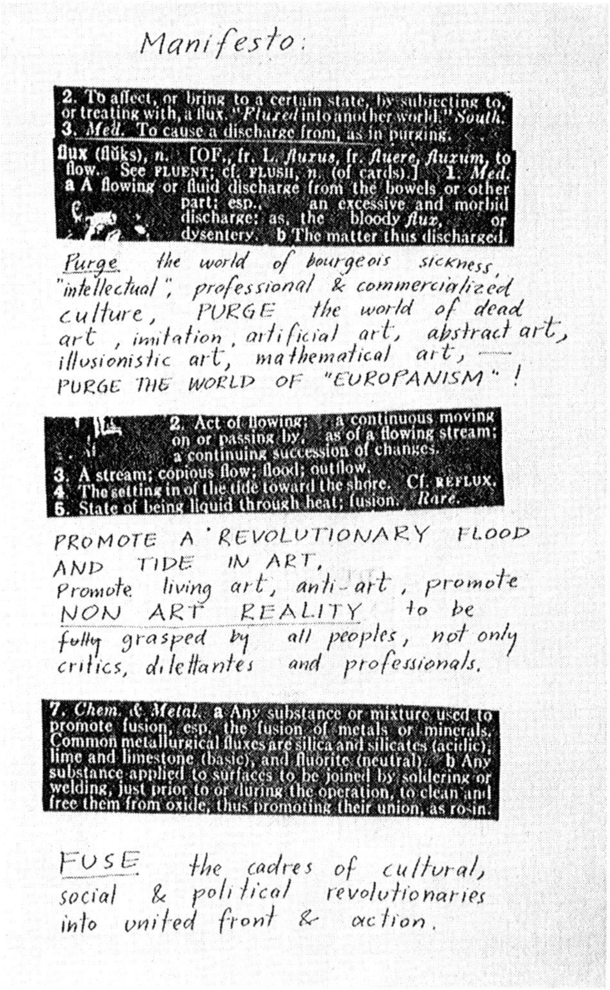

Manifesto:

2. To affect, or bring to a certain state, by subjecting to, or treating with, a flux. "*Fluxed* into another world." *South.*
3. *Med.* To cause a discharge from, as in purging.

flux (flŭks), *n.* [OF., fr. L. *fluxus*, fr. *fluere*, *fluxum*, to flow. See FLUENT; cf. FLUSH, *n.* (of cards).] **1.** *Med.* **a** A flowing or fluid discharge from the bowels or other part; esp., an excessive and morbid discharge: as, the bloody *flux*, or dysentery. **b** The matter thus discharged.

Purge the world of bourgeois sickness, "intellectual", professional & commercialized culture, PURGE the world of dead art, imitation, artificial art, abstract art, illusionistic art, mathematical art, — PURGE THE WORLD OF "EUROPANISM"!

2. Act of flowing; a continuous moving on or passing by, as of a flowing stream; a continuing succession of changes.
3. A stream; copious flow; flood; outflow.
4. The setting in of the tide toward the shore. Cf. REFLUX.
5. State of being liquid through heat; fusion. *Rare.*

PROMOTE A REVOLUTIONARY FLOOD AND TIDE IN ART, Promote living art, anti-art, promote NON ART REALITY to be fully grasped by all peoples, not only critics, dilettantes and professionals.

7. *Chem. & Metal.* **a** Any substance or mixture used to promote fusion, esp. the fusion of metals or minerals. Common metallurgical fluxes are silica and silicates (acidic), lime and limestone (basic), and fluorite (neutral). **b** Any substance applied to surfaces to be joined by soldering or welding, just prior to or during the operation, to clean and free them from oxide, thus promoting their union, as rosin.

FUSE the cadres of cultural, social & political revolutionaries into united front & action.

28 George Maciunas, *Manifesto,* 1963. Offset on paper, 8¼ × 5⅞ in. Photo by the Walker Art Center; courtesy of the Gilbert and Lila Silverman Fluxus Collection, Detroit.

a more systematic basis by which the authors would be compensated for the performances of their work. It would also strengthen Fluxus 'propaganda' activities, demonstrations, festivals, infiltrations and coordination of activities with useful people in other countries."[18] George Brecht wrote to Maciunas requesting elaboration: "What is Fluxus 'propaganda'? What kind of 'demonstration'? 'infiltration'? Co-ordination of what kind of useful people in what kind of activities?"[19] Maciunas responded with the policy statement outlined in number 6. Many Fluxus members, interpreting (or misinterpreting) the position taken in *Fluxus News-Policy Letter* number 6 as too narrow, responded angrily. Jackson Mac Low wrote a lengthy critique dated 25 April 1962:

> I'm not opposed to serious culture—quite the contrary. I'm all for it & I hope & consider that my own work is a genuine contribution to it. . . . No blunderbuss attack against culture (serious or otherwise) as a whole . . . will do anything to remedy what's wrong in the present situation. I am not at all against art or music or drama or literature, old or new. I'm against the overbalance of museum culture . . . as against present-minded and presently "useful" cultural activities and would certainly like to see the balance tipped the other way, but I would not want to eliminate museums (I like museums).[20]

Other letters to Maciunas—from Dick Higgins, Nam June Paik, and German Fluxus artist Tomas Schmit, among others—echoed Mac Low's sentiments.[21] Maciunas wrote to Higgins and Alison Knowles expressing his opinion of these responses: "I do not understand your statement (& Jackson's) that 'there is no point in antagonizing the very people and classes that we are most interested in converting.' [illegible]sm that is very clearly directed . . . can reduce the attendance of the masses to these decadent institutions."[22]

In this context, to "understand" would have meant to accept the complaints about *Fluxus News-Policy Letter* number 6 and the oppressive relationship it described between cultural institutions and the apparently unenlightened public. Mac Low's criticism of the policy newsletter suggests, however, that this relationship is not necessarily—not always—oppressive, and that it can be effectively criticized without destroying it. Criticism of the policy newsletter counters the image of political consensus traditionally understood as the operating principle of both Fluxus and the historical avant-garde. According to this formula, art transforms unstructured social criticism into a highly structured political critique aimed directly at the institutions of art.[23] It is a defensible, if problematic, way to understand the historical avant-garde, but it is ill suited to understanding Fluxus.

Not surprisingly, responses to newsletter number 6 embrace multiple political views. Maciunas wrote to Emmett Williams, Daniel Spoerri, and Robert Filliou that "Brecht blew his top off because proposals were getting too terroristic and aggressive, Henry Flynt thought they were too 'artistic,' too much 'serious culture' as he calls it. Jackson Mac Low thought they were not serious enough. Each is pulling in different directions like Paik's piano piece."[24]

They would pull in different directions once again when the demonstration flyer against Stockhausen used the same language as *Fluxus News-Policy Letter* number 6. The flyer called on all radical thinkers to protest Stockhausen in the interest of nonracist revolutionary thinking (see Fig. 27). The logic behind this call identified Stockhausen with the philosopher Theodor Adorno's antiethnic claims for the separation of modern art and all forms of popular culture, including jazz music. Maciunas probably knew, or at least should have anticipated, that this language would raise—and perhaps exacerbate—the conflicts created a year earlier by the newsletter.

George Maciunas charted these conflicts in a diagram that he titled "Fluxus (Its Historical Development and Relationship to Avant-Garde Movements)" (Fig. 29), which marks the expulsion of several artists at precisely those years when they challenged his leadership of Fluxus. Within the section labeled "Fluxus Group" (above the year 1961, marked at the bottom of the diagram); a vertical line indicates that Jackson Mac Low, Tomas Schmit, and Emmett Williams were no longer members as of 1963, the year of the *News-Policy Letter* controversy. Another round of exclusions—of Philip Corner, Dick Higgins, Alison Knowles, Ben Patterson, Nam June Paik, and Takehisha Kosugi—occurred in 1964, the year of the Stockhausen incident.

The section on the far left of the diagram records Fluxus history in terms of running jokes, art movements such as collage and concretism, and the historical avant-garde, among other things[25]—activities and movements outside painterly modernism, which had defined ambitious art in the 1950s. This history prefigures the exclusion from Fluxus of artists who either chose a nonlinear relationship to the historical avant-garde or denied the relationship altogether.

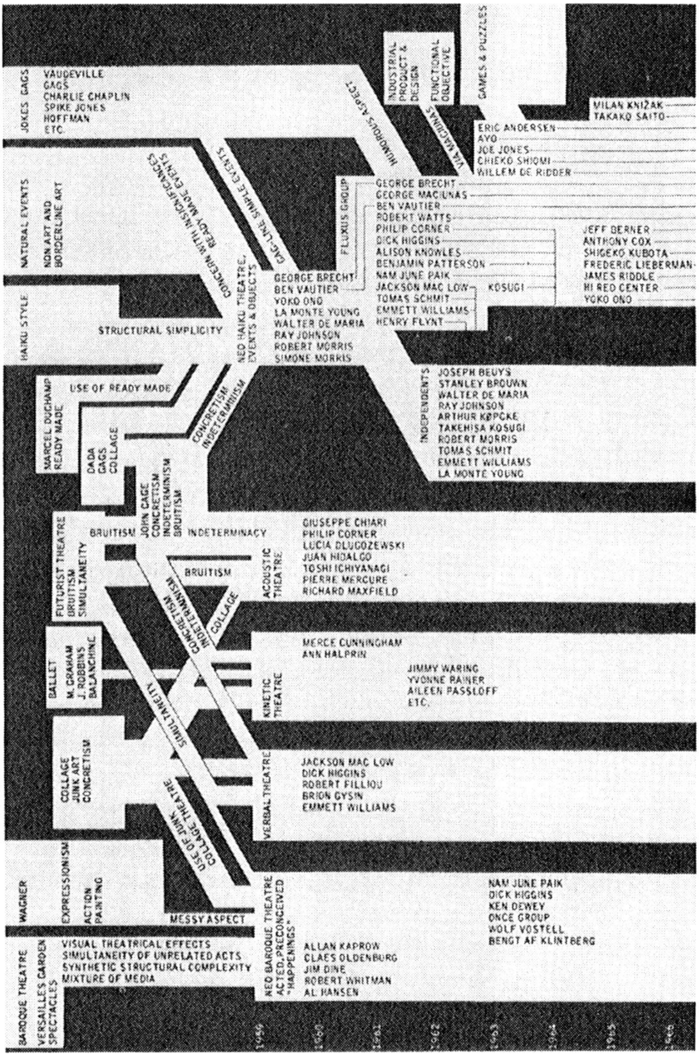

29 George Maciunas, "Fluxus (Its Historical Development and Relationship to Avant-Garde Movements)," 1967; text and design by George Maciunas. Offset on paper, 17⅜ × 6 in. Courtesy of the Gilbert and Lila Silverman Fluxus Collection, Detroit.

In its time lines and historical charts, Maciunas's diagram records the survival of the fittest: the historical avant-garde and other pop cultural elements such as vaudeville endure. Yet as Stephen Jay Gould eloquently notes in *Full House,* the linear graphics characteristic of evolutionists' charts make variations within trends virtually unrepresentable, as the abrupt terminations in Maciunas's evolutionist chart illustrate.[26] Given the technical limitations of the linear chart, it is not surprising that it fails to represent the subsequent participation of all of the eliminated artists in later Fluxus performances and publications. That the excluded artists continued to work with other Fluxus artists, including Maciunas, suggests the impossibility of Maciunas's purging Fluxus so as to reshape it on the model of the historical avant-garde, for Maciunas never had the power to permanently expel anyone or to restructure Fluxus. Thus, although his graph is misleading as a snapshot of Fluxus and of the artists actually working in the group, it does indicate Maciunas's own ideological position and Fluxus's uneven adherence to the avant-garde model.

For those who define Fluxus in relation to Maciunas, his activist vision, his causal conception of the relation between the historical and the contemporary avant-garde, and his ability to define that relationship for any given member in a sense "determine" Fluxus membership. This diagram, therefore, graphically presents Fluxus to the world as a historically validated form of avant-garde activism that is consistent with Maciunas's own view of the historical avant-garde. It also justifies Maciunas's historical paradigm for or definition of Fluxus, which continues to prevail in American exhibitions and catalogues. According to this model, the objects in the Fluxkits, many of them designed by Maciunas according to the artists' specifications, merely negate the costly paintings and gallery distribution system that sells them. From the perspective of a methodology that describes art in terms of left-leaning politics, the objects and performances of Fluxus affirm the avant-gardism associated with that political framework.

For this reason the question "Is Fluxus a neo-avant-garde?" is usually answered in the affirmative, with the "Purge Manifesto" and Maciunas's historical diagram cited as evidence of the dadaism of Fluxus and its apparent attack on existing attitudes about art. But the answer should be yes *and* no, depending both on what the avant-garde is or has been and on which Fluxus artist is considered.

For some theorists, the avant-garde is a utopian space of hopefulness within the modernist project, one where critical attention is paid to the aims of universal justice and equality, moral progress and happiness.[27] Thus Matei Calinescu described the origin of the avant-garde in "romantic utopianism with its messianic fervor," which was then "follow[ing] a course of development essentially similar to that of the older and more comprehensive idea of modernity."[28] Insofar as the multiplicity of Fluxus exemplifies the Enlightenment ideals of democracy and pluralism, self-expression and mutual tolerance, and the significance of objective research (information) and subjective response (experience), Fluxus can certainly be described as avant-garde.

However, Calinescu describes the historical avant-garde in terms that fit only the part of Fluxus called its common front. Both the avant-garde and modernism

> rest originally on the same linear and irreversible concept of time and, as a consequence, are faced with all the insoluble dilemmas and incompatibilities involved in such a time concept. . . . Less flexible and less tolerant of nuances, it [the avant-garde] is naturally more dogmatic—both in the sense of self-assertion and, conversely, in the sense of self-destruction.[29]

Dogmatism, ideological self-assertion, intolerance of nuances, occasional purges, and a linear time line all belong to Fluxus; again, this means that it can properly be described as avant-garde, or neo-avant-garde. But only in part. The rubric "neo-dada," often attached to Fluxus, proceeds from the common front definition as constructed by Maciunas. The apparent clarity of the familiar term *avant-garde* has led to the widespread acceptance of this historicist model of Fluxus. Indeed, metonymically Fluxus has been dismissed (or supported) as just so much harking back to (or affirming of) the historical avant-garde.[30]

At the other extreme are theories that argue for the autonomy of the avant-garde, with its effectiveness directly proportional to its refusal of worldly commitments. Clearly, Fluxus cannot be validated as avant-garde by reason of autonomy. Both in controversies like those of the Stockhausen concert and newsletter number 7 and in the social and experiential connections made by the works themselves, Fluxus is deeply committed to the world.

The most-often-cited theorists of the avant-garde, Renato Poggioli and Peter Bürger, disagree on whether the avant-garde is an institutional critique of the art world or of affirmative culture more generally. Both, however, conceive of the avant-garde as activist. According to Poggioli, it is "a movement . . . constituted primarily to obtain a positive result, for a concrete end. The ultimate hope is naturally the success of the specific movement, or on a higher, broader level, the affirmation of the avant-garde spirit in all cultural fields. . . . We shall define it as *activism* or the *activist moment.*"[31] And in Bürger's formulation, "With the historical avant-garde movements, the social subsystem that is art enters the stage of self-criticism."[32] For both Poggioli and Bürger, the historical avant-garde was a broad-based critique of culture aiming at its transformation and therefore committed to some form of political activism.

Neither the humanist nor the activist definition of avant-garde activity, however, is suited to the deeply ambiguous social and ideological structure of Fluxus as evinced in the Stockhausen and newsletter controversies and in Brecht's statement that "there has never been any attempt [in Fluxus] to agree on aims and methods." Indeed, both definitions, on their own, can be criticized as overly narrow on several fronts.[33] If, in the end, Fluxus is ambiguous in its relation to the avant-garde, a new framework, one that can accommodate the avant-garde *and* the experiential nature of Fluxus, needs to be proposed for exploring the movement more holistically. This would counteract the approach critics have taken in the past, looking at Fluxus as either a neo-avant-garde footnote to the historical heroic avant-garde or as mere chaos: an empty, angry tirade or merely a corny, anti-art joke. Such responses constitute a failure of imagination, one that explains in part the obscurity of Fluxus.[34]

Another return to the early history of Fluxus can help us further establish the nature of Fluxus experiences, thus permitting a shift from the negative dialectics common to all but one of the theories of the avant-garde presented thus far. It may be possible to retrieve from this experiential framework something besides mere reactive strategies, something more coherent and life affirming. Yet in this we take a risk: by refusing to apply established art theories to our subject, we lose a certain sense of control over aesthetic experience and the artistic process, potentially becoming mere masters of crazy wisdom. That is a necessary risk, however, if we are to awaken to the full aesthetic dimension of Fluxus.[35]

Something Unnameable

> [We must] open our eyes and ears each day seeing life as excellent as it is. . . . To accept whatever comes regardless of the consequences, is to be unafraid or to be full of that love which comes from a sense of at-oneness with whatever.
>
> —John Cage, *A Year from Monday*, 1967

George Brecht's statement at the beginning of this chapter that the connection between Fluxus artists "is something unnameable" reflects a desire to keep Fluxus open to discussion, to describe Fluxus in terms of what *is* happening rather than what *has* happened, and to free it of the material and conceptual bondage of systematic analysis. The decision to keep the matter open to discussion, to not name it, resonates strongly with Cage's instruction "to accept whatever comes."

Cage's admonition also goes some way toward explaining the empirical basis of much Fluxus work. He certainly had a strong influence on several Fluxus artists, offering them a philosophical direction that corresponds closely to the experiential framework of the Event and the Fluxkit.

As unfashionable as this empirical character may be now in academic circles, Cage's exhortation "to open up our eyes and ears each day" nevertheless has its philosophical proponents. Cage was a student of the famous lay theologian of Zen Buddhism Daisetz Teitaro Suzuki, whose many books include the influential *Essays in Buddhism* and *Living by Zen.*[36] Cage studied informally with Suzuki at Columbia University and elsewhere in the late 1940s and early 1950s, where Suzuki "settled on the seventh floor of Philosophy Hall, under the watchful eye of a framed photograph of the American pragmatist philosopher John Dewey."[37] Both American pragmatism and Zen Buddhism are radically empiricist, based in the principles of direct sensory perception of everyday life and the sense of connectedness to the world that results, and in a commitment to attaining that sense of connectedness by using what is at hand.

The same empiricism and pragmatism lie at the core of many Fluxus Events, as in the examples shown in Figure 30. Mieko Shiomi's *Wind Music* (1963) is typical:[38]

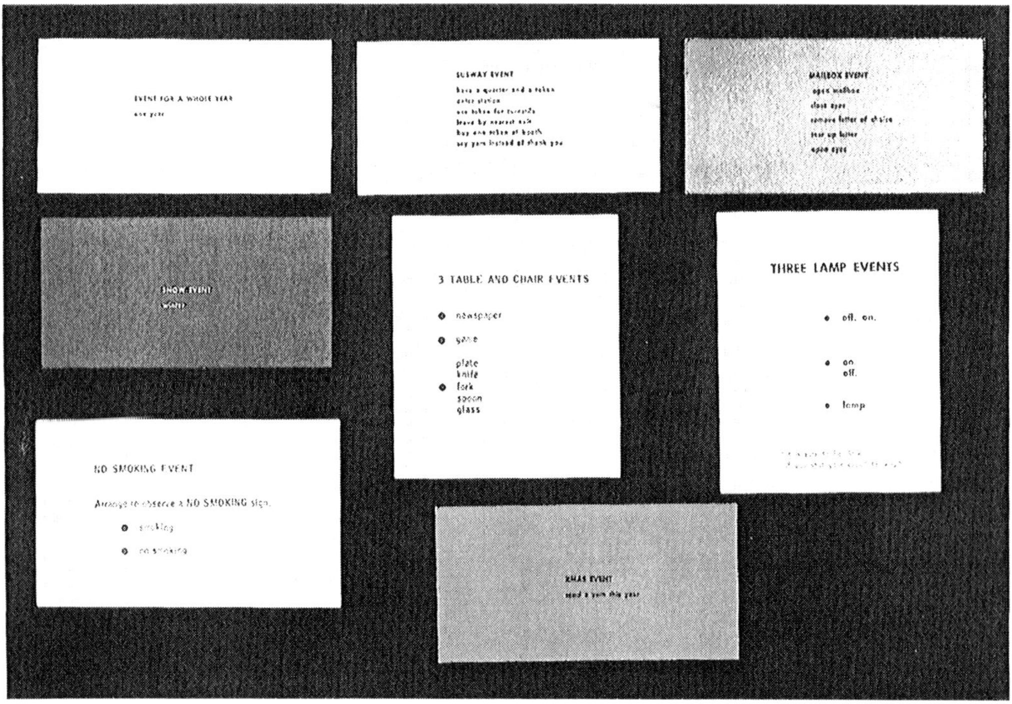

30 George Brecht and Robert Watts, Event score cards; dates vary. Offset on paper; sizes vary. Courtesy of the Library, Getty Research Institute, Los Angeles.

1. Raise Wind.

2. Be Blown by wind.

3. Wind at the beach, wind in the street, wind passing by a car.

Typhoon.

Or Ken Friedman's *Fruit Sonata* (1963), which instructs merely "Play baseball with fruit," the result being a pulverized fruit mash that makes for good, messy fun—and may be a good thing to do with bad fruit. Brecht's *No Smoking Event* likewise calls simply for the audience to observe a No Smoking sign (Fig. 31). Finally, Robert Watts's *Two Inches* (1963), which instructs, "A two-inch ribbon is stretched across the stage or street and then cut," has a result that is both visually beautiful, based in everyday materials and natural happenstance, and multisensory (Fig. 32).

None of these works necessarily involves an audience. Each, through use of readily available materials—wind, fruit, ribbon, scissors—creates sensory awareness of both the materials themselves and the situation. The results can be quite beautiful: The wind passes around the performer, and the ribbon curls gracefully to the ground, gently gliding on unseen air currents. The fruit piece, in contrast, has a certain situational humor.

Cage described his work in terms appropriate to these Events, as well as to Suzuki's teaching: "Each moment presents what happens, everything is present in the foreground."[39] And in the final sentence of his influential essay collection *Silence* (1961), he writes: "It behooves us to see each thing directly as it is, be it the sound of a tin whistle or the elegant [mushroom] *Lepiota procera.*"[40] To experience "each thing directly" means to forgo all systems of objective and subjective analysis, to become sensitized to the world and to unmediated experience.

Cage's notorious silence should be understood primarily as a product of this Zen availability to experience. More specifically, that silence functions as a space for primary experience within the normally "filled" space of music. One well-known story in particular supports this interpretation. In 1952, Cage entered the anechoic chamber at Harvard University, a room as free of reverberations and outside sound as was possible at the time (99.8 percent). It would allow Cage to experience absolute silence, a quality with which he had already experimented extensively in several works, including *Sonatas and Interludes* (1946–48), *A Flower* (1950), *Two*

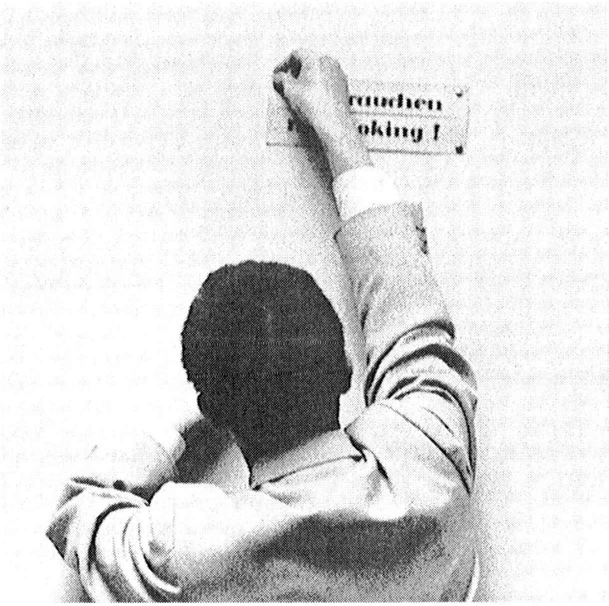

31 George Brecht, *No Smoking Event,* 1962. Performed by Nam June Paik at the Concert Partitur, Wiesbaden, Germany. Photo by George Maciunas; courtesy of the Gilbert and Lila Silverman Fluxus Collection, Detroit.

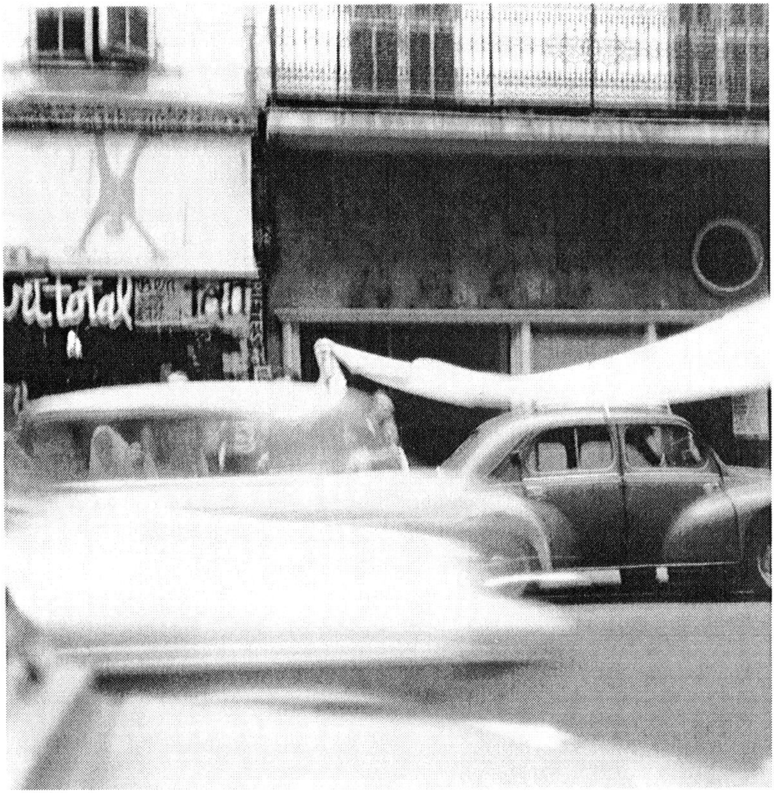

32 Robert Watts, *Two Inches,* Nice, France, 1963. Ben Vautier's shop is in the background. Photo by George Maciunas; courtesy of the Gilbert and Lila Silverman Fluxus Collection, Detroit.

Pastorales (1951), and *Imaginary Landscape #4* (1951). Expecting to hear pure silence, instead Cage "heard two sounds, one high and one low. When I described them to the engineer in charge, he informed me that the high sound was my nervous system in operation, the low one my blood in circulation. Until I die there will be sounds. And they will continue following my death. One need not fear about the future of music."[41] In other words, since there is no silence, there is no pure music (pauses are full of sound, and sound consists of intervals). Indeed, the ambient sounds of the environment themselves constitute music: music is all around. Cage wrote his notorious *4′33″*, a piece in three silent movements, in 1952 following the anechoic chamber experience. For the duration of the piece (specified in the title), no sound is played or projected into the performance space. As virtually every scholar of Cage to date has noted, this composition can be understood as allowing ambient sounds in the environment of the listener to be heard as music.

For Cage, direct perception meant depersonalizing the composer's work, such that sound itself became unmediated in the extreme. The expressive interpretation of musicality by a performer or composer was unacceptable—hence his criticism of Stockhausen's continued investment in the tonal structure of Western music. As he put it in his famous "Lecture on Nothing," "I have nothing to say and I'm saying it and that is poetry as I need it. This space of time is organized. We need not fear these silences,—we may love them."[42] And elsewhere: "I don't want it [my music] to mean anything. I want it to be.... No thing in life requires a symbol, since it is clearly what it is."[43] These were the ideas he offered his 1958–59 class on experimental composition, which included Brecht, Kaprow, Hansen, Higgins, Mac Low, and Florence Tarlow.

Graphic representation of this experimental freedom could take many forms, depending on each participant's personal vision. One well-known attempt is the circular "Intermedia Chart" by Dick Higgins (1995; Fig. 33). His diagram is dynamic in that it differentiates between types of work without an evaluative schema of "fittest" forms. As this model shows, human experience is diverse, resulting in diverse work and therefore productive of the as yet unknown.

Higgins's chart depicts intersections between Fluxus and other artistic efforts as overlapping circles that appear to expand and contract in relation to the "Intermedia" framework that encompasses them. It is an open framework that invites play. Its bubbles hover in space, rejecting an art/anti-art historical framework

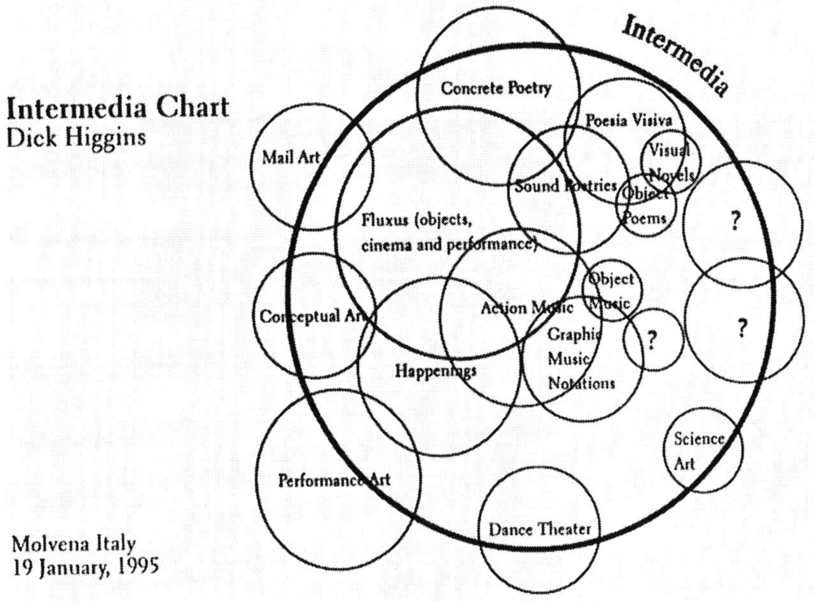

33 Dick Higgins, "Intermedia Chart," 1995. Postcard, 5 × 7 in. Courtesy of the Estate of Dick Higgins.

such as Maciunas used in his time line (see Fig. 29). The circles in a sense embrace the social formations and artistic experiments of various groups of culture makers that evolved out of the Cage class and other related efforts.

In its fluidity, the "Intermedia Chart" accommodates a wide range of individual experiences of historical circumstances: the 1959–60 New York Audiovisual Group formed by Al Hansen and Dick Higgins; Mac Low and LaMonte Young's extension of the experimental musical notations magazine *Beatitude East* as a self-published book, *An Anthology,* in 1961; the two 1961 performance series at Yoko Ono's loft in lower Manhattan and George Maciunas's AG Gallery on Madison Avenue—these all elaborated on the experiential formats associated with Brecht's Events and the Cage class generally and appear on the chart in that overlap between the Fluxus circle and action music, concrete and sound poetry, mail art, Happenings, conceptual art, and so forth. Each participant would have a different view of how these circles overlapped, while the circles containing question marks seem to invite consideration of additional relationships.

As I described in Chapter 1, European Fluxus was similarly open to the possibilities of the movement (even before its official naming by George Maciunas in 1962). In addition to the fertile Cologne context, which by 1961 was the site of collaborative efforts by Fluxus artists Wolf Vostell, Benjamin Patterson, and Nam June Paik and which that same year saw the performance of Brecht's pieces by Cage and David Tudor at the atelier of Mary Bauermeister (see Fig. 8), Wuppertal hosted the first Fluxus-titled exhibition at the Galerie Parnass in 1962 and was home to the Verlag Kalender/Ebeling and Dietrich, which produced *Kalenderrolle* numbers 1 and 2 (rolled texts, as opposed to folios, containing experimental poetry, music, and visual art) in November 1961 and June 1962, respectively. These productions, which are represented as concrete, sound, and visual poetry on the chart, brought together an international assortment of Fluxus artists, including Paik, Patterson, Dieter Roth, Emmett Williams, and LaMonte Young, each of whom would have a unique place in concrete poetry, graphic music notation, action music, and Happenings. Clearly, any one artist or group of artists might inhabit many circles to varying degrees, representing a diversity almost unrepresentable on the teleological time line suggested by Maciunas.

Intermedia

Given the flexible nature of Fluxus, it should come as no surprise that Fluxus artists have continued to work together for over forty years, exploring a broad constellation of expressive modes.[44] Among these, print was of particular importance. In 1964 Dick Higgins, exasperated by Maciunas's delays in issuing a collection of texts, *Jefferson's Birthday,* founded a publishing house which he called the Something Else Press (SEP).[45] That press published many books by Fluxus artists as well as an inexpensive series of pamphlets under the Great Bear imprint, widely available in art book shops, galleries, and grocery stores, and through the mail. In 1966, in the first newsletter for this press, the term *intermedia,* the ostensible subject of the "Intermedia Chart," first surfaced in a new context.

Dick Higgins borrowed the idea from Samuel Coleridge (1812), for whom it meant "in the field between the general idea of art media and those of life media" and "between media"—in other words, a dynamic interstitial space between media forms and between art and life structures.[46] Rather than merely multiplying existing media categories, like multimedia (as in opera, which discretely combines theater with music and dance) or mixed media (as in illustrated stories, presenting complementary images and words), intermedia actively probes the spaces between the different media. (The term, an appropriate one for understanding Fluxus, has since spread into common art parlance and changed meaning, becoming associated with hi-tech art.)

Consider, for example, Robert Watts's Event *F/H Trace,* which takes classical music and turns it on its head, poking fun at high-minded musicians (Fig. 34). During a bow—which *is* the piece, rather than coming at the end of the piece—Ping-Pong balls fall out of a horn. By this simple means, *F/H Trace* crosses over from music into games of chance; reflections of childhood, in the high-pitched, happy sounds of balls hitting the floor; and (of course) vaudeville humor. And yet the work is formally pared down, such that no single element is extricable from the rest.

The *2nd Gatha* (1961), by Jackson Mac Low (see Fig. 6), subjects words to a pictorial logic as the eye traces letters in many directions over the page. Coursing in multiple directions, the visual and linguistic parts do not separate neatly; rather,

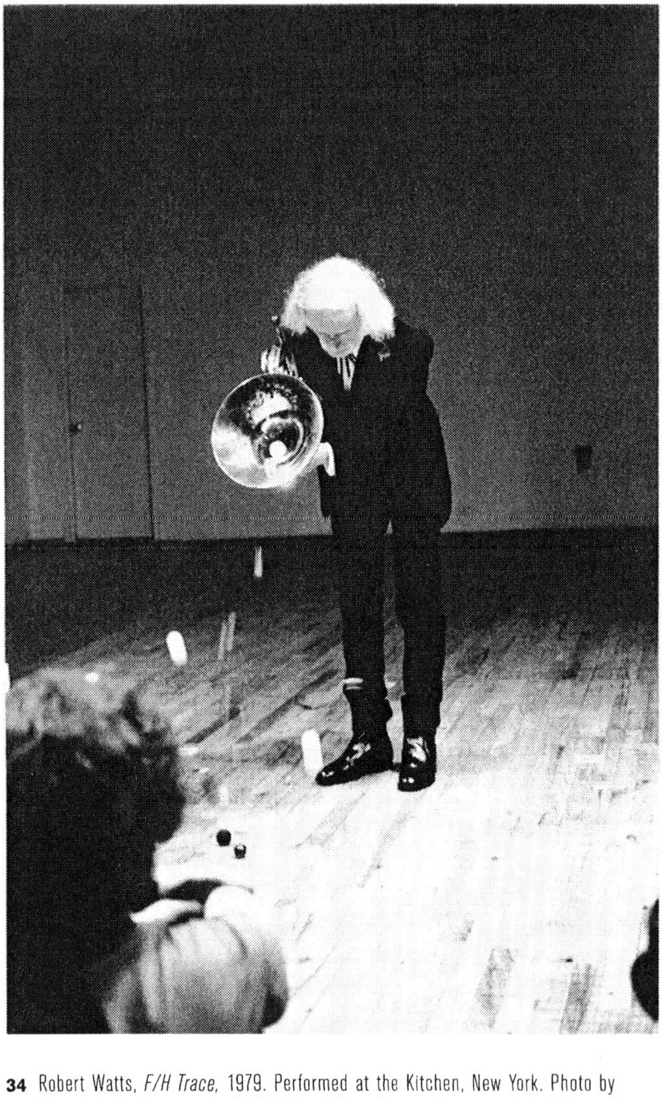

34 Robert Watts, *F/H Trace,* 1979. Performed at the Kitchen, New York. Photo by Manuel A. Rodriguez; © 1988 Robert Watts Estate. Courtesy of the Robert Watts Studio Archive, New York.

the visual poem functions as an intermedium between image and text. The effect is even more pronounced when the written text is transformed into sound: invigorated by speech and spontaneous performance decisions, the *Gathas* operate between art media (image and text) as well as between art and life media (image-text and improvisational utterance).

George Brecht's *Word Event* (1961; Fig. 35) is typical of Fluxus intermedia art:

> WORD EVENT
>
> Exit.
>
> 1961

Realizations range from looking at an exit sign or acting on it, to having a performative or theatrical relation with others observing the sign, to using this piece as a means by which the artists might leave a performance.

Another example of intermedia is Fluxus artist Emmett Williams's *Alphabet Symphony*, where each letter of the alphabet is a prompt, such that *j* stands for "smoke a joint," which the performer reads and then enacts, documenting the performance in a series of photographs. The photograph intermediates between a live performance, static portraits, and a range of twenty-six life activities. While scripted as text, the *Alphabet Symphony* generates sound experiences (of the lighter, the inhalation), thus intermediating also between text and music. The work's intermedialism resides in the fact that no one mode is causally independent of the others: there is no sound without the text, no document without the performance.

As these examples suggest, *intermedia* is an unstable descriptive term, predicated as it is on the dynamic exchange between traditionally distinct artistic and life categories. This elastic quality does not, however, render the term vague. On the contrary, like a mathematical expression, it is extraordinarily precise, for it relies on structurally codependent relationships. "Intermedia" art, then, is not so much a thing as a function, allowing for almost limitless artistic formations and experiences.

The intermedia function, by paring down existing fine-art categories that developed within specific political and philosophical contexts, interacts with numerous philosophical, discursive, and political traits. The Norwegian art historian Ina Blom

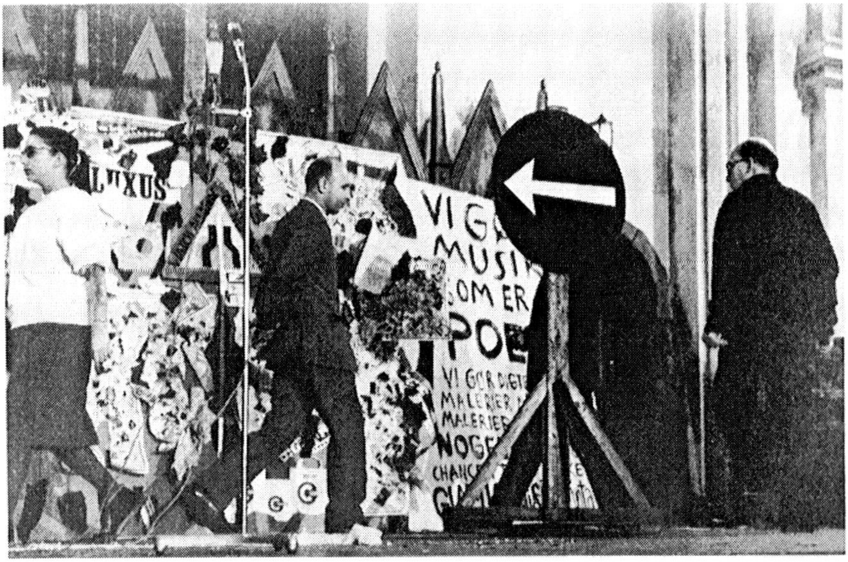

35 George Brecht, *Word Event* (*Exit*) or *Direction,* Nikolai Church, Copenhagen, 1962. The two men shown are Eric Andersen and Emmett Williams. Photo by Sisse Jarner; courtesy of Eric Andersen.

has called this range of effects the "intermedia dynamic."[47] Significantly, even though secondary systems of knowledge (art, music, poetry, theater) contribute to the intermedia function, it is the life media (spontaneous decisions, the relationship to the environment, and the physical parameters within which the work occurs) that keep it always within the primary informational, or experiential, modality. As Higgins put it in his essay introducing the term,

> Much of the best work being produced today seems to fall between media. This is no accident. The concept of the separation between media arose in the Renaissance. The idea that a painting is made of paint on canvas or that a sculpture could not be painted seems characteristic of the kind of social thought—categorizing and dividing society into nobility with its various subdivisions, untitled gentry, artisans, serfs and landless workers—which we call the feudal conception of the Great Chain of Being. . . . However, the social problems that characterize our time, as opposed to the political ones, no longer allow a compartmentalized approach. . . . Thus the Happening developed as an intermedium, an uncharted land that lies between collage, music and theatre. It is not governed by rules; each work determines its own form and medium according to its needs.[48]

In some ways, this passage is tinged with the same causality and idealism as Maciunas's linear model. However, the revolutionary, class-based activism of both the historical avant-garde and Maciunas's protests is ill matched to the organic mode described here. The activist formula, in which dominant culture is the enemy, participates in an old order or "Great Chain of Being." Intermedia experience, in contrast, looks to a new world system, where strict categories and causalities are unclear—or even "absolutely irrelevant."

A 1962 graphic by Higgins, "Essay on LaMonte Young" (Fig. 36), is a good example of the weakening of categorization and causality. The top half depicts the philosophical roots—ones consistent with experience and pragmatism—of LaMonte Young's music, much of which explores the effects of space on tonal sound via compression and expansion, and extreme (dayslong) durations of sounds. In the center we find the "elegant empiricists" Kant and Hegel, Bakunin and Durutti, with nature (atomic power, sun and soil, grass, cow, and ghee; ocean and fish) on the left and Rousseauism and Early Transcendentalism (Emerson, Thoreau, Nansen,

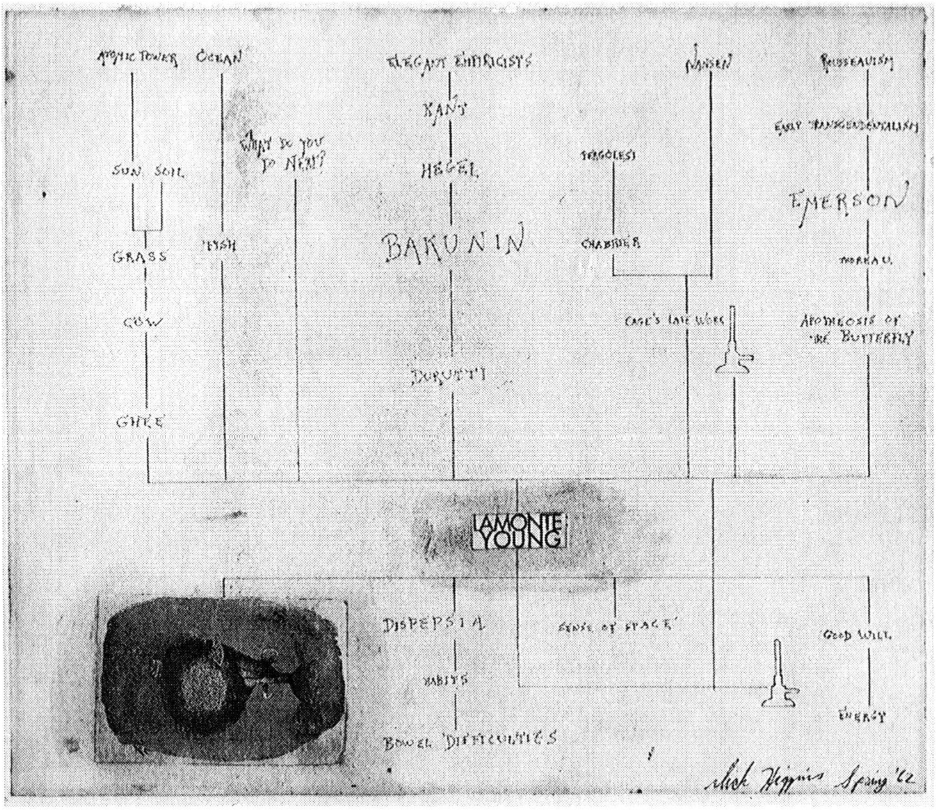

36 Dick Higgins, "Essay on LaMonte Young," 1962. Collage, 18 × 21 in. Photo by Brad Iverson; courtesy of the Gilbert and Lila Silverman Fluxus Collection, Detroit.

Pergolesi, Chabrier, late Cage, and the Apotheosis of the Butterfly) on the right. At the bottom, however, words signifying nature and philosophical attention to nature become a picture of a blowfish, primary physical states (dyspepsia, habits, and bowel difficulties), and abstractions (sense of space, good will, and energy). In this chart, the philosophical traditions that pass through the artist (here, Young, but the same applies to virtually all Fluxus artists) are transformed into primary experiences spatially conceived and combined in Fluxus intermedia work.

The constructive (as opposed to deconstructive) thrust of the intermedia function is underscored in its projection toward a new synthesis. "The importance of efficiency of [Higgins's] Intermedia essay," writes Blom regarding its effect, "did not reside in its actual argumentation or description, but in its character as an affirmative, its positive naming of a principle and an attitude."[49] That affirmative aspect of intermedialism gained rapid acceptance.[50] By 1967, a year after Higgins revived the term, Franconia College in New Hampshire had initiated its Intermedia Program, which included a day of performances featuring Fluxus regulars Dick Higgins, Alison Knowles, and Philip Corner and sometime participants Carolee Schneemann and James Tenney.[51] Also in 1967, the New York State Council on the Arts offered grants for an Intermedia Festival;[52] Schneemann received one, though no core Fluxus artists qualified.[53] The term first appeared in the popular press early in 1968 in *Newsweek:* "There is an artform that fits no conventional category. It is neither painting nor sculpture, film nor drama. It might be called intermedia."[54]

Thus, intermedia work reverberates with multiple systems of thought, even as it is structured to privilege primary experience. In this regard intermedial work in general, like the Event in particular, is not unique, since all art is both material and communicative. Every artwork contains both primary and secondary aspects.

For the historian, what is at issue is the degree to which a given form of experience—primary or secondary—can be manifested. The majority of Fluxkits and Events have an intermedial structure and also trigger primary experiences. Interpretations of this work, then, which necessarily depend on secondary structures of knowledge, may be called right or wrong only in the degree to which they retain a connection to the work's basis in direct perception. Interpretations that rely exclusively on any one discursive mechanism (such as calling a work merely anti-art) will be more "wrong," in this sense, than elastic analyses. For example, Brecht's *Keyhole Event* (see Fig. 1) might be placed variously between text and image, theater and image or text, all three of these and life—each of these a far more accurate approach than calling it simply "anti-art." Similarly, when Emmett Williams, in Copenhagen in 1962, ate peanuts for an hour while others performed scored Events around him, that was an action not only between life and performance, but also between the mundane body and self-conscious artist: he was hungry and happened to be performing live. Higgins's chart allows for these experiential passages as the floating bubbles overlap, intersect, pass over *and through* each other. The point is to enjoy the possibilities, not to hammer them down.

Yet most people, critics and supporters alike, tend to favor the ideologically narrow, linear model of Fluxus associated with Maciunas's time line, ignoring the thrust toward experience that I consider the defining aspect of Fluxkits and Events. Although this interpretation is not entirely incorrect, subjection of all of Fluxus to this framework violates the integrity of the artists and their work.

The fact that dialogue about Maciunas's version of Fluxus was not limited, through newsletters or flyers, to the group itself only furthers this violation. Publicly, Maciunas propagated his ideas through demonstrations and even magazine advertisements in which he aligned the name Fluxus with the avant-garde anti-art rhetoric of no skill requirements and revolutionary iconoclasm.[55] As self-appointed spokesperson for the group, Maciunas was able to push his common front line quite effectively: "Maciunas' proclaimed anti-art stance and his insistence on 'art nihilism' enabled him to engage in the very serious struggle of discrediting the meaning-filled art object and of championing the action-oriented events, performances, and publications that were being produced as Fluxus."[56] Even today, anti-art, art nihilism and "discrediting the meaning-filled art object" remain the defining terms for critics, despite the testimonials and work of the participating artists themselves. Comparison of early and recent criticism indicates that the anti-institutional antics applauded today only frustrated critics in the 1960s. That sensibility, though shared by some Fluxus artists, is far from universal, in part because it excludes the movement's radically materialist component and hands-on aspect.

Although contemporary theory, which tends increasingly to explore sophisticated extra-artistic avenues, has furthered self-awareness within the discipline of art history, it does little to enhance artistic experience itself. Thomas Crow states the problem in *The Intelligence of Art:*

> The highly technical theories of language and signification deployed by the enthusiastic convert are not subject to modification in the course of his or her work; this particular vocabulary of paraphrase cannot be remade by the art historian's particular use of it—which is another way of saying that the *work of art itself has no independent claim or comeback against the mode of explanation made of it. . . .* The power, they would be right to observe, is all on one side.[57]

Given that art objects are the physical result of human experience being subjected to an aesthetic process, they embody human paradoxes: there is "a gap, a zero point, or a disruptive substitution taking place inside a work of art from which issues a continual turning over or transformation of its defining elements."[58] Since any one time or place is unique, the internal logic of great art is likewise unique, informed as it is not merely by the established discourses that seem to circumscribe it, but more importantly by artists' critical engagements with these discursive fields and their own life experiences, which may not be contained within existing knowledge structures. Artistic intelligence cannot be mapped onto any preexisting model of the mind, of human culture, or even of art history. Artistic intelligence, rather, must engage in a "continual turning over" of its own premises as these interact with life lived.[59]

This process enables one to think about art (or more specifically, Fluxus) not as conflicted, but as motivated by a process of transformation, or flux. The various models for diagramming Fluxus, for example, favored variously by different members of the group, seem on their surface irreconcilable. Yet no one model is entirely right or wrong. Rather, each is better or worse suited to the experience of Fluxus by more or fewer artists or viewers. This apparent illogic constitutes one aspect of Fluxus's artistic intelligence. Fluxus transforms the avant-garde (as institutional critique, as iconoclasm) to become, in part, its opposite: aesthetic experience. In Crow's terms, the avant-garde and the experiential take a cyclical turn, with the iconoclastic being exchanged for the experiential.

Historically, however, descriptions of Fluxus have focused on its avant-garde dimension, thus limiting its broader value and isolating it from other, overlapping, movements of the 1960s. As a result, Fluxus has been largely written out of the history of its times. This willful neglect continues today. Yet the experiential dimension and intermedia function of Fluxus have influenced other fine-art movements, such as Happenings, pop art, and conceptual art, as Chapter 3 will demonstrate.

EXPERIENCE IN CONTEXT

Fluxus, Happenings, Conceptual and Pop Art

3

Experience as Art

On 3 and 4 December 1976 in a storefront at 3 Mercer Street, Fluxus artist Geoffrey Hendricks staged a two-day performance and installation construction involving body hair removal and labeling (Fig. 37). The piece was called *Unfinished Business: Education of the Boy Child* and included the artist's eight-year-old son, Bracken Hendricks.

The work stemmed in part from a conversation Hendricks had had some months earlier with the mail artist Ray Johnson about removing his then legendary chest-length beard. By coincidence, the day after that conversation Johnson received a beard in the mail from a student at the Rhode Island School of Design, Scott Mednick. Johnson forwarded the beard, which was to serve as a means of identifying each other if the two men were to meet (though of course that function was now destroyed), to Hendricks.

The first day of the public performance featured a range of educational activities. Dick Higgins taught

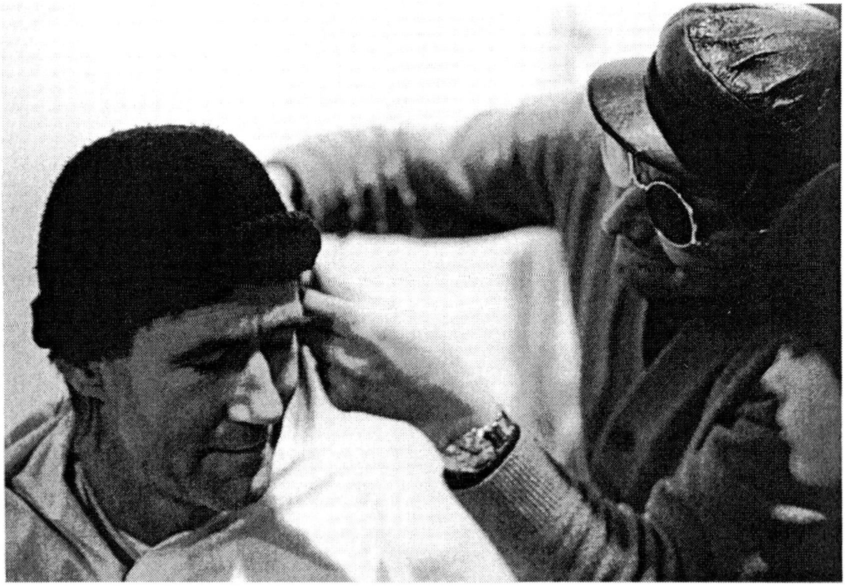

37 Geoffrey Hendricks, *Unfinished Business: Education of a Boy Child*, 1976. Performed 3–4 December at 3 Mercer Street, New York City. Here, George Maciunas cuts Geoffrey Hendricks's hair; "the Boy," Bracken Hendricks, looks on from far right. Photo by Robert Wickendon; courtesy of the artist.

Bracken—"the boy child"—a song; Geoffrey, Bracken, and the now beardless Scott Mednick cut wood, made instruments, and bundled sticks in the window; and the Boy learned how to make a woodcut print.[1] The second day saw the ceremonial shaving of the beard. The Boy gathered signatures and locks of hair (for which a lock of beard could be had in exchange) from people in the audience. The hair, properly labeled, was tied to Hendricks's chair. After the beard was removed, he shaved. George Maciunas then gave him a haircut (see Fig. 37), putting Ray Johnson's signature black knit cap on his head and cutting around it. The result was a pageboy cut.

This performance work had roots in a variety of connected movements: Happenings, Fluxus Events, conceptual (language) art, and art environments. It was, equally, an experience in the life of Bracken: his "education" as initiator of a public exchange and as attendant to his father is played out literally (not just symbolically). The experience is simultaneously art- and nonart-based, for him and for all the participants.

In *John Dewey and the Lessons of Art,* Philip Jackson argues that to experience *as art* is not the same as having an artificial experience; art, after all, is itself a form of reality.[2] The artist is simply selecting elements from the world and putting them together in singular ways to enhance experience. As the Fluxus artist Philip Corner put it in December 1992, responding to a request for materials from *The Seoul of Fluxus* (Korea): "Why waste time and effort trying to nail down Fluxus?... Fluxus is a piece of reality (sitting silently throwing pieces-of-reality to the audience)."[3] Thus the audience experiences chosen bits of reality as art, liberated from both the expectations of normative artistic practice and the weight of expository mechanisms.

Despite its empirical character and reputation to the contrary, Fluxus is better served by an "art for art's sake" attitude than by viewing it as a "cipher" standing for something else. With few exceptions, Fluxus works have no specific communicative purpose, nor, unlike pop and conceptual art, are they informed by a particular conceptual system. Indeed, it is when Fluxus experiences are subjected to systematic interpretive methodologies that the greatest distortions in the project and group dynamic immediately appear. Rather, the meaning of Fluxus experiences lies in their simultaneous engagement with and withdrawal from everyday life, in their substitution of art and anti-art with life (as art).

John Dewey wrote that art "enables us *to forget ourselves by finding ourselves* in the delight of experiencing the world about us in its varied qualities and forms."[4] Fluxus is well suited to this model. In the words of Henry Martin, Fluxus "seems to affirm our existence as autonomous minds or conscious perceivers, while yet refusing us to indulge our sense of ego."[5]

Fluxus experiences sensitize the perceiver to the life world by creating a special place—called art—for the sensitization to occur. Thus, even though reality is experienced as art and vice versa, the two remain distinct. A rubber ball, for example, may be art at one location, but not at another. Without the designation *art,* that rubber ball—Corner's "piece-of-reality"—would probably not be considered noteworthy.

Yet with each attempt to pin the distinctions down, the boundaries shift. This situation is not unique to Fluxus. Pop art, for example, has an experiential aspect that academic analysis has virtually ignored, instead continuing to interpret the art as a cipher—a secret or disguised form of symbolization—for a system outside itself.[6] The same can be said of the reception of conceptual art. It is time for the experiential mode to be reinjected into interpretation of the art of the 1960s, and in particular those movements with which Fluxus has had extensive contact.[7]

Fluxus, Fluxus, Everywhere

In 1989 the New York–based Emily Harvey Gallery announced a retrospective "Fluxus and Company" group show with this press release:

> Fluxus artists created new forms of art that are now major fields of practice. Henry Flynt named and pioneered concept art. Dick Higgins named and developed intermedia. Nam June Paik gave birth to video art. Fluxus composer La Monte Young developed the music on which the entire school of minimalist composition is based. Fluxus poets Jackson Mac Low and Emmett Williams created a vast body of work that has been the foundation for several forms of literature and art, including concrete poetry, sound poetry and poésie visive. . . . Performance art, artists' books, multiples and mail art were dramatically influenced by

artists such as Alison Knowles, George Brecht, Joseph Beuys, Ben Vautier and Jean Dupuy.[8]

With this statement, Fluxus is presented in relation to various better-known art movements, particularly ones of the 1960s and 1970s. As I will demonstrate in what follows, these other movements, like Fluxus, have tended to be seen not for their experiential value; rather, they have been described almost exclusively in the hypertextual terms attacked by Dissanayake (see Chapter 1) and Crow (see Chapter 2).

On Higgins's "Intermedia Chart" (see Fig. 33), the relationships between Fluxus and like-minded art movements are represented by overlapping circles, a graphic mode that does little, however, to demonstrate the precise nature of those relationships. One thing that can be said is that the connections are not based merely in stylistic influence. Rather, as or like reality, Fluxus work (like the community itself) is complex, structured on many levels: stylistic, experiential, sociohistorical, and ideological. Thus its relations to the "now major fields of practice" are likewise pluralistic.

In this chapter I offer a preliminary sketch of the complex relationships between Fluxus and three other major movements of the 1960s and 1970s: Happenings, conceptual art, and pop art. Unfortunately, space does not allow exploration of such offshoot movements as mail art, visual and sound poetry, video art, or minimalist composition vis-à-vis Fluxus. Those directions remain ripe for future investigation.

Happenings

As early as 1958, Kaprow explained how Happenings developed almost seamlessly from action painting:

> I developed a kind of action-collage technique, following my interest in [Jackson] Pollock. These action-collages, unlike my constructions, were done as rapidly as possible by grasping great hunks of varied matter: tinfoil, straw, canvas, photos, newspaper, etc.... Their placement in the ritual of my own rapid action was an acting-out of the drama of tin soldiers, stories and musical structures, that

> I once had tried to embody in paint alone. These parts projected further and further from the walls and into the room, and included more and more audible elements. . . . I immediately saw that every visitor to the environment was part of it. . . . I offered him more and more to do until there developed the Happening.[9]

A year later, Kaprow documented this lineage photographically by including pictures of Pollock painting in his *Assemblages, Environments, and Happenings.*[10]

In fact, the seed for this historical narrative was sown already in 1952, when Harold Rosenberg, in "The American Action Painters" in *Art News,* described the painter as a performer: "At a certain moment the canvas began to appear to one American painter after another as an arena in which to act—rather than as a space in which to reproduce, redesign, analyze or 'express' an object, actual or imagined. What was to go on the canvas was not a picture but an *event.*"[11] Action painters, noted Rosenberg, introduced the body into the work in real time and with concrete motions. The images they created can thus be read as physical traces of their movement over the canvas. Extraneous materials such as cigarette butts and incidental marks such as paint can lines and coffee stains remind the viewer of the artist's physical presence.

The critical mainstream strongly disagreed with Rosenberg. Clement Greenberg, for example, ridiculed Rosenberg's idea that the abstract expressionist gesture belonged to the "same reality [as] breathing and thumbprints, love affairs and wars."[12] Hilton Kramer attacked Rosenberg for looking to a theatrical model for painting: "painting being painting, and not the theater, what does he mean by 'an arena in which to act'?"[13]

For many artists, however, abstract expressionism did exactly what these critics said it did not: it was a sort of performance dedicated to exploring day-to-day reality. It is therefore possible to describe Kaprow's Happenings as the practical answer to Kramer's question, "what does he mean by 'an arena in which to act'?" They are precisely an "acting-out," a movement beyond the attempt "to embody in paint alone." The "action" of painting has been substituted with the actions of theater and then life.

In light of Kaprow's description of Happenings evolving naturally from abstract painting, it is not surprising that most art criticism from the period simply applied the evaluative terminology of action painting, with its individual, athletic gestures, to the group heroics of the Happening performance. A description of Happenings from 1965, for example, is typical: "the accent [is] still upon action—flashing neon lights, nude movies, optical effects, moving objects."[14] Action remained the definitive core value in art at the time.

There is not space here to consider Happenings in depth.[15] However, one detailed example is necessary to give an idea of their narrative action. For this, Kaprow's *Calling,* which took place on 21–22 August 1965 (the year of the above critic's comment) in New York City and at a farm in New Jersey, serves admirably. Kaprow describes the first day:

> On three different street corners in New York, a participant was waiting. . . . Each carried a paper bag which contained aluminum foil, muslin, and a ball of cord . . . at 4:30, cars stopped near each of them, and their names were called. They got into the cars. As they were driven randomly about the city . . . the three people were covered with aluminum foil. At 4:50 each car parked, all occupants except the foil-wrapped figure got out, the car was locked and a coin placed in the meter.

The cars drove to different locations, and were replaced by three other cars. After more shuffling and another transfer of passengers, "the three cars drove about the city until 5:45, when they were scheduled to deposit their wrapped passengers at Grand Central Station. . . . When the third package arrived, a large crowd had already gathered, and the other two participants had begun calling out each other's names." The participants then removed their wrappings and proceeded to phone booths, where they dialed the first drivers, who answered the phone only after fifty rings, said simply "Hello," and then hung up. The next day, in New Jersey, participants either wandered in the woods listening for voices and calling their co-participants' names or hung upside down in muslin bags from trees.

> For perhaps ten minutes the names of the five hanging people were the material for a random vocal symphony sounding from various locations and with various volumes and qualities. Finally the pauses in the calling grew longer and the voices stopped. The five people who had been stripped of their clothing still hung in their uncomfortable positions. After a moment, a sound was heard among the trees indicating that someone had begun to leave. The hanging people swung down, and everyone moved slowly and quietly out of the woods.[16]

Calling exemplifies the sequentially strict, action-oriented (and therefore narrative) nature of the Happening. Occurring only once, the Happening was logistically complex. Contrast this with the brevity and repeatability of the typical Event score.

At first glance, then, the Happening as a performance form seems not to represent a significant break with the reigning paradigm of artistic taste. It was enough like painterly action and narrative theater to be comprehensible to the general public. Hans Robert Jauss explains that such work, which succeeds immediately in its context, "can be characterized by an aesthetics of reception as... precisely fulfilling the expectations prescribed by a ruling standard. It satisfies the desire for the reproduction of the familiarly beautiful; confirms familiar sentiments; sanctions wishful notions; makes unusual experiences enjoyable as sensations; or even raises moral problems, but only to solve them in an edifying manner as predescribed questions."[17] Despite their apparent distance from the "ruling standard" of the painted canvas, in short, Happenings are "familiarly beautiful" because of their actionism, with its concomitant emphasis on narrative. They confirm, moreover, the "familiar sentiments" and "wishful notions" of American freedom and individualism while ignoring the more pressing problems of the day. This interpretation goes some way toward explaining the critical and popular success of Happenings as mass experience.

However, the account of Happenings as evolving largely from the action of action painting misses something essential (as Kaprow's eventual withdrawal from a clearly defined art practice indicates).[18] Jauss is helpful here as well: "The distance between the actual first perception of a work and its virtual significance, put another way, the resistance that the new work poses to the expectations of its first audience, can be so great that it requires a long process of reception to gather in that which was unexpected and unusable within the first horizon."[19]

Kaprow describes both Happenings and Fluxus art as "avant-garde lifelike art," as opposed to "avant-garde artlike art," a phrase that, in introducing the principle of lived experience, distances Happenings from the painterly standard. What did it feel like to hang upside down from a tree? Was the wrapped passenger afraid of suffocation or anonymous violence? Did the phone rings seem like an eternity? Was it frustrating to be hung up on? What does the title *Calling* refer to: the phone call, the calling in the woods, human communication, or the artist's calling or vocation? About this life-experiential dimension of Happenings Kaprow is explicit: "Despite formalist and idealist interpretations of art, lifelike art makers' principal dialogue is not with art but with everything else, one event suggesting another. If you don't know much about life, you'll miss much of the meaning of the lifelike art that's born of it."[20]

To put the thrust of interpretation behind the painterly origins of Happenings is to miss the "principal dialogue" of the art form, its conception in terms of "everything else." *Calling* was concerned with artistic activity, but only in part. It also summoned up the audience's experience of telephones, taxis, mass transportation, urban congestion, trees, voices, and being upside down. The neat characterization of Happenings as developing linearly from action painting thus fails to account for "everything else": experience beyond mere artistic reference.

Far from consisting of "individualistic" acts, participation performance (Kaprow's term) involves a range of experiences, since "participation in anything is often a question of motive and use."[21] The implications are clear: the vitality of various locations (the street, the woods, Grand Central Station), combined with a sense of art and experience from and in life, as well as the negotiated concordance with the artist, would generate both different and similar experiences for the participants. In Kaprow's words, "Their prior investments of time, energy and values were called into some (serious) question by what they did."[22]

By 1973 Kaprow was writing lucidly about the life-experiential basis of Happenings, in particular as they related to Events: "Nontheatrical performance does not begin with an envelope containing an act (the fantasy) and an audience (those affected by the fantasy). By the early 60s the more experimental Happenings and Fluxus events had eliminated not only actors, roles, plots, rehearsals, and repeats but also audiences, the single staging area, and the customary time block of an hour or so."[23] These similarities help to explain why some spectators saw little difference between a Fluxus concert and a Happening.[24] Actions in both performance types could be interpreted as painterly, or as an anti-art liberation *from* the painterly—or as neither. The full attention demanded by Fluxus Events and Happenings could then extend beyond those arenas, causing a simple walk in the woods to be enhanced by a new heightened awareness of every sight, every sound, every smell, taste, and texture.

A French artist associated with Happenings, Jean-Jacques Lebel, had brief contact with Fluxus in 1961–62 while visiting New York with the poet-critic Alain Jouffroy (who subsequently met Maciunas and was an organizer of the Paris Fluxus in 1962). There they met Kaprow, Higgins, and others associated with Happenings and Fluxus; held an exhibition at the March Gallery; participated in activities at Claes Oldenburg's Store; and gave a reading at the Living Theater[25]—a range of activities within a community that was later pried apart into the distinct, if overlapping, movements depicted in the "Intermedia Diagram." Lebel describes the links between Fluxus and Happenings thus:

> Anyone who recognizes the formidable libidinal, polytechnical, multidirectional and often "delayed-action" uprising of the Sixties and especially the people who lived this experience—can hardly be surprised [at seeing] Fluxus and Happenings grouped as a subject of a single manifestation. After all, Fluxus and Happenings were contemporaneous—Happenings surfacing only slightly earlier—and a good many artists swam happily in both of the currents of this great single stream. The difference, finally, if there is a difference, lies in their programmatic intentions.[26]

The "program" Lebel refers to here, of course, is the disputed activist political agenda associated with Maciunas.

In addition to possible (if disputed) "lifelike art" parallels between Happenings and Fluxus, several Fluxus artists have described a lineage similar to that cited by Kaprow as the basis for Happenings, with roots in abstract expressionism. In a 1957 essay titled "Chance Imagery," for example, George Brecht points to the power of the chance-oriented, or "natural," process of action painting. For Brecht, Pollock introduced the ordinary into art: "His paintings seem much less manifestations of one of a group of techniques for releasing the unconscious (as the Dada experiments seemed), than they do of a single, integrated use of chance as a means of unlocking the deepest possible grasp of nature in its broadest sense... and, to get away from the idea that an artist makes something 'special' and beyond the world of ordinary things."[27] Dick Higgins likewise describes a translation of natural terms between Fluxus, Happenings, and abstract expressionism: "The lives of objects, their histories and events were considered somehow more realistic than any conceivable personal intrusion on them. Many would see this as a reaction against what is considered the personal, intuitive nature of Abstract Expressionism. . . . I would rather regard the impersonality of Fluxus not as a reaction against this element of Abstract Expressionism, but . . . as a translation of it into different terms and formats."[28]

Like Kaprow, Brecht and Higgins both suggest that the performative element of much of Fluxus, as well as its direct relationship to audience and object, evolved from the performative and ordinary aspects of abstract expressionism. This shared lineage suggests that much connects Happenings to Fluxus, not only socially (as participating in each other's work suggests) but also in terms of something "somehow more realistic" than a merely painterly basis could provide.

However, Brecht's and Higgins's statements are not representative of Fluxus as a whole. Most Fluxus artists distinguish their work from Happenings precisely by way of the Event's placement in an objective reality. For example, the German Fluxus artist Tomas Schmit wrote:

> Every time I hear Fluxus and happening spoken in one breath or see them put together in a title for an exhibition, or even thrown together in one and the same pot, I shudder as if I saw a carp fuck a duck: these two things have very little in common and very much that keeps them apart: the term "happening" was first used by Kaprow for a certain form of performance namely, the *expressionistic, symbolistic, voluminous opera-type-of-thing.* Fluxus on the other hand was the name of a group of people, a group of activities, a sort of movement. . . . They were completely *unsymbolistic, anti-expressionistic, not informal but form-free, extreme simple events, actions, zen exercises, boredom pieces, etc.*[29]

The dichotomy is clear: the expressive and symbolic elements of Happenings, which align it with the action in action painting, are opposite in character to the "unsymbolistic," "anti-expressionistic," "form-free" elements of Fluxus.

Schmit's performance work is, in its antiexpressive simplicity, typical of most Fluxus Events of that time. His *Zyklus,* which appeared on many early Fluxus programs, consists of a simple instruction: "Water pails or bottles are placed around the perimeter of a circle. Only one is filled with water. Performer inside the circle picks the filled vessel and pours it into the one on the right, and then picks the one on the right and pours it into the next one on the right, etc., till all the water is spilled or evaporated."[30] Through performance, a nonart activity—an everyday experience—is offered up as an art event. Unlike the majority of Happenings, *Zyklus* is neither site specific nor dependent on a particular performance situation, whether theatrical or nontheatrical. Thus, even though *Zyklus* requires a restricted interpretation of a set of directives—"water pails or bottles are placed around the perimeter of a circle"—while most of Brecht's Events do not, in each case a range of possible realizations is generated, including the time needed to bring the piece to a conclusion. The open-endedness of the Event, which may be a publicly performed instruction, a primarily private experience, a read score, or all (or none) of these, is what separates it from the established formal aspects of fine-art media.

Brecht's Events were sometimes sent around in letters to artists and could be performed in virtually any situation with any number of people, just as *Zyklus* could be performed by anyone using any vessel for virtually any duration. While much recent Fluxus performance is more elaborately scripted than the earlier Events, and may allow for the traditional dynamic between performer and audience, it continues in general to be flexible, non–site specific, based in chance, and simply scored. These qualities set the open ended, form-free Event firmly apart from the Happening, with its communicational structure of "concordance," requiring agreement between a clearly identified author and performer (which includes the participatory audience).

This delineation of roles is particularly true of very early Happenings (1959–62). The first Happening dates to 1959. Called *18 Happenings in Six Parts,* it specified certain participants, including Allan Kaprow, Red Grooms, Sam Francis, George Segal, Rosalyn Montague, Shirley Pendergast, Lucas Samaras, Janet Weinberger, and Dick Higgins, as well as time intervals (for example, "Between part one and part two there is a two minute interval"). In addition, this Happening maintained the authorial division normally associated with a proscenium space, as indicated by such directives as "You have been given three cards. Be seated as they instruct you."[31] In these respects, the first Happening was more like traditional theater than were Brecht's Events or the subsequent Happenings of the 1960s.

As group identification stabilized, however, the two art forms became more, not less, alike. Later works by Kaprow, such as *Fluids* (1967), which resulted in a rectangular wall of ice, were less theatrical, whereas Fluxus performances became increasingly complex, as exemplified by Geoffrey Hendricks's *Unfinished Business* with its detailed instructions: the removal of hair, the building of an installation with that hair, the act of labeling, and so forth. Thus, when Kaprow noted that in Events "the absence of instruction leaves no doubt about their appeal to ambiguous use,"[32] he is clearly referring to early Events—in this case, indeed, to Brecht's *Two Elimination Events* from 1961.

TWO ELIMINATION EVENTS

· empty vessel

· empty vessel

The piece, Kaprow points out, has elements of both performance and conceptual art, since "the repeated word empty" can be taken

> as a verb or adjective; the two identical phrases can refer to two empty containers that should be accounted for somehow or can be taken as instructions that two containers be emptied. As a Conceptual piece, the work invites participants to consider that these possibilities may be simply thought about. The title's key word, *elimination,* suggests a reductive attitude that can be assumed toward them... it could allude to the "empty" (but full) state of Zen.[33]

The Event scores shown in Figure 30 illustrate further ways in which Events mediate between performance and conceptual art.[34]

The distinction between Fluxus Events and early Happenings helps to explain the overwhelmingly negative response Fluxus received in the American press. Happenings had set the tone for art performance in the lower Manhattan art scene of the late 1950s, and American critics seem to have been expecting the same when they attended performances by Fluxus artists. The experiential and informational thrust of Fluxus was a disappointment and duly criticized. A critique of Dick Higgins's "Saint Joan at Beaurevoir" in the *Village Voice* was typical, with the reviewer comparing the piece to "happenings," which "are wild and joyous and semi-accidental.... [This] was not. It was studied, painstaking, almost frozen—at unendurable length."[35]

Although later Happenings reverberated more closely in the experiential dimension with Fluxus Events, the die had been cast. Negative reviews of Fluxus works tended to stress their lack of liveliness ("Fluxus is boring"). For reviewers, the informational content was insufficient to constitute interesting concepts as well, as is amply demonstrated by accounts linking Fluxus to conceptual art.

Conceptual Art

Sometime Fluxus participant Henry Flynt coined the term *concept art* in 1961: "'Concept Art' is first of all an art of which the material is concepts, as the material of, e.g., music is sound. Since concepts are closely bound up with language, concept art is a kind of art of which the material is language."[36] The term's applicability to Fluxus seems obvious: it is particularly well suited to the Event score, a textual presentation of a concept that may or may not have a performative dimension (as in Nam June Paik's score "climb into the vagina of a live whale").[37] Given that some of the first conceptual art was produced by Fluxus artists in the form of Event scores, and the term coined by a Fluxus associate, the nearly total absence of Fluxus from almost all histories of conceptual art is remarkable.

Lucy Lippard's rich memoir *Six Years: The Dematerialization of the Art Object from 1966 to 1972* is typical. She describes Fluxus as irrelevant for later conceptual art: "Around 1960 Henry Flynt coined the term 'concept art,' but few of the artists with whom I was involved knew about it, and in any case it was a different kind of 'concept'—less formal, less rooted [than conceptual art] in the subversion of art-world assumptions and art-as-commodity."[38] A few pages later, however, she writes that "while GAAG's [Guerilla Art Action Group's] almost Dada letters to President Nixon ('Eat What You Kill') and other world leaders were in the spirit of the general 'Conceptual movement,' their blood-and-guts performance style and their connections to Europe, via Fluxus and Destruction Art, separated them from the cooler, Minimal art–oriented Conceptual mainstream."[39] These observations reflect the multiple nature of Fluxus: Fluxus was both too political and not political enough (or more accurately, not focused enough on a clear political objective) for the "cooler, Minimal art–oriented Conceptual mainstream," which Lippard describes as "a fellow traveler with the political ferment of the times."[40]

The art critic Peter Frank departs from standard accounts of conceptual art like Lippard's when he says that "Conceptual Art started when some people [i.e., George Brecht] . . . took Happenings, applied to them the Zen lessons learned from John Cage and came up with Event."[41] The artist/critic-cum-curator Robert Morgan, in his essay "Idea, Concept, System," describes this prehistory in a bit more depth:

Conceptual Art as a term and as a phenomenon in the New York art world in the late '60s was a mainstream affair. On the other hand, the term "concept art" comes from an entirely different vantage point, much earlier on, a point which has been acknowledged in the '80s by [conceptual artist] Sol Lewitt. The Fluxus movement, largely instigated and organized through the efforts of George Maciunas between 1961 and 1963, is where the earlier notion of "concept art" took hold.... This is not to suggest a cause-and-effect relationship; but some major conceptualists have, when pressed, admitted that Fluxus did constitute a "proto-conceptual" movement.[42]

These accounts raise crucial questions. What is the connection between concept art and conceptual art? How did Fluxus come to be at odds with later conceptual art? And perhaps most important, why has the story linking Fluxus with conceptual art not been told?

Lippard suggests that conceptual art of the heroic period (1966–72), which met with comparative commercial success (Morgan's "mainstream affair"), used formally minimal styles of representation. Indeed, most histories of conceptual art describe the movement in modernist terms as a reaction, realized through a formal reduction of means, to abstract expressionism. For example, Seth Sieglaub, a publisher of, and dealer in, conceptual art, speaking of exhibition catalogues, said: "When art does not any longer depend on its physical presence, when it becomes an abstraction, it is not distorted and altered by its reproduction in books. It becomes 'PRIMARY' information, while the reproduction of conventional art in books and catalogues is necessarily (distorted) 'secondary' information. When information is PRIMARY, the catalogue can become the exhibition."[43] "Primary" information here is analogous to primary, or minimal, form; it does not refer to the multisensory, pragmatic knowledge discussed by Dewey, but to esoteric, disembodied, scientific knowledge as a kind of Platonic essence. In conceptual art of the mainstream, works avoided physicality (on which all previous artistic production allegedly depended) as much as possible, striving instead for the "higher" plane of ideas. Thus it reinforced the idealist philosophical paradigm that posits a clear separation between pure thought and experiential body. According to this framework, and borrowing the logic from Heidegger and Levin in Chapter 1, the ontological thought that is typical of Fluxus becomes, if not impossible, at best physically corrupted from the outset, since Fluxus offers embodied primary experiences as concepts, whereas conceptual art is strictly disembodied.

The conceptual artist Joseph Kosuth, in the essay "Art after Philosophy," describes the move to a disembodied aesthetic in the same terms as Sieglaub, placing *idea* in opposition to material basis of its form.[44] Once the work was thus polarized, it followed that conceptual art should assume a comparatively nonphysical character. In contrast, according to Kosuth, formalist art "is only art by virtue of its resemblance to earlier works of art. It's a mindless art."[45] It was this "mindless" (read: physical or bodily) manner of artistic production, he argues, that made a scientific approach necessary: "In art's unique character is the *capacity to remain aloof* from philosophical judgments. It is in this context that art shares similarities with logic, mathematics and, as well, science."[46]

This aloof character, which Kosuth aligned with minimal form, produced, through rejection of the material world, a "cool" asceticism—an aesthetic, moreover, that contrasted sharply with the formalist characterization of abstract expressionism (that other current to which conceptual art ostensibly constituted a reaction) as emotionally and materially interconnected, that is, non-aloof. It should come as no surprise, then, that mainstream conceptual works resemble scientific documents: stark photographs, unadorned texts, single objects of scrutiny, and so forth (Fig. 38). This definition of conceptual art, like its ensuing aesthetic limitations, dominates the art world's view of the conceptual, not only because of its consistent style but also because it resonates with a dominant (hegemonic?) notion of the idea as disembodied.

As discussed in Chapter 2, Fluxus produces situations that, by staking out the physical side of cognition, erode the subject/object, form/idea division typical of Western metaphysics. Flynt's notion of concept art, in which all realms of an individual's experience are expressible through the "material of language," is especially useful in considering this work, which resists the overdetermined poles of mainstream conceptual art and abstract expressionism. In allowing for a range of language experiments that stand in opposition to the pseudoscientific, idealist model of human thought proposed by Kosuth, Flynt's idea can be located to a certain degree in the cluster of experiments typical of early Fluxus.

Flynt recalls that "Jackson Mac Low began transferring Cage's chance procedures to poetry—yielding a more computational or artificial concrete poetry."[47]

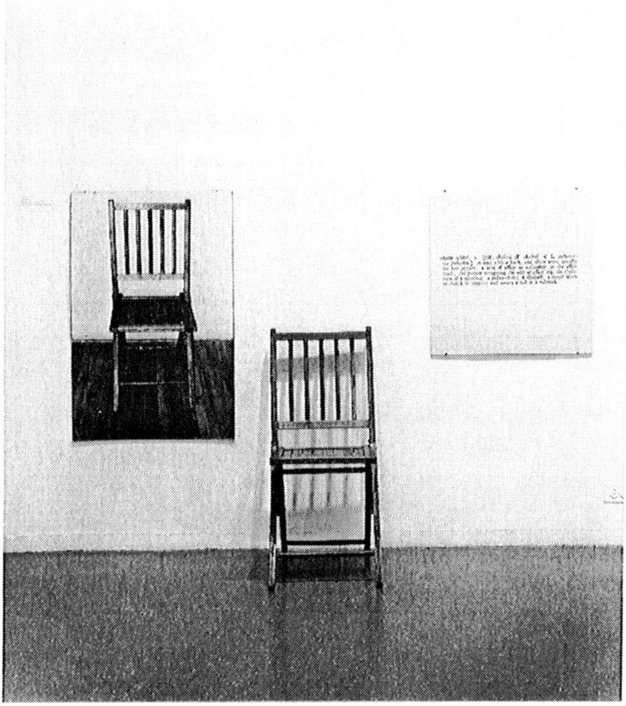

38 Joseph Kosuth, *One and Three Chairs*, 1965. Wooden folding chair, photographic copy of a chair, dictionary definition of a chair. Photograph © 2001; courtesy of the Museum of Modern Art, New York, Larry Aldrich Foundation Fund.

In so doing, Mac Low made a possible (and systematic) link between linguistic structures and their opposite, Cage's anarchistic operations of chance and indeterminacy. For Cage, the throw of dice or toss of a coin might determine the duration or nature of a sound, or the structure of the piece itself. Similar principles allow the performer to determine aspects of a piece normally controlled by the composer.[48] Thus, while Mac Low's *2nd Gatha* (see Fig. 6) arranges words in a grid, the actual sequence of words spoken in performance is derived by chance. In other words, the language units interact both with the indeterminacy of life processes, as in some (late) Happenings and (early) Events, and with the study of the relationship between language and ideas in the abstract. These living, pragmatic senses of language, which are typical of Fluxus, lie outside the mainstream conceptual artists' aloof scientism and determinism, even as Mac Low's poetry has a conceptual basis.

The performances of Yoko Ono likewise run counter to the disembodied idea of mainstream conceptual art. Typical is the Event *Cut Piece* (1961), a striptease of sorts, but instead of watching a woman undress, the audience is called upon to remove her clothing with scissors—a disconcerting actualization of voyeuristic language ("I undressed her with my eyes"). Unlike Brecht's Events, this work is clearly about the person of Ono and the specific identity of each audience member who engages (or not) in the act of cutting. As a comparatively ego-based piece, it runs counter to the anti-egoistic basis of the typical Event. Nevertheless, *Cut Piece,* which is performed frequently in concerts of historic Fluxus work, certainly belongs to the transactional domain linking Events and conceptual art.

Although not Event based, Alison Knowles's books—including *Bean Rolls* (1962; Fig. 39), *Big Book* (1967), and *The Finger Book of Ancient Language* (1982; Fig. 40)—also relate text directly to the body, but minus an egoistic aspect. Because the books engage a person in exploration without awareness of time or place, their performativity is simultaneously conceptual and Event-like. In *Bean Rolls,* for example, the many scrolls are individually unrolled and read, the can is held in the hands, and the beans spill out onto the floor or can be rattled in the can. Each reader determines the sequence of actions and of pages read. Similarly, the *Big Book* is actually walked and crawled through, and the *Finger Book* offers tactile languages from around the world. All offer a sensory alternative to the purely

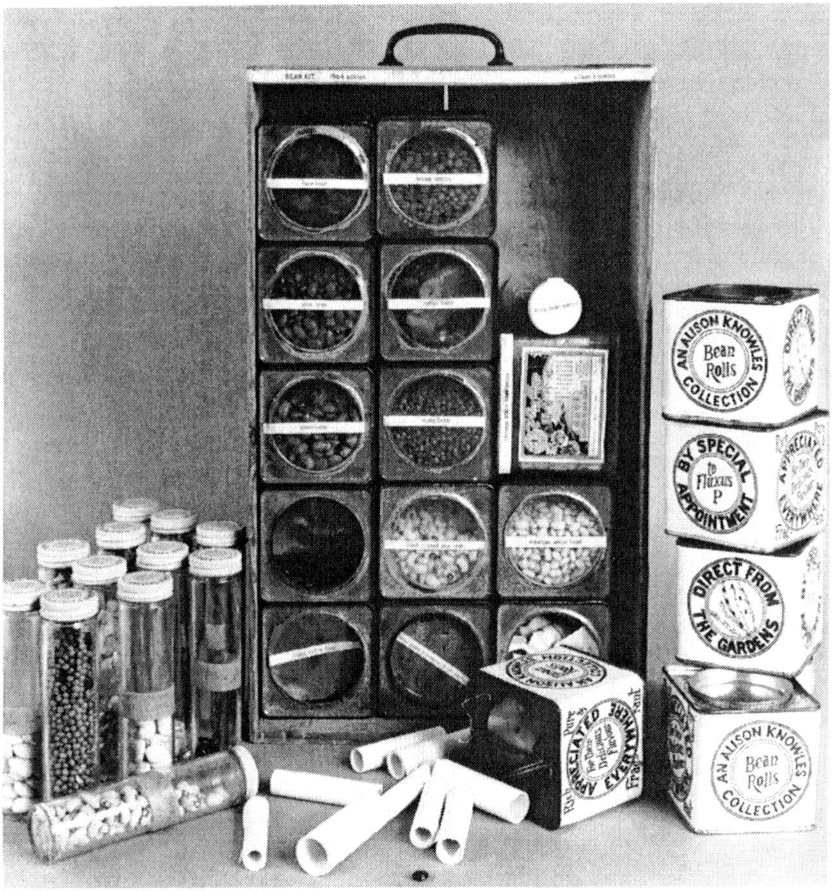

39 Alison Knowles, *Bean Rolls*, 1964. Knowles's boxes are in the foreground and to the side; George Maciunas's version is in the background. Photo by Brad Iverson; courtesy of the Gilbert and Lila Silverman Fluxus Collection, Detroit.

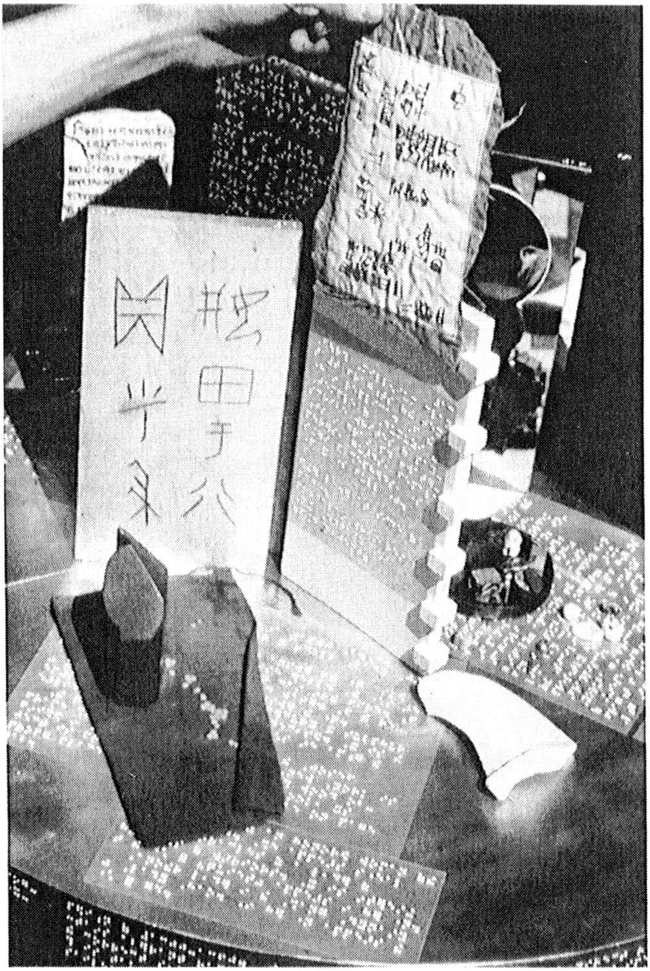

40 Alison Knowles, *The Finger Book of Ancient Language,* 1982. Mixed-media interactive book on 11-in. spine and aluminum base. Courtesy of the artist.

cerebral, or disembodied, definition of language in the idealist sense, as exemplified by mainstream conceptual art.

Relatedly, the Japanese Fluxus artist Mieko (sometimes Chieko) Shiomi realized gentle and beautiful "spatial poems" that likewise bound words to nonverbal material. She set pins documenting word use into maps, sprinkling a graphic image of the globe with words as they were used by friends at diverse locations. Her *Spatial Poem No. 1 (word event)* (1965; Fig. 41), for example, instructs the viewer to "write a word (or words) on the enclosed card and place it somewhere. Please tell me the word and the place, which will be edited on the world map." What the piece is, whether travel log, performance, conceptual art piece, or mapping exercise, differs depending on where one enters into it. Shiomi's spatial poem, like Brecht's Events, Mac Low's poems, Ono's *Cut Piece,* and Knowles's books, is without doubt "Concept Art" in Flynt's sense. "The material *is* language," and the language is material.

Fluxus work, in the end, is a concept art, but not a conceptual art in the commercial sense, since it rejects the minimalist form and linguistic scientism outlined by Sieglaub, Lippard, or Kosuth. Following this distinction, Fluxus becomes concept in a broader, more physically inclusive sense—one could even say a physically charged intellectual sense.

Pop Art

In 1964, the Fluxus artist Robert Watts initiated a project against mainstream conceptual art: "The idea occurred to copyright 'Pop Art,' thereby taking the term off the market and preventing its use, perhaps in anticipation of its extensive consequent use as a marketing label on a variety of products."[49] This attempt required a search of all the variations on the term *pop* with the U.S. Patent Office, which mandated that a term could be copyrighted only by product type. Watts wrote a letter to his lawyer, Arthur Jacob, requesting a search of the records of manufacturers of everything from apparel and luggage to food and recreational equipment for previous uses of the term.[50] The papers that arrived showed trademark registrations—P.O.P., POPS, and POP, among others—for prepared pork, candy, soda, firecrackers, and all manner of other products. Not only did the popular imagery these goods relied on (where a picture of a pig meant pork, or a bottle signified

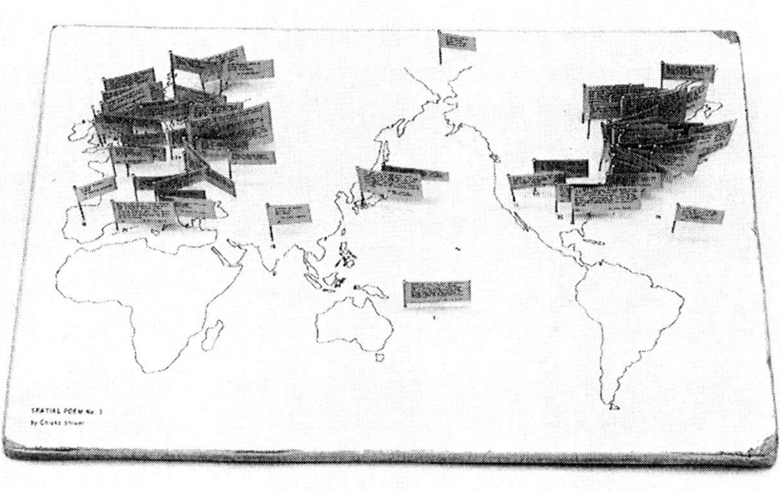

41 Mieko Shiomi, *Spatial Poem No. 1 (word event),* 1965. Map on fiberboard, masking tape, pins, offset on cards, $11\frac{7}{8} \times 18\frac{1}{8} \times 3\frac{3}{8}$ in. Photo by Brad Iverson; courtesy of the Gilbert and Lila Silverman Fluxus Collection, Detroit.

soda) themselves resemble the icons of pop art, but the overall project satirized the prevalence of pop art in the high-art mainstream as the very term *pop art* was turned into a brand name indistinguishable from any other name-recognized commodity. In attempting to copyright the term, Watts, who had been included in several early pop art exhibitions but no recent ones, was assuming ownership of it, or trying to. In so doing, he was perhaps making allegiances with other pop artists even as he demarcated territorial overlaps between Fluxus and pop.

For example, the year of this work, 1964, is the year Andy Warhol is said, with the film *Sleep,* to have invented static cinema. In fact, however, it is quite possible that the Fluxus artist Jackson Mac Low came up with the idea first. Mac Low, who worked with LaMonte Young on *An Anthology* (1963), has described his invention of the film form in part as a response to the static music of Young, in which electronic equipment sustains a constant sound indefinitely.[51] Mac Low also cites *Tree Movie,* which calls for a tree to be filmed using time exposure over the course of years, as an earlier experiment in static cinema, one that Warhol's circle may have appropriated:

> I had thought for a long time that it was merely a parallel development, thinking that "Sleep" had been made prior to the January 1964 Fluxpaper, + that [Nam June] Paik and [Eric] Anderson [*sic*] were merely being friendly partisans in insisting that "Tree Movie" was the egg from which all those golden-egg-laying geese [hatched]. But our friend Jonas [Mekas] demonstrated the time sequence to me pretty convincingly at a Christmas party at Carol Berge's last year: Jan. 1964 "Tree Movie" Pub'd in Fluxpaper; Feb. 1964, I gave copies of the Fluxpaper out at a rehearsal for a program of simultaneities (20 Fe[b]. '64, I think) at the Metro; April 1964 "Sleep" produced. I had given copies to, among others, Warhol's pal Gerry Malanga.[52]

Confusing matters, the musician John Cale, a friend of Warhol's, worked with LaMonte Young from the late 1950s to about 1964. They collaborated on Young's *The Tortoise Droning. . . ,* a piece that was still evolving in 1968, when Howard Junker described it thus: "He begins his performance before they [the audience] arrive, partly to give the impression that his 'theatre of eternal music' has always been going on. Indeed his current composition, 'The Tortoise, His Dreams and Journeys,' has been performed in an ever changing essentially static form on various occasions since 1964."[53] Perhaps Cale introduced Young's duration idea into Warhol's circle as music, and someone else independently made the extrapolation to film. A related example of interaction between Warhol's circle and Fluxus is *Police Car* (1964), a film by John Cale comprising an underexposed segment of flashing patrol car lights, which appeared on a 1964 reel of Fluxfilms assembled by George Maciunas.

In any event, the nearly simultaneous appearance of *Tree Movie* and *Sleep* testifies to intensive interaction between artists and groups of artists, even as it raises a possibly unacknowledged debt to Fluxus. At the very least, the situation demonstrates that authorship is not always clear-cut.

Collaboration also marked musical experimentation. LaMonte Young, for example, helped Cale turn his viola into an experimental, and then a rock, instrument.[54] Called the Dream Syndicate, their project of 1963–64 relied on two electronically amplified voices and an amplified violin and viola. The idea was to hold the same notes unbroken for two hours; for example, Young might hold the deepest bass note, Cale the middle three tones on the viola, and Marian Zazeela (Young's wife) the final, high-pitched note on the violin. Of this experience Cale commented: "That was my first group experience—and what a one! It was totally new! I mean, tapes as art objects!... The indians knew this monotone... but they use totally different sounds."[55]

Shortly thereafter, Cale brought static music into pop culture (with a later member of the Dream Syndicate, Angus MacLise). The droning viola undertone of their band, the Velvet Underground, derives from the Dream Syndicate. Later, Fluxus and the Underground would come together in public performance at least once, at a benefit concert held for the alternative-scene paper *East Village Other.* John Wilcock (who published the paper and was an important supporter of pop art) invited George Maciunas's participation with these words: "The East Village Other is having a Benefit Party & Ball at the Village Gate, mostly for Art D'Lugoff's benefit at the end of March. We're having Warhol's Velvet Underground, the Fugs, underground movies etc etc and I'd like to have every turnon thing that I can think of taking part somehow which naturally includes Fluxus."[56] As the rock-music historian John Rockwell puts it, speaking of this cultural connection more generally, "there was a kinship between minimalism and structuralism on the one hand and a stripped down, abstracted rock & roll on the other."[57]

Like the layered circles of the "Intermedia Chart," Happenings, conceptual art, and pop art overlap one another and Fluxus in close alliances. Yet as with conceptual art, Fluxus has been largely written out of the history of American pop art, again because it did not—as pop art, like Happenings and conceptual art, to a certain extent did—"precisely fulfill... the expectations prescribed by a ruling standard."[58] As Christin Mamiya observed in 1992, "many... collectors saw Pop Art as an affirmation of a society based on commodity exchange"[59]—something that could not be said of Fluxus. Thirty years earlier, in *A Symposium on Pop Art,* the critic Dore Ashton stated: "To the extent that interest in objects and their assemblage in non-metaphorical terms signifies a reduction in individual choices, pop art is a significant sociological phenomenon, a mirror of our society. To the extent that it shuns metaphor, or any deep analysis of complex relations, it is an impoverished genre and an imperfect instrument of art."[60] Clearly, the form of pop these analysts describe is the banal, clean, graphic art associated with its most famous practitioners—Warhol, Lichtenstein, and Oldenburg—and not art derived from popular culture and materials more generally.

In contrast we can look to an essay by Thomas Kellein, "Fluxus—an Addendum to Pop?" which appeared in the 1991 catalogue *Pop Art: An International Perspective.* Kellein, who includes Fluxus under the rubric "Euro Pop," thus distancing it from American (mainstream) pop art, writes: "Where the Pop Artists analytically probed the aesthetics of mass media and the mass market, Fluxus aspired to be an accumulation of goods in its own right, distributed subversively through massive 'Headquarters' and 'Mail Order Houses.' What Fluxus wanted was not an artistic encapsulation of the consumer society but a direct sales strategy organized by artists themselves."[61] For Kellein, because Fluxus developed critical strategies (such as independent "mail-order warehouses"; Fig. 42) against "the aesthetics of mass media and the mass market," it should be considered part of a distinct, politically motivated European phenomenon, separate from the capitalist-oriented American pop movement. Historically, however, the ideas of independent distribution and the mass market were not so compartmentalized; they commingled extensively in both New York and Europe.

In New York, for example, where according to Kellein the pop artists merely analyzed and appropriated a mass consumer style, Claes Oldenburg's *Store* (1961–62) played a key role in the history of pop art, Happenings, *and* Fluxus.

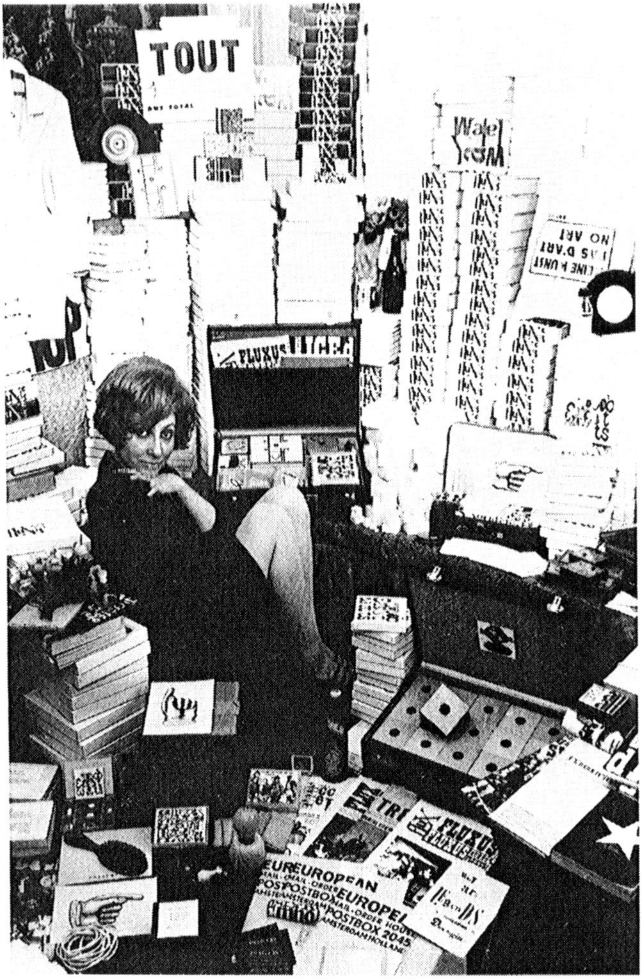

42 Willem de Ridder, *European Mail-Order Warehouse/Fluxshop,* 1964–65. Photo by Wim van der Linden; courtesy of the Gilbert and Lila Silverman Fluxus Collection, Detroit.

From a storefront on the lower east side of Manhattan, Oldenburg offered up plaster and papier mâché models of everyday "crap" (his term) that were sold cheap. At the same time *The Store* launched indoor and street performances and established itself as a place to meet and talk for the local art community. (On his return from Europe in 1963 Maciunas, too, ran a distribution venue and performance space from his loft on Canal Street, the Fluxhall. From this space he produced and marketed—through the *Fluxus Newsletter*—Fluxus editions.)

Interestingly, Fluxus's Something Else Press produced a book about Oldenburg's project, called *Claes Oldenburg's Store Days* (Fig. 43). The opening remarks of the able editor, Emmett Williams, highlight the sense of performance embodied in *The Store* ("[it] was on the one hand a real place where real sales were made, and on the other a set of ideas whose reverberations are still being felt")[62] and the experience of being there, qualities that resonate beyond the traditional confines of pop art and extend toward Fluxus. Oldenburg himself described the experiential dimension of the project thus:

> The original idea of The Store was a simple one—to fill a space with objects such as those in any kind of store, but this was not satisfactory as I proceeded...
>
> one's own body the form of change
> keep form even after making, in a situation of change
> not only mechanical but psychological
> moving sculptures are often all fixed
> mine are not
> the law of my work is time
> change[63]

As "a situation of change," *The Store* has implications for Fluxus as well, as an experiential exploration of the everyday—a defining dimension of pop art.

Oldenburg eventually joined the world of major galleries, public commissions, and museum shows. Before all that, though, there was *The Store,* a scene of experimentation and independence from those very structures to which his later work would hew. These same characteristics mark the work of Fluxus artists, especially ones beyond New York. Yet what I want to emphasize here is that the principle of independent proprietorship and distributorship was hardly excluded

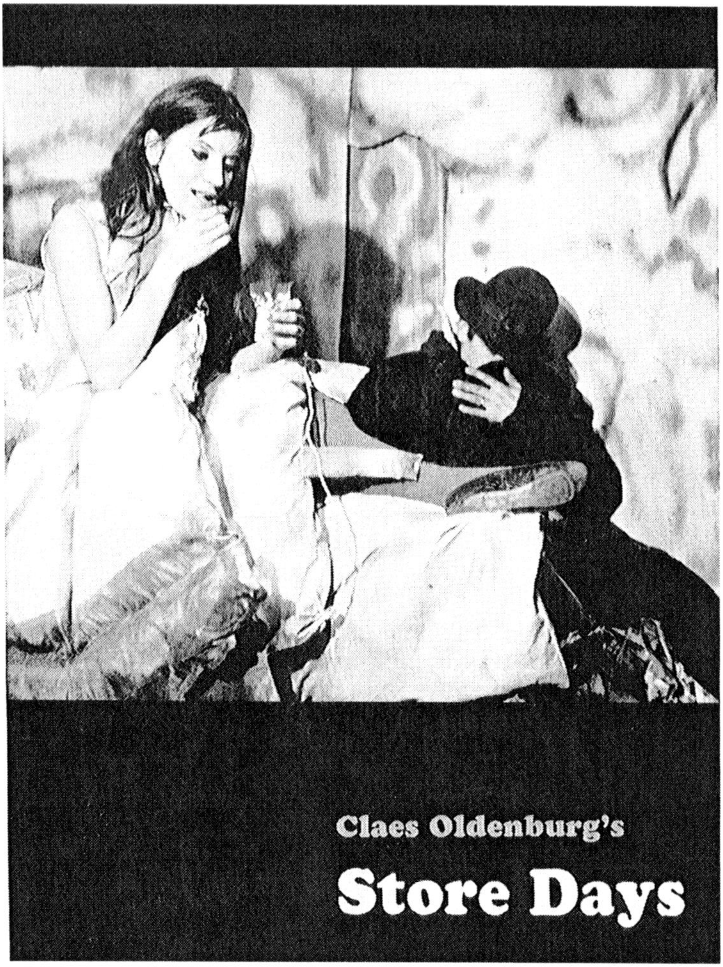

43 *Claes Oldenburg's Store Days,* ed. Emmett Williams (New York: Something Else Press, 1968). Courtesy of the Estate of Dick Higgins.

from pop art or Fluxus in America. Nevertheless, this principle was associated very strongly with Fluxus in Europe, where there are many more examples.

During the Festival of Misfits in London in 1962, Ben Vautier became a living sculpture, taking up residence in a gallery where he ate, slept, waved at passersby (especially ladies emerging from the salon next door who paused to examine their coiffures in the window), wrote, and conversed with the curious (Fig. 44). The space, Gallery One, was packed full of Vautier's text panels and other novelties (Fig. 45), which he also sold through his store in Nice. In both *Living Sculpture* and his shop, the artist was engaged in a conceptual exchange with the audience that included both public performances of everyday experiences and the transformation of these into words or slogans that could be written on things as artworks for sale.

Similarly, from 1965 to 1968 in Villefranche-sur-Mer, France, the French artist Robert Filliou and American expatriate George Brecht were selling "useless" ideas and objects in their store, the Cédille qui Sourit (the Smiling Cedilla, or "Store of Useless Knowledge"; Figs. 46 and 47). As Figure 46, a double exposure, shows, sitting around and talking, having drinks, or cavorting was as much a part of the project as the merchandise inside (which included Maciunas's Fluxus materials, a few of Vautier's objects, beaded jewelry, and a few odds and ends). The store was also documented in a book by Something Else Press, called *Games at the Cedilla; or, The Cedilla Takes Off* (1968).

Similarly, in Denmark in 1971, Eric Andersen set up a supermarket of Anonymous Merchandise in Århus. This idea was later reprised in a collaborative "catalogue" of objects conceived with Knud Pedersen and offered for sale at a temporary, but real, market, the "Good Buy Supermarket" (Fig. 48), a venue for Fluxus multiples mass-produced for "Excellent '92," a Fluxus reunion celebration.[64].

The most frequently cited example of a pure Fluxshop in the "accumulative" and "subversive" sense is Willem de Ridder's Amsterdam-based *European Mail-Order Warehouse/Fluxshop* (1964), which existed in de Ridder's living room for only one evening.[65] Despite being almost entirely temporary and imaginary, this Fluxshop—thanks to an often reprinted photograph (see Fig. 42)—has become a standard conceptualization of Fluxus sales practices.[66]

In *Pop Art: An International Perspective,* the art historian Evelyn Weiss reports that in Germany, Fluxus and pop art were interdependent throughout the 1960s:

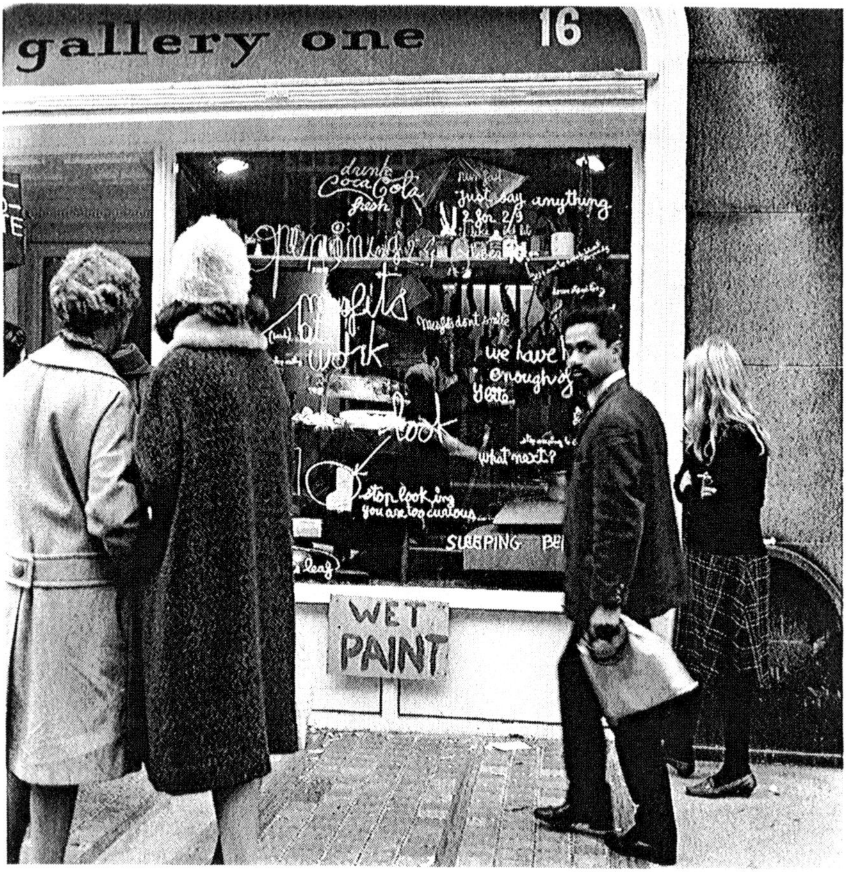

44 Ben Vautier, *Living Sculpture,* 1962. Looking toward the storefront, Gallery One, during the Festival of Misfits, London. Photo by Bruce Fleming; courtesy of the Gilbert and Lila Silverman Fluxus Collection, Detroit.

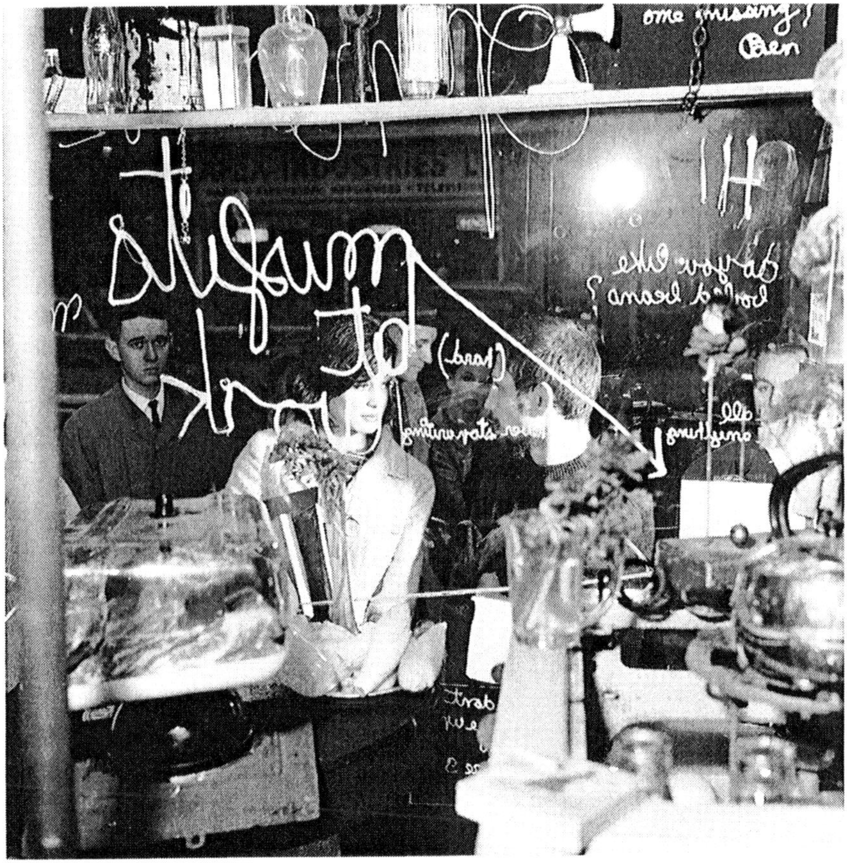

45 Ben Vautier, *Living Sculpture*, 1962. Looking through the storefront window to the outside. Photo by Bruce Fleming; courtesy of the Gilbert and Lila Silverman Fluxus Collection, Detroit.

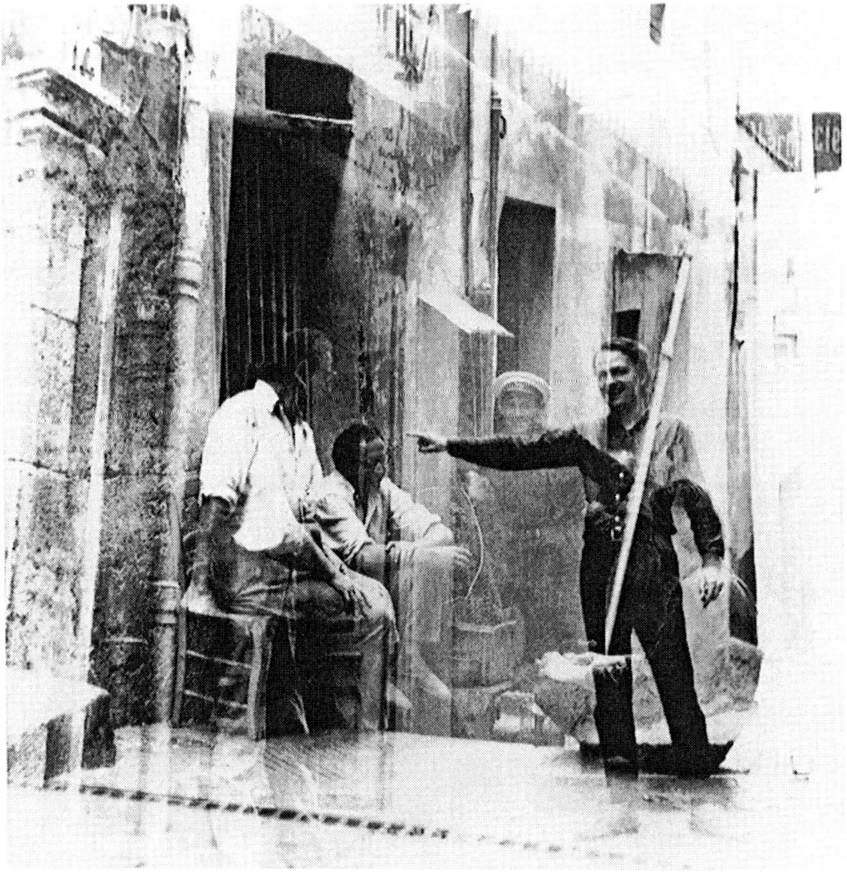

46 George Brecht and Robert Filliou, La Cédille qui Sourit (Store of useless knowledge), Villefranche-sur-Mer, France, 1967. Double exposure with Robert Filliou, [unknown], and George Brecht (pointing). Photo by Jacques Strauch and Michou Strauch-Barelli; courtesy of the Gilbert and Lila Silverman Fluxus Collection, Detroit.

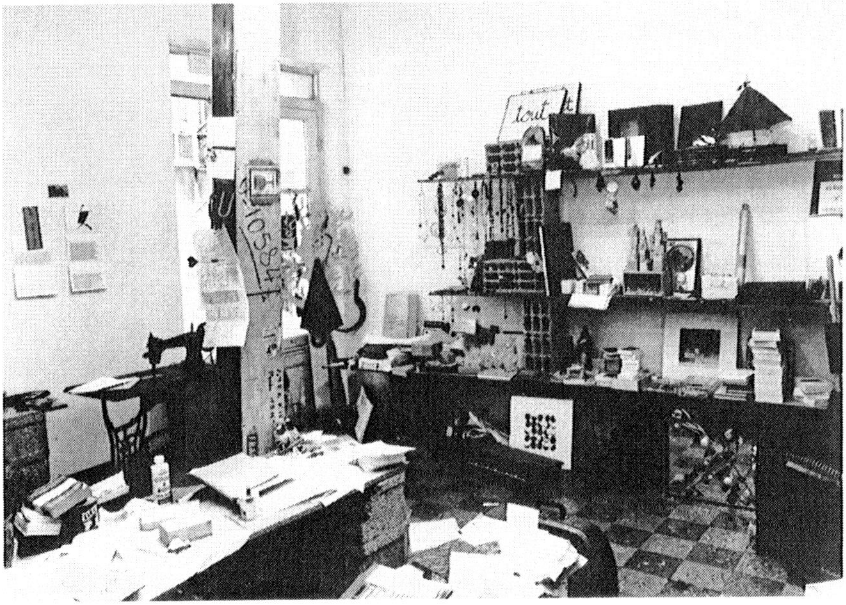

47 George Brecht and Robert Filliou, La Cédille qui Sourit, Villefranche-sur-Mer, France, 1967. Interior. Photo by Jacques Strauch and Michou Strauch-Barelli; courtesy of the Gilbert and Lila Silverman Fluxus Collection, Detroit.

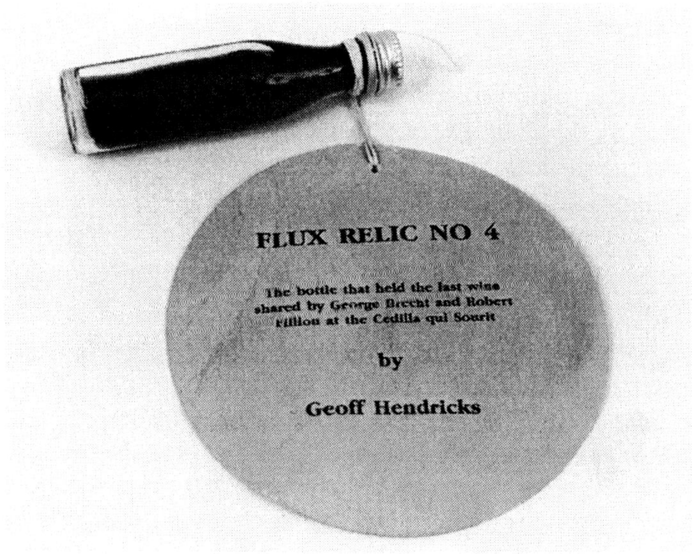

48 Geoffrey Hendricks, *Flux Relic No. 4*, 1992; produced for Good Buy Supermarket, Nikolai Church, Copenhagen, organized by Michael Berger, Knud Pedersen, and Eric Andersen. "Last Bottle of Wine from the Cedilla Store." Courtesy of the artist.

> Pop Art came up against a number of emerging European trends, with which, for a time, it coexisted in a kind of symbiosis. In addition to Nouveau Realisme in Paris, in Germany there was a concentration on Happenings and a particularly strong representation of the Fluxus movement. As its name suggests, this was an unorthodox and *unprogrammatic* movement that defied ossified artistic forms and institutions (museums, galleries, and exhibitions included), combining incongruous *real* elements with music, actions and pictures in a Surrealistic and sometimes intentionally confusing way.[67]

Weiss, almost uniquely among historians of the period, demonstrates that cross-influences were at work between pop art and Fluxus in France, England, and America as well. As the following examples illustrate, Fluxus artists and pop artists had many kinds of associations, not only in terms of distribution venues, which exhibit pragmatic parallels, but also in terms of the way their art was received in the United States and Europe.

The Festival of Misfits, which took place in London from 23 October to 8 November 1962, was organized by the nouveau realist/pop artist Daniel Spoerri, who had social and professional connections to the group. Participants included Americans (Higgins, Knowles, Maciunas, Patterson, and Williams) as well as French Swiss (Ben Vautier), French (Robert Filliou), Danish (Addi Køpcke), and English (Robin Page) Fluxus artists with a range of artistic associations. Although Spoerri collaborated very little with Fluxus after this point, he did subsequently coproduce *L'Optique Moderne* (see Fig. 11) as well as an edition of "snare pictures" (documenting cutlery and dishes left from a meal that had been glued down in place; Fig. 49) with Maciunas. Later, Spoerri, with Maciunas, Watts, and Peter Moore, spoofed the fetishization of experiential acts with *Monsters Are Inoffensive*—here, the tableware is alive as hands and body parts reach through and around the settings, imaginarily animating the inanimate (Fig. 50)!

On 24 October 1962 in connection with the Festival of Misfits, the Institute of Contemporary Art (ICA), a strong supporter of early pop art in England, hosted a Fluxus concert, "The Misfits Fair" (in which many pieces by artists not in attendance were performed by friends present). The critic Arthur Penrose and pop artists David Hockney, Joe Tilson, and Richard Smith were all in the audience, perhaps lured by the reputation of such contributors as George Brecht (also in attendance),

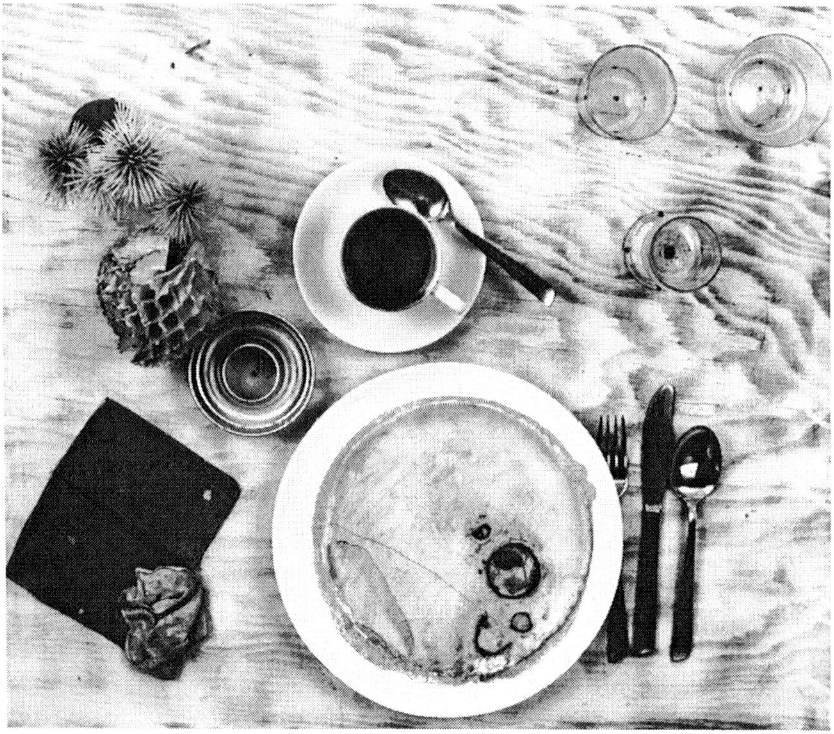

49 Daniel Spoerri, *Meal Variation No. 4, Jack Youngerman,* from *Twenty-nine Variations on a Meal,* 1964. The original mounted meal, from which Maciunas made an edition printed on linen, 21 × 25 in. Photo by Nancy Anello; courtesy of the Gilbert and Lila Silverman Fluxus Collection, Detroit.

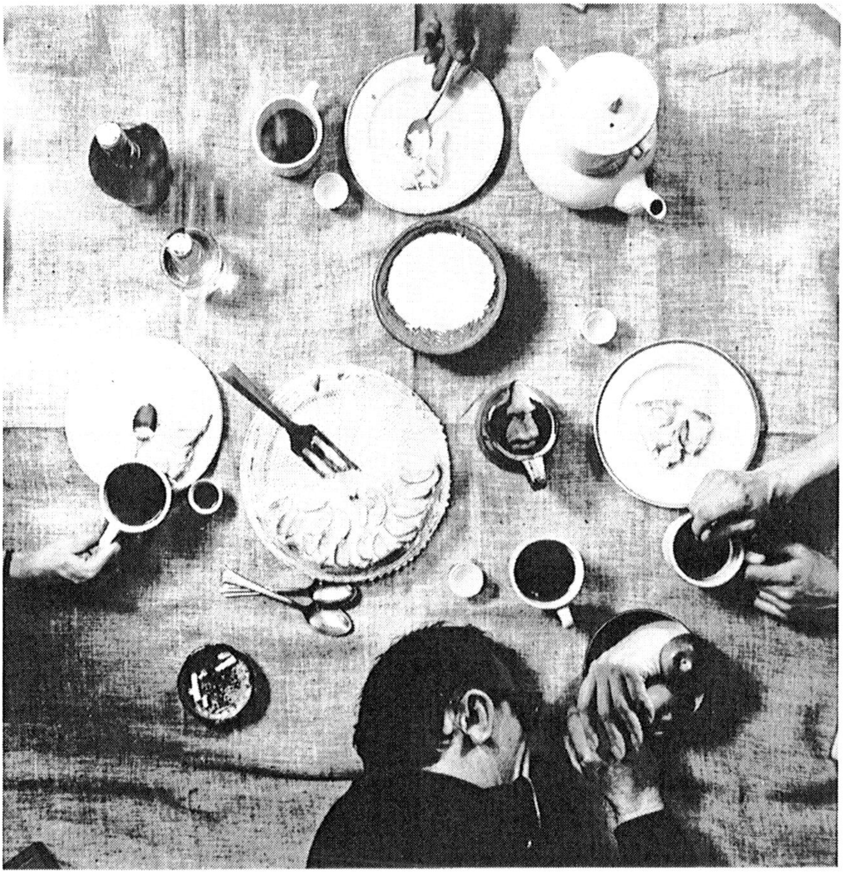

50 Robert Filliou with George Maciunas, Peter Moore, Daniel Spoerri, and Robert Watts, photograph intended for projected edition, *Monsters Are Inoffensive,* 1967. Edition would have consisted of photo laminate, vinyl surface tabletop, 36 × 36 in. Photographer unidentified; courtesy of the Gilbert and Lila Silverman Fluxus Collection, Detroit.

Robert Watts, and Al Hansen as American pop artists.[68] This pop connection was likely reinforced by several events. For example, Brecht and Watts, together with "Misfit" Dick Higgins, had performed during 1959 and 1960 at New York's Reuben Gallery, a venue associated with pop artists Red Grooms, George Segal, Claes Oldenburg, and James Dine.[69] On 29 February 1960, Higgins and Hansen had taken part in the Judson Church performance series called "Ray Gun Specs" along with Grooms, Kaprow, Oldenburg, and Robert Whitman. Also in 1960, George Brecht and Robert Watts were included in "New Forms—New Media," an important show in the history of pop art,[70] and late the next year Watts was represented in the Museum of Modern Art's "Art of Assemblage" exhibition.[71]

Following the Festival of Misfits and back in the United States, Brecht and Watts were included in the "Popular Image" exhibition at the Washington Gallery of Modern Art in April 1963, but they were excluded when the show moved to London's Institute of Contemporary Art that October.[72] This was a decisive moment for both groups. The ICA show substituted in Allan D'Arcangelo, Robert Indiana, and Mel Ramos, artists with a comparatively spare graphic style. Cleaned up and mass produced, this art lacks the experiential component of much early pop and of the Fluxus work that was often associated with pop art in its earliest guises.

A fascinating affiliation between Fluxus and pop art occurs in Al Hansen's *Venus* collages (see Fig. 7), produced from about 1960 to 1995. In most of them Hansen appropriates Hershey bar wrappers to reference oral sensuality ("Lick me," "like me," and "oh" over the crotch) and graft it onto the visual art tradition of Venus-making. These Venuses' "licked" wrapper surfaces evoke both classic Venuses (of Botticelli, for example) and, with their accentuated hips and thighs, primitivistic fertility goddesses such as the Venus of Willendorf. Some of Hansen's Venuses are made of cigarette butts or matches, likewise conjuring up lewd associations with orality and a strong libidinal force. Although these collages, especially those made with Hershey wrappers, clearly partake of a pop art context, the banal association with consumerism is complicated by the overlay of 1960s sexual mores, art-historical references, and the flavor of chocolate.

Alison Knowles's graphic series *Identical Lunch* (Fig. 51), which shows people eating the identical lunch above a Star-Kist logo, also strongly references consumerism. As in the Hershey Venus, the trademark is overlaid with a reference to the act of eating. The work brings the performer into contact with mass imagery

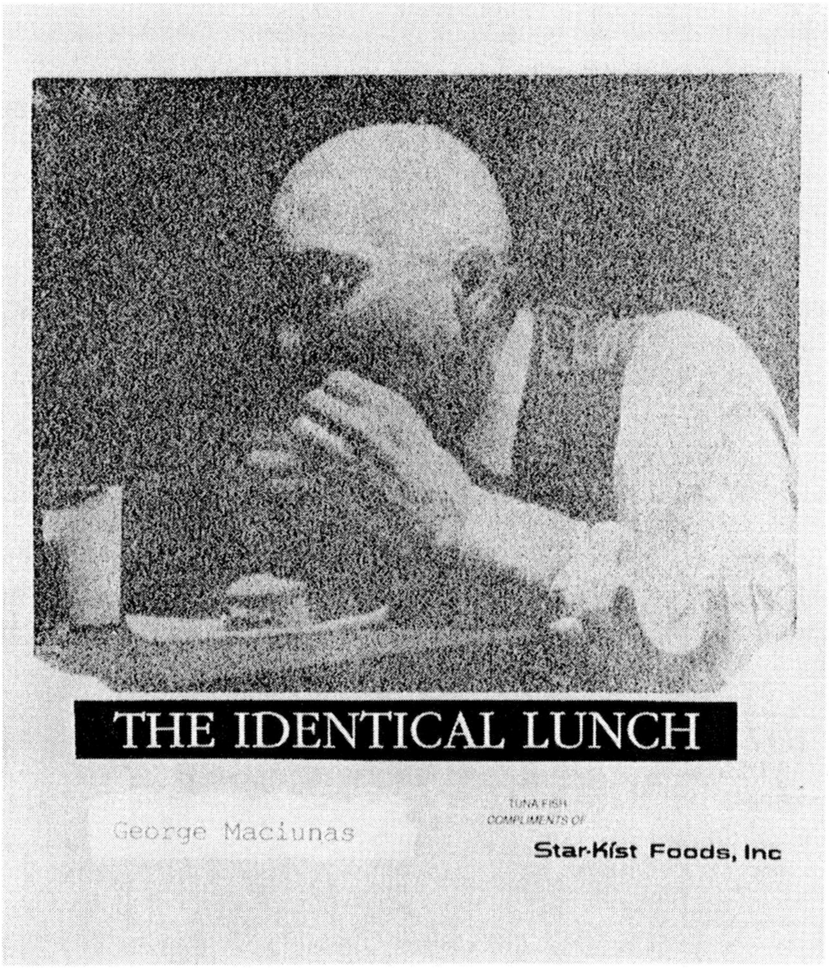

51 Alison Knowles, *The Identical Lunch,* 1970 (2d ed., 1990). Four-color silk-screen graphic on canvas, 17 × 17 in. Courtesy of the artist.

and (paradoxically) with the private ritual of eating the relatively unchanging lunch—"a tuna fish sandwich on whole wheat toast with butter, no mayo, and a cup of buttermilk or the soup of the day." This "identical" lunch is not identical at all. It varies by place, by time, by distance between the performer and the plate, and by taste. As in the ritual described in Chapter 1, the participants shown in the graphic are having an interpersonal and variable experience, whose link to mass culture is never overtly represented by mainstream American pop art.

In another work that is both conceptual and pop but that, by insinuating itself into the nonart marketplace, is at the same time fundamentally at odds with the purist definitions of those terms, Robert Watts, continuing his 1964 attempt to copyright the term *pop*, made a piece of black Swiss cheese and engraved it with the name of his new business, Pop Art Productions.[73] He also designed T-shirts, a "cucumber table," "genital underwear," and stick-on tattoos, which were later produced under the name Implosions, Inc., with George Maciunas and Herman Fine (Figs. 52 and 53).[74]

Watts also created counterfeit money and artists' postage stamps—which, like the quasi-bureaucratic machines that dispensed them (Fig. 54), belonged to the project of at once affirming and subverting popular culture. In this case, "popular culture" is the money bureaucracy: the banks and the post offices. Thus, Watts's currency and stamp work has specific applications for both consumerism and mail art as art forms and democratizing practices. By making his own money and stamps and offering a means of distribution, Watts realized the possibility for mass culture as well its deregulation. The work stands opposed to the government-regulated monetary and postal exchange in particular and economies of production and consumption in general. In a world where time "is" money, making one's own has liberating potential.

Also referencing pop culture, *The Scissors Brothers' Warehouse Sale* graphic (*Blink;* see Fig. 12) was produced on a number of items besides an artist's canvas.[75] At the Scissors Brothers' Warehouse Sale, run by the artists George Brecht, Robert Watts, and Alison Knowles, these items were sold cheap, while the forty-two identical prints sold for between $40 and $400, the final price remaining concealed until the buyer had committed to the purchase.[76] Brecht and Watts reversed this random pricing process in *Delivery Event,* also from 1963, where the

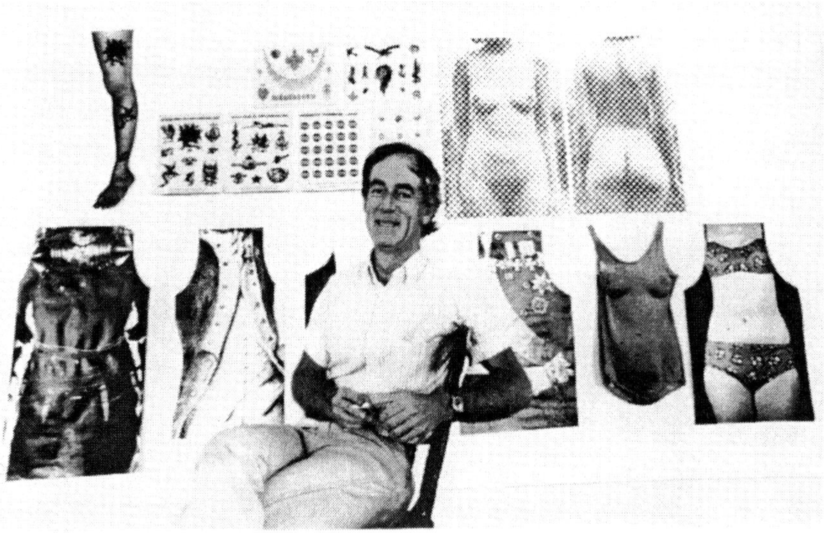

52 Robert Watts, shown with materials for *Implosions, Inc.*, 1967. Photographer unidentified; © 1988 Robert Watts Estate. Courtesy of the Robert Watts Studio Archive, New York.

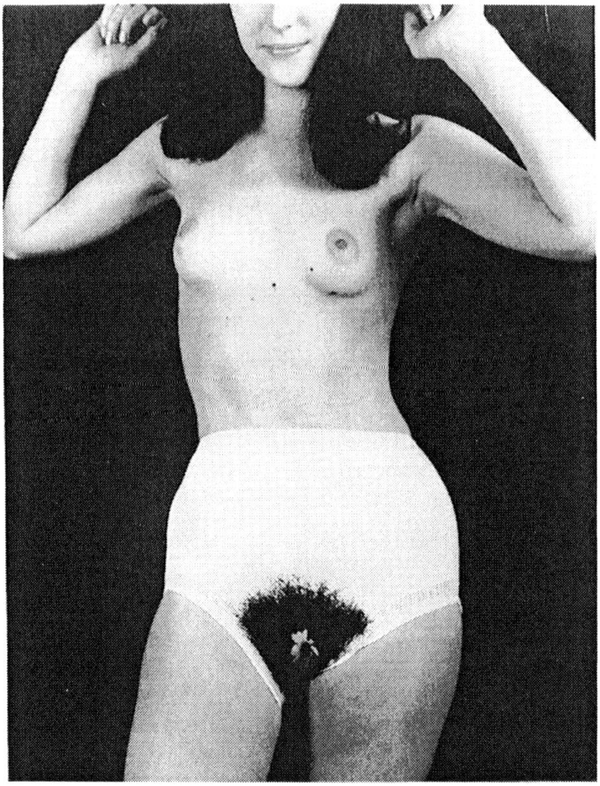

53 Robert Watts, *Female Underpants*, 1965. Photo by the artist; © 1988 Robert Watts Estate. Courtesy of the Gilbert and Lila Silverman Fluxus Collection, Detroit.

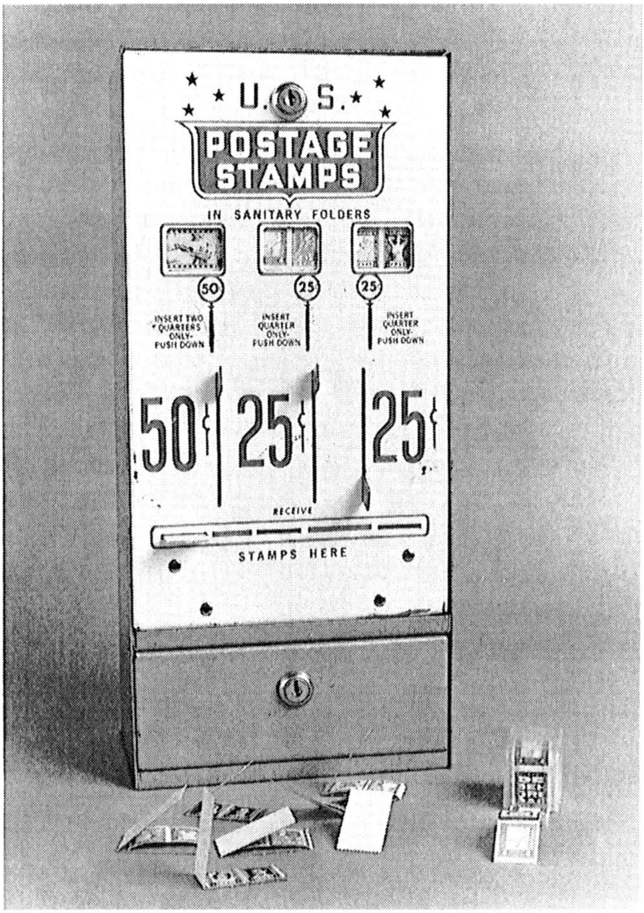

54 Robert Watts, *Stamp Dispenser,* 1963 (remade 1982). Commercial stamp dispenser, offset on gummed paper, cardboard folders, 17½ × 8¼ × 6⅝ in. Photo by Brad Iverson; courtesy of the Gilbert and Lila Silverman Fluxus Collection, Detroit.

price paid determined what would be delivered to the purchaser. Items ranged from wall stickers to green aluminum hooks and paperweights.

That same year, 1963, George Maciunas produced *Water Yam,* the boxed edition of Brecht's first Event scores (see Fig. 3). This object, which with its standardized form, peel-away label, and instructional format resembled an introductory science kit or set of reading primers, conforms to Maciunas's use of print materials in the Fluxkits and to the principle that the kits should be cheap, disposable, and unprecious. The cards themselves, however, are much like Brecht's earlier hand-printed Event cards, which aped typesetting.[77]

The high cost of culture is problematized in the cheap materials and low cost of both *Water Yam* and, somewhat differently, *Blink* and *Delivery Event. Water Yam,* which sold for about $2, suggests a manufacturer's commitment to low cost and mass production, whereas the random pricing of the forty-two silk-screened *Blink*s and the anonymity of objects associated with the final prices paid in *Delivery Event* refer to arbitrary values in art and fashion. These works thus represent different objectives for their makers—one apolitical or anarchic, the other Marxist/activist—though each uses similar popular elements: found labels, iconic images, a sign aesthetic, and innovative pricing.

Whether at the level of the mass-produced food system or the streamlined aesthetics of the public sign, Knowles, Hansen, Brecht, and Watts negotiated spaces between a popular sphere and an individual, concrete experience of eating, licking, pouring, playing, and so forth. Thus, while some pop art—especially those elements that mined consumer icons, made static films, engaged a sense of chance, or made independent distributorships—reverberates with aspects of Fluxus, the banality of most mainstream American pop art stands far removed from the experiential dimension of Fluxus pop. The same is true of conceptual art, despite its strong linkages with Fluxus textual experiments. In the end, both pop art and conceptual art have a reflexive relationship with Fluxus at the level of practice, a relationship that is as varied and complex as those movements. The influence of Fluxus in terms of its dynamism, and particularly in terms of the visceral and empirical side of Fluxus experiences, is discounted in historiographic analyses of pop and conceptual art. This lack of inclusion does as much damage to these "new forms of art," as Harvey described them, as it does to Fluxus.

GREAT EXPECTATIONS

A Reception Typology

4

American histories and surveys of performance art from the 1960s to the 1990s emphasize its gestural and expressionistic aspects, even interpreting the centrality of the body as a "performative of the subject."[1] In other words, performance activates the artist's subject identity. Although this model undoubtedly pertains to many Happenings and to the most visceral strains of political performance, it is demonstrably at odds with the typical experiential Fluxus event and Fluxkit, both of which present depersonalized, or primary, information. The performance historian's analysis of gesture and action in the service of a political agenda may explain why the many histories of performance give Fluxus scant coverage, or none at all. There are a few noteworthy exceptions, including Owen Smith's work and that of Kristine Stiles, whose recent scholarship demonstrates a tidal shift in the reception of Fluxus.

This chapter, in contrast, emphasizes texts and exhibitions that, implicitly or explicitly (both in the art world and in the journalistic mainstream), have given Fluxus its generally accepted definition in the United States as a centrally organized, activist, and American avant-garde movement.

Recent exhibitions, criticism, and archival analysis here have channeled Fluxus toward Robert Morgan's "mainstream affair," in which art moves from underground contexts into commercial galleries and, finally, large museum shows and art expositions. This cultural movement of Fluxus in the past decade or so has to a greater or lesser extent eclipsed its experiential component. With objects locked away in vitrines (a perhaps unavoidable situation, if the objects of Fluxus are to be preserved), interaction is impossible. The original purpose of the object as an experiential trigger is obfuscated, and the work merely becomes an attack on the other framed objects that surround it (for indeed, Fluxkits-underglass do *look* like anti-art).

When curators permit new work by Fluxus artists to be interacted with, they go some way toward addressing this problem. The *In the Spirit of Fluxus* exhibition of 1993, for example, which was cocurated by Liz Armstrong and Joan Rothfuss, included an interactive sounding doorway by Alison Knowles and a household-appliance concert room by Yoshi Wada. Such installations are the exception, however. Until recently, when Fluxus was codified, its experiential dimension—its core component, the one thing that marks most Fluxus work—was largely inaccessible.

Art historians, curators, and critics should know better. Artists who reference experience in their works must be taken at their instruction: it is that simple. Before developing a reception typology for Fluxus, then, I would like to explore a few ways in which Fluxus artists have presented their own work.

One example is the 1962–63 piece *Galerie Légitime* by the French artist Robert Filliou (Fig. 55). The *Galerie* consisted of a felt hat containing a rubber-stamped cloth; two handmade boxes (one of manila paper, one of orange paper), also rubber-stamped; a typewritten score in the orange box; two small coins; journal pages stapled and cut into the shape of a face; and various other objects appropriate for handling. Filliou would demonstrate and discuss the contents of his hat to curious passersby. Occasionally work by other artists might be included, as in 1962 when Ben Patterson and other participants in the Misfits Fair (see Chapter 3) contributed.

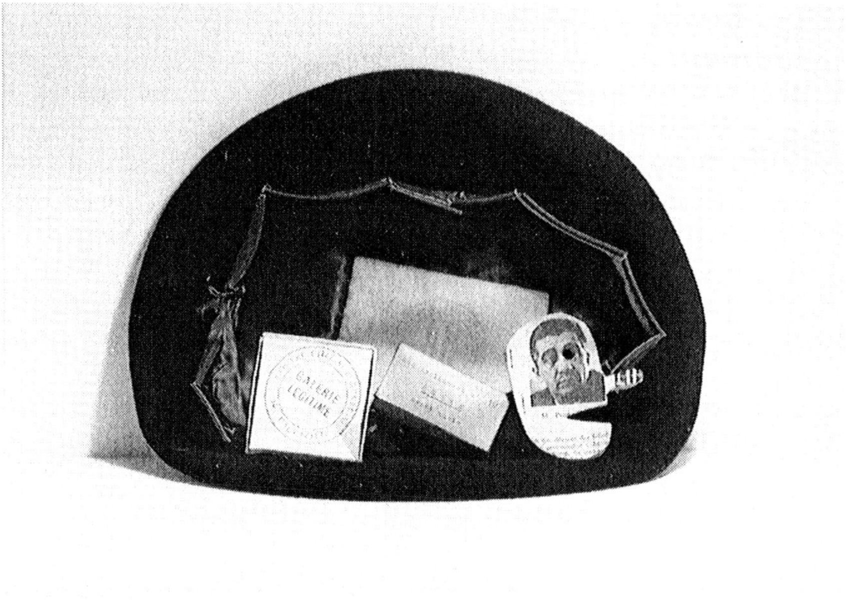

55 Robert Filliou, Galerie Légitime, 1962–63. Wool beret with mixed media. Photo by Paul Silverman; courtesy of the Gilbert and Lila Silverman Fluxus Collection, Detroit.

In the view of Fluxus as a negative dialectic, the *Galerie* is an institutional critique that rejects the organizational and viewing habits of galleries and museums (hence its name). This interpretation is not wholly incorrect. It is, however, incomplete, for it is *experientially* incorrect. Viewing the piece simply as an antigallery, antimuseum statement leaves little room for the conversations that arose with passersby, the careful handling of the boxes, the appreciation of the texture of the paper. There is much in Fluxus, and particularly in the work of Filliou, a retired mathematician, practicing Buddhist, and self-proclaimed one-eyed lapsed Huguenot, that supports this more anthropological reading, a reading very much at odds with the standard critical and art-historical frames of explanation. Proper analysis of this work would have to include many sources of information and would most likely end up being highly iconological, steeped in myriad chains of meaning irrelevant to Filliou's intent. The *Galerie*'s value as a testimony to everyday experience lies precisely in that quality: the impossibility of accounting for every contemporary or future meaning of the work.

Part of the problem of fitting the work within a particular framework of expectations, discursive strategies, and artistic intentions lies in its title. It is a gallery of some sort. But it is also a hat. And it is a changing assemblage of objects. In the end, the ontology of this remarkably open-ended piece lies in the responsibility of visitors to experience it for themselves.

Thirty years later, this responsibility of the audience constituted the curatorial thrust behind the Danish-German-American Fluxus anniversary festival "Excellent '92." The celebration began at Michael and Uta Berger's amazing Fluxus collection, the Fluxeum (housed in a converted church), in Wiesbaden-Erbenheim on 22–24 November and then traveled to the Nikolai Church in Copenhagen for performances on 26, 28, and 29 November (organized by Eric Andersen and Knud Pedersen, a friend to Fluxus since the first Danish festival in 1962).[2] An additional concert of historic works occurred on 27 November at the Malmø (Sweden) Konsthalle. During this same time, Larry Miller also organized several evenings at the Judson Church in New York. Fluxus artists from Denmark, England, France, Germany, Sweden, Japan, and the United States participated at the European venues, including Eric Andersen, Philip Corner, Geoffrey Hendricks, Dick Higgins, Joe Jones, Bengt Af Klintberg, Alison Knowles, Ann Noël, Ben Patterson, Willem de Ridder, Mieko Shiomi, Ben

Vautier, and Emmett Williams, and in New York Miller and Carolee Schneemann performed. New and old works were incorporated, so that whatever Fluxus was for a given artist at that moment determined that person's contribution.

A highlight of "Excellent '92" was Andersen and Pedersen's "Good Buy Supermarket," an inexpensive venue for mass-produced Fluxus multiples conceived in the tradition of Maciunas's Fluxhall, Ben Vautier's store, Andersen's Anonymous Merchandise market, and the Cédille qui Sourit.[3] Beyond the stipulation that each multiple offered in the supermarket should be mass producible, artists were free to determine the style and content of the objects they contributed. Shopping bags bore the "Excellent Festival" brand name, and UPC symbols appeared on all the art sold. A surging throng of shoppers snapped up the inexpensive (about $10 on average), mass-produced objects; mauling the shelves for bargains and storming the cash registers, they more closely resembled hordes after a food embargo than genteel art aficionados.

This mob scene testifies positively to the cultural significance of Fluxus in today's somewhat moribund art world. What's more, the variety of objects offered for sale speaks to the international character and range of approaches in Fluxus. Some pieces resembled recent objects by the participating artists, others were reminiscent of historic work, and many pieces drew on both present and past. Geoffrey Hendricks, for example, best known for his "sky paintings" (Fig. 56), produced a "Sky and Earth" card multiple for the Good Buy Supermarket as well as a series of fictional Fluxrelics, including a shrink-wrapped cigarette butt smoked by Joe Jones, a safety pin from one of Nam June Paik and Charlotte Moorman's stripteases, and the last bottle of wine from the Cedilla Store (see Fig. 48). New works that were continuous with historic multiples included Alison Knowles's beanbag *Pocket Warmer* for fingers, which harked back to her *Bean Rolls* of 1963, rolled texts stuffed into a square canister among dried beans. The variety of items offered for sale in the Good Buy Supermarket makes it clear that the Fluxus multiple, though related to the typical Maciunas multiple, such as his Fluxkits (see Fig. 5), is at the same time distinct from that model.

According to Peter Frank, "The Fluxus 'manner' as preached and promulgated by Maciunas emphasized a stylized and rarefied version of Intermedia characterized by wit, game-playing, reduced means and formats and enigmatic expression"; that manner, however, "constituted only one facet of Fluxus."[4] For example, whereas

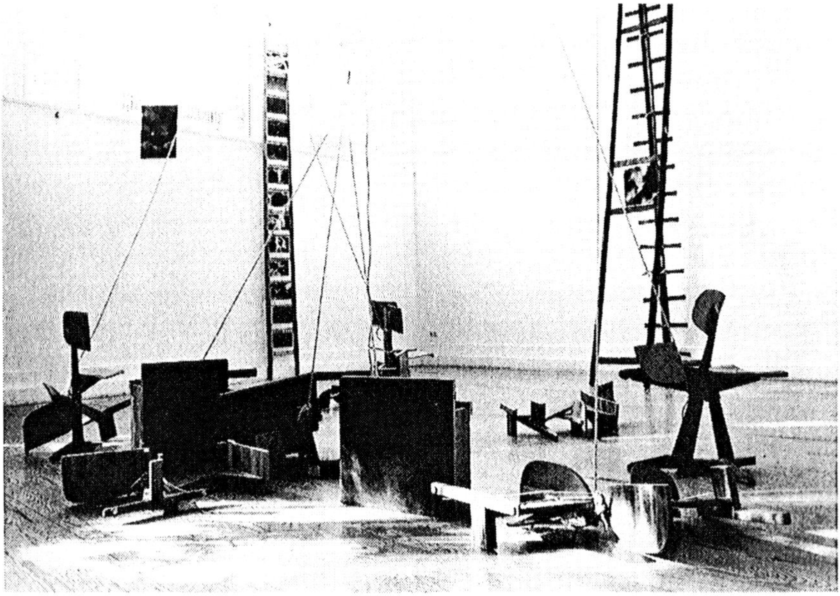

56 Geoffrey Hendricks, *Quarter*, 1992. Mixed-media installation at Fluxus Da Capo Festival, Kunsthaus, Wiesbaden, Germany. Photo by Iosif Kiraly; courtesy of the artist.

the Maciunas-type Fluxkit does not necessarily identify the authors of its various parts, the creators of the multiples produced for the Good Buy Supermarket were named on the label, a gesture toward authorial integrity that does not, however, violate the integrity of Fluxus as a multifaceted whole, a site of interacting and changing ideas. Similarly, the Fluxkit was hand-assembled, allowing a one-of-a-kind distinction to be made. In contrast, the Good Buy multiples were all mechanically shrink-wrapped, emphasizing their mass production and mass availability more successfully than any sales context invented thus far by Fluxus.

The performance formats created for Excellent '92 were similarly open ended and available to a diverse audience. The festival opened at the Bergers' Fluxeum on 22 November with an "à la carte" approach. Audience members sat at small tables, where a two-page, formal menu listed various Events, both old and new, by the range of Fluxus artists present and costing from $2 to $20. Ben Patterson, acting as headwaiter, then circulated among the spectators, took their orders, and directed the artists to the various tables to perform the selected Events.

The diners were witness to their own selections and others' as performances occurred throughout the space. Tinkling, mechanically rhythmic music made by rotary-motorized rubber bands on violins and Superballs on tom-toms and other drums in the choir loft of the Bergers' church-museum announced that someone had "ordered" Joe Jones's "Big Band" of self-propelled musical instruments (see Fig. 25). Meanwhile, Dick Higgins on a ladder pouring water into a basin meant that someone had ordered George Brecht's *Drip Music* (see Fig. 2). Two live hens strutted in another part of the room—Ben Vautier's *Hens*—and Alison Knowles appeared with a new work, shaking a metal tray full of beans and toys as she walked around the room. In the midst of this apparent chaos were people sitting at tables listening to Sony Walkmans, carrying out instructions recorded by de Ridder to (among other things) "suck on your finger," "stick your finger in your ear," "lift your chair over your head," or "stand on your chair."

Experiential coherence was afforded by the fact that audience members controlled what was ordered and from whom and had direct contact with the artist, sometimes even as co-performers. The artists, moreover, performed in one another's pieces and talked about them, further bolstering the coherence of the event. In the engagement of audience interest and breadth of experience presented, as well as in its emphasis of the communal, experiential nature of Fluxus, the à la carte format made for the most successful evenings of the Excellent festival.[5]

Given the open-ended nature of Fluxus as exemplified by the Excellent festival, which meandered between rational and not, structured and not, mediated and not, and among multiple senses, this description stands vulnerable to the accusation that it merely mystifies experience. This is a risk that I have attempted to allay while still creating the space for experience in a broad epistemological sense here. What remains is to explore how Fluxus has come to mean what it has in various contexts—either as art or as something else. For example, the *Galerie Légitime* might be an anti-art gallery for one viewer, a fashion statement for another, a cabinet of curiosities for a third, and a garbage can for a fourth, while the à la carte format might register as dinner theater for one viewer, an occasion for conversation for another, avant-garde disturbance for a third, and a cosmic blitz for a fourth. These readings are not incompatible, merely variously descriptive; they give the best Fluxus work meaning in terms of the range of experiences and discourses it is able to summon up.

The primary experience Fluxus engenders gains meaning from the discourses it evokes. All art has a primary aspect and a discursive aspect—the issue is where the experience occurs on this continuum. The critical establishment, however, has favored the latter. From the point of view of a high-art mainstream, for example, Fluxus has been primarily understood as a rejection of abstract expressionism (specifically, its painterly basis), an interpretation that does little to address its primary, experiential aspect. That Fluxus was lambasted in the early days for being excessively boring (read: untheatrical), ugly (read: unpainterly), and ideological (read: un-American) indicates expectations predicated on a particular reading of art produced during the cold war and associated with the loose category of formalism. As this chapter will demonstrate, reception of Fluxus over the past thirty years, which is marked by a remarkably consistent tone of denigration or appreciation along these lines, lies squarely in the perceptions and misperceptions of the early years.

Fluxus Nostalgia

As early as the mid-1970s, the American press had come to regard Fluxus as a historic movement, even though the artists continued to produce as a group. Thus located in the past, Fluxus became a living memory of the idealism of the sixties. In

1977, for example, Maciunas's project "Seattle Week" received coverage that reinforced a nostalgia-based definition of the group, both by telling of his "founding" of Fluxus in 1961 and by describing the adherence of Fluxus to the historical avant-garde. One critic wrote in the *Seattle Times* that Fluxus "serves to remind us we [should] accept and stop questioning... our lives. Anyone may conduct a Fluxfest event. The Movement has been holding events in New York City, Europe and Japan since 1961."[6] A week later, another *Times* article described the philosophical basis of Fluxus work in pure Maciunas terms, as anti-art and anticommodity; not only that, but in its anti-one-upping avant-gardism it was, the reviewer noted, intentionally opaque.[7]

A review in the *Seattle Post-Intelligencer,* while not embracing the anti-art aspect of Fluxus, reflects this shift toward Fluxus as nostalgic history as well. Focusing on the movement's attention to commodification, the writer R. M. Campbell says that "Fluxus is concerned with enjoyment, with good things; it is benign. It is also disposable.... It all seems disturbingly American: do it, create it, dispose of it."[8] Although in Campbell's view disposability becomes the endpoint of Fluxus ephemerality, the Event structure itself refutes this interpretation. In fact, the performative elements of virtually every Event—those things that promote flux as a necessary, far from precious mode of experience—not only reject disposability but emphasize regeneration and reuse of objects and experiences. The deceptively simple "no smoking" sign in Brecht's Event (see Fig. 31) contains *two* options—to smoke and not to smoke—and permits a recycling of the sign system (and the object itself) as art. Thus Campbell goes one step further than the *Times* critics quoted above, eliding the social and political claims of Maciunas's idea of Fluxus even as he confuses ephemerality and disposability.

By the time Maciunas died in 1978, the art press had almost completely accepted a nostalgic and historicist view of the political aims of Fluxus and its role in spurring a generational coming-of-age. Subsequent reviews praised Fluxus exhibitions and concerts as testimonials to Maciunas's perspective or criticized them for compromising that sacred formula. In either case, the constant element is a distancing of the present from the idyllic or naive early 1960s.

Typical of positive evaluations is a 1979 article in *Flash Art International* that provides a gleeful account of a Fluxus memorial concert for Maciunas consisting of thirty-three primarily classic 1960s Events in New York City (see Fig. 34).[9] A dozen or so artists, including Philip Corner, Ken Friedman, Geoffrey Hendricks, Dick Higgins, Alison Knowles, Larry Miller, Peter van Riper, Yasunao Tone, and Robert Watts,[10] performed such short pieces as *Snowstorm No. 1* by Milan Knizak (who was not present), in which "paper gliders are distributed to an idle and waiting audience,"[11] and *Wall Piece for Orchestra*, an unusually non-ego-based and lovely Event by Yoko Ono (also not present): "Hit a wall with your head," where the performers came in single file and quite close to a wall and then gently tilted their heads into it.[12] As this concert proved, said the reviewer, "the Fluxus spirit and George Maciunas are still very much alive."

In the *SoHo Weekly News*, Elin von Spreckelsen comments on the same concert: "It was clear by the audience's responses that the pieces are viable today. They show their contribution to the opening up of ideas and the commonplace acceptance of conceptual art today.... Looking at the pieces in 1979, one *nostalgically* can see how Fluxus ideas journey in both the art world and in mass humor."[13] While the author references 1960s-based definitions of the group (logically enough, given that this was a memorial concert for Maciunas), she does not appear to completely buy into the Maciunas myth when she states that "it is typical of Fluxus to have one artist step outside of his own artistic identity to become a performer in another artist's piece." Thus the matrix or communal nature of Fluxus performance is shown to override the apotheosis of the individual (even, perhaps, Maciunas himself). Later, Spreckelsen differentiates the reception of Fluxus in Europe and that in the United States: "Unlike the Happening which started during the same time, Fluxus never received commercial success.... [although as an] alternative to traditional gallery art, it did catch international attention in the artistic world outside of the United States. Here, unpublicized and unconsumed, it continues to live in its unofficial way." Perhaps Spreckelsen is suggesting that Fluxus was structurally predisposed to fail in the United States, whereas in Europe the avant-garde tradition created a context better able to support related work.

Writing about the same concert, critic and longtime enthusiast of Fluxus music Tom Johnson adopted a curiously passive point of view:

> I would like to comment on George Maciunas, the self-proclaimed patron saint of the New York Fluxus Group, and on the tabloid Newspaper celebrating his death that I purchased at the concert. I would like to discuss the recent work by

> Alison Knowles that was also included in the program. And I would like to go into detail about particularly memorable performances.... But it seems preferable to focus on [the] 60s pieces.

Just why the nostalgic, historicist point of view is "preferable" is unclear. The review does not cover recent work, and it is typical of writing from this period. Perhaps this statement provides a clue:

> What was Fluxus? It was a genre of performance art that happened 10 years before the term was coined. It was a form of dada that happened 30 years after dada. It was what happened when young followers of John Cage gathered together in the early 60s. It was a style that drew minuscule audiences and no critics when it was alive. And it is a matter of some nostalgia today.[14]

A similar historicizing of a bygone Fluxus dominates an article on George Maciunas that appeared in *Artforum* in 1982: "The man who ran Fluxus almost single-handedly for 13 of its 16 years was also the person responsible for 'the Fluxus look,' and as identifiable as that look is, it was based on a set of not-purely-aesthetic principles that permeated everything Maciunas did."[15] Like many artistic innovations, the Fluxus graphic style practiced by Maciunas was the result of necessity. As the author of this article rightly points out, the crowded letters, minimal margins, and odd formats that Maciunas used arose from his need to conserve funds. Where a border was not needed in a commercial graphic-design job, Maciunas designed it for a Fluxus graphic and then cut it off and used it for a Fluxus piece. These objects, with their identifiable style, quickly assumed non-utilitarian meanings and contributed significantly to a Maciunas = Fluxus perspective on the group—a perspective that determines the contents of the largest collection of Fluxus materials in the world.[16]

The Silverman Fluxus Collection

The Gilbert and Lila Silverman Fluxus Collection—located in Detroit and New York and curated by Jon Hendricks, a friend of George Maciunas, who sometimes collaborated with him, and a vocal supporter of Fluxus since the mid-1960s—is the only major collection in the world that holds uncompromisingly to the Maciunas-based paradigm for Fluxus.[17] In an article from 1983, Hendricks writes: "At its inception, Fluxus was intended by George Maciunas to be a publication.... A significant aspect of Fluxus, which is perhaps frequently felt, but seldom written about, is its concern with social politics." He then provides "several quotations taken from George Maciunas' letters to various Fluxus artists which clearly demonstrate the underlying political purpose of Fluxus."[18] The perspective that Maciunas alone inspired the formation of Fluxus and was responsible for its political agenda has determined the content of five catalogues associated with the Silverman Collection (two of them presented to the public as "definitive"), as well as some misattributions.[19] As is typical of the process of artistic canonization, the collection's "Fluxus"-titled objects and Events narrowed increasingly in scope as "non-Fluxus" work (meaning work not "intended by George Maciunas" to be part of Fluxus) was progressively excluded.[20] At the same time, the production quality of each catalogue rose as increasingly prestigious venues sponsored the exhibitions.

For example, the first catalogue, *Fluxus Etc.*, was produced in 1981 by the Cranbrook Academy of Art in Bloomfield Hills, Michigan, using cheap newsprint and no-gloss card stock. It is comparatively open in its inclusion of materials that fall outside Hendricks's strict definition of Fluxus (to which he attributed much of the group's energy)—that is, in what he calls "etc." The flyer accompanying the book and exhibition notes that although "the group was held together by George Maciunas [who] designed, edited, published and produced the Fluxus editions—year boxes, books, newspapers, films and broadsides..., the movement's strength was its diversity and independence of the many artists involved."[21] *Fluxus Etc., Addenda I,* a collection of writings, followed the Cranbrook catalogue in 1983. Also produced on newsprint, it contains no declarative statement but privileges Maciunas: roughly 90 percent of the book reproduces newsletters and proposals written almost exclusively by Maciunas, while the remaining 10 percent is a transcript of a deathbed interview between Maciunas and Larry Miller.

The third publication issuing from the Silverman Collection, *Fluxus Etc., Addenda II*, appeared a few months later under the auspices of the Baxter Art Gallery in Pasadena, California. Its production values are still higher, with the print appearing on a better grade of paper and the glossy red heavy-stock cover featuring Maciunas's Purge Manifesto (see Fig. 28). This catalogue contains an introduction, written by gallery director Jay Belloli, that describes the collection's establishment "in 1978 (unfortunately shortly before the death of George Maciunas)," which marks the end of Fluxus and, effectively, the termination date of the collection's holdings. This final edition of the *Etc.* catalogues marks the culmination in the preliminary phase of the process of equating Fluxus with Maciunas and packaging Fluxus in increasingly luxurious publications.

Though not a catalogue per se, a later (1995) publication by the commercial house Thames and Hudson, unambiguously titled *Fluxus,* belongs to this same lineage, in part because Hendricks coauthored it, in part because sixty-five of the ninety-six images derive from the Silverman Collection (of the rest, twenty-nine are from Archiv Sohm, Staatsgalerie Stuttgart, and two from the Onnasch Collection of Museu d'Art Contemporani de Barcelona).[22] The lead essay, Thomas Kellein's "I Make Jokes! Fluxus through the Eyes of 'Chairman' George Maciunas," offers the reader quotations that seem to undermine the absolute category of "chairman," though the work depicted reasserts the dominant paradigm of Fluxus as outlined in English-language publications.

The same model determined the publicity for larger museum shows, and thus (indirectly) the reviews of those shows. A 1983 exhibition flyer for the Neuberger Museum at the State University of New York at Purchase, for example, presented this version of Fluxus:

> Fluxus was an international art movement founded by George Maciunas in the early 1960s. Inspired by such art movements as futurism and dada, the artists, poets, musicians and dancers who embraced Fluxus were held together by the idea of an art for every man, a non-academic art, which encompassed satire and humor in order to poke fun at materialism, "fine art," and even itself through a series of exhibitions, festivals . . . etc.[23]

The *New York Times* reviewed the show, making the predictable observation regarding the paradox that marked Maciunas's anti-institutional stance and the work's institutional viability: "One of the ironies of our time is that throwaway art becomes archivable, collectible, pricey (A Fluxus Year Box. . . . would now fetch $250) and institutionally embraceable."[24] Given the institutionalization of the historical avant-garde, the fact that Maciunas's Fluxus is called "institutionally embraceable" should come as no surprise. Irony notwithstanding, this observation is based on a misattribution of the group's relationship to institutions, as described in Chapter 2. The first Fluxus-titled concerts occurred in a museum in Wiesbaden, Germany, after all. A reviewer of the same exhibition at its Pasadena, California, venue took note of the transformation of Fluxus from a disorganized social alliance into a movement befitting the basic tenets of modernist art history, stating that "The practice of art history abhors a messy drawer in the art kitchen... so the territory of the utter chaos known as Fluxus has begun to be straightened out."[25] This straightening out seems to require the transformation of Fluxus from an open-ended, experiential movement into a rigidly codified political one. The irony may lie, not in the institutionalization of an anti-institutional movement, but in the programmatic revision of an experiential one.

A show in 1988 at the Museum of Modern Art suggests the success of this art-historical project. The accompanying publication, *Fluxus: Selections from the Gilbert and Lila Silverman Collection*, contains an essay by MoMA book curator Clive Phillpot on Fluxus in the mid-1980s. In it, he defines Fluxus by way of the Purge Manifesto produced by Maciunas before the first Fluxus-named festival in Wiesbaden in 1962 (the document also appears on the verso of the catalogue's title page). As in *Addenda II*, therefore, the manifesto is physically and conceptually fused with the name Fluxus. Phillpot writes: "The aims of Fluxus, as set out in the Manifesto of 1963, are extraordinary, but connect with the radical ideas fermenting at the time."[26] The fact that the manifesto was unsigned appears to be irrelevant.

The Museum of Modern Art show, which virtually guaranteed movement of this version of Fluxus into the mainstream of art-historical consciousness in the United States, was instigated in part by the projected publication of the first deluxe coffee-table book on Fluxus, *Fluxus Codex,* by the Silverman Collection and Harry Abrams. In November 1987 Hendricks wrote to Riva Castleman, curator of prints and drawings at MoMA:

> In the Fall of 1988, Harry N. Abrams will publish *Fluxus Codex*, a massive study of Fluxus products documenting every known work, whether made or planned. There has been consistent lack of understanding about this international movement which was predominantly centered in America.... I would like to discuss with you the possibility of a small Fluxus show at the Museum of Modern Art next Fall that would coincide with the publication of *Fluxus Codex*.[27]

The affirmative response came from Clive Phillpot, whose MoMA library had exhibition space.

Critics either praised the exhibit by reference to a nostalgic and politicized model of the 1960s or criticized it for lacking vitality. The venue itself even brought about differences of opinion. A review in *Artforum* stated: "The do-it-yourself wackiness of the objects might have been lost in an over-aestheticized setting, but that is no reason to marginalize the work by stuffing it into the vestibule of a library."[28] Robert Morgan saw things differently: "One of the delights at seeing this exhibition is that it's in the Library of the Museum of Modern Art and not in the regular exhibition space. This makes the show somewhat of an adventure. One gets the opportunity to hunt, to peer around the card catalogues and to look between the shelved books on reserve. Fluxus emphasized such an approach." In addition, Morgan addresses the problem of Maciunas's role in Fluxus: "Through it all it was clear that George Maciunas was the central figure. His relationship to Fluxus was comparable to Breton's relationship to Surrealism."[29]

Like the MoMA catalogue and *Addenda II*, the *Fluxus Codex* accepts the Maciunas-based paradigm for Fluxus. The book, which reproduces two photos of Maciunas's studio from 1969 on a spread immediately preceding the title page, serves as a catalogue raisonné of Fluxus projects linked to Maciunas by production or mention in a newsletter. The introduction by Robert Pincus-Witten explains that "Fluxus' resident Genius was George Maciunas. . . . Fluxus begins with the foundation of Fluxus press in 1961–2, abruptly terminating in May of 1978 when Maciunas dies."[30] Although it contains no scholarly or interpretive writing, the collection's stringent stance creates a uniform aesthetic that obscures the idiosyncratic nature of Fluxus as it has been understood by the majority of its artists. Bruce Altschuler notes this problem in his critique of the *Codex* for *Arts* magazine: "Restricting Fluxus to Maciunas related material . . . creates an arbitrary division within the work of many artists. More importantly, to follow Maciunas in taking a narrow view of Fluxus is to limit our understanding of its significance."[31]

At about the same time, other American institutions that so far had embraced a community-based, multiple understanding of Fluxus now abandoned that vision. The Jean Brown Collection at the Getty Center for the History of Art and the Humanities, for example, was radically restructured in the late 1980s to accommodate the Maciunas-based organizational model. Free-form artists' files were reorganized in relationship to Maciunas's newsletters and projects. "Other" material was appended to files outside the system. Although this reconfiguration reflected Brown's understanding of Fluxus as Maciunas's project,[32] it did not accurately reflect the collection itself, which, according to archivist Eric Vos, included many "non-Fluxus events etc., containing non-Fluxus work by Fluxus artists."[33] Brown, indeed, viewed herself as a nexus within a larger community.[34] In reorganizing the Brown collection, then, Vos adopted an approach quite different from Brown's: "The demarcation of Fluxus as a group of artists (rather than as a canon of works) has meanwhile been 'codified,' with Jon Hendricks's Fluxus Codex.... [Therefore] the Fluxus Codex formed the basis of the organization of this series."[35] Without a doubt, this restructuring will affect how scholars experience the archive and how they will arrange information.

This Maciunas-centered schema also determined the core narrative of "In the Spirit of Fluxus," which opened at the Walker Art Center in Minneapolis in February 1992, and then followed an extensive itinerary, including the Whitney Museum of American Art in New York; Museum of Contemporary Art in Chicago; Wexner Center for the Visual Arts in Columbus, Ohio; San Francisco Museum of Modern Art; Santa Monica Museum; and Fundació Antoni Tápies in Barcelona. As the most visible and largest such exhibition to date, "In the Spirit of Fluxus" has defined Fluxus for most people for the immediate future. Moreover, its acceptance at these major institutions reflects a shift in the ruling standard of taste in favor of critical art forms. The Maciunas-based paradigm, with its emphasis on cost-effectiveness, political idealism, and collective identity, sat comfortably astride that shift. Nevertheless, the focus on Maciunas had an enfeebling, oppressive effect in the end. As one reviewer put it, "I strolled around and looked at all the crappy junk gathered in editions: bottles, jars, spectacles, plastic mickey mouse toys. Something was very wrong. It was as if someone was telling you a really corny joke and you almost laughed but didn't want to expend the energy.... Fluxus is the art of victims, and its secret dreariness and oppressed sensibility waft up to the viewer from beneath the gag."[36]

In contrast, and to the curators' credit, risks were taken in the inclusion of the two contemporary works named at the beginning of this chapter as well as at the symposium that accompanied the opening, "Fluxus Publicus." There, Fluxus scholar Karen Moss described several "Fluxus West" California projects that fell outside the scope of the show; Eric Andersen discussed Fluxus in Europe, before, during, and after Maciunas; and Alexandra Munroe examined the broad context of Fluxus in Japan. In this manner, the exhibition organizers made space for dissension, which occurred in heated debates following the lectures. However, the dominant narrative reigned in the exhibition catalogue, *In the Spirit of Fluxus.*[37] With the exception of Kristine Stiles's elastic and experientially broad analysis of the Event, "Between Water and Stone," and Andreas Huyssen's "Back to the Future: Fluxus in Context," each essay in that volume confirmed the standard point of view, which in turn was supported by the majority of artifacts on exhibit. Reflecting the strong object basis of Fluxus exhibitions in this country since Maciunas's death, only one Fluxus performance, by Emmett Williams, occurred during the entire opening weekend.[38]

Williams's performance may be linked to the publication of *My Life in Flux—and Vice Versa,* an account of thirty years of Fluxus activity from the perspective of one of its most gifted artists.[39] As such, the book offers a humorous, personal, and highly informative series of recollections. Even as he sees Fluxus through the lens of Maciunas's leadership, Williams provides anecdotes of present-day events and traces productive friendships, such as with the poet Robert Filliou, that endured long after Maciunas's death. This book was followed five years later by an equally amusing and detailed series of writings by Maciunas's friends and colleagues, edited by Williams and his wife, Ann Noël, called *Mr. Fluxus: A Collective Portrait of George Maciunas* (Fig. 57).[40]

Williams's first contact with Fluxus came at the very start. Shortly before the first Fluxus-titled festival in Wiesbaden (where he was living) in 1962, he had received a letter from his friend LaMonte Young, from the international concrete poetry and experimental music scene, inviting Williams to submit work to the journal *Beatitude East,* a project that would eventually become *An Anthology,* designed by Maciunas and comprising new music, concrete poetry, and ideas that would be central to Fluxus generally. Responding to Williams's questions about Maciunas and the projected Wiesbaden concerts, Young wrote: "He is a very good swindler and money hustler and hard worker and an expert at type photo-offset work—he will probably give very good concerts once the series gets going. He has much energy."[41] This letter suggests that Williams's association with Maciunas was nearly simultaneous with the naming of Fluxus, although his relationship to other

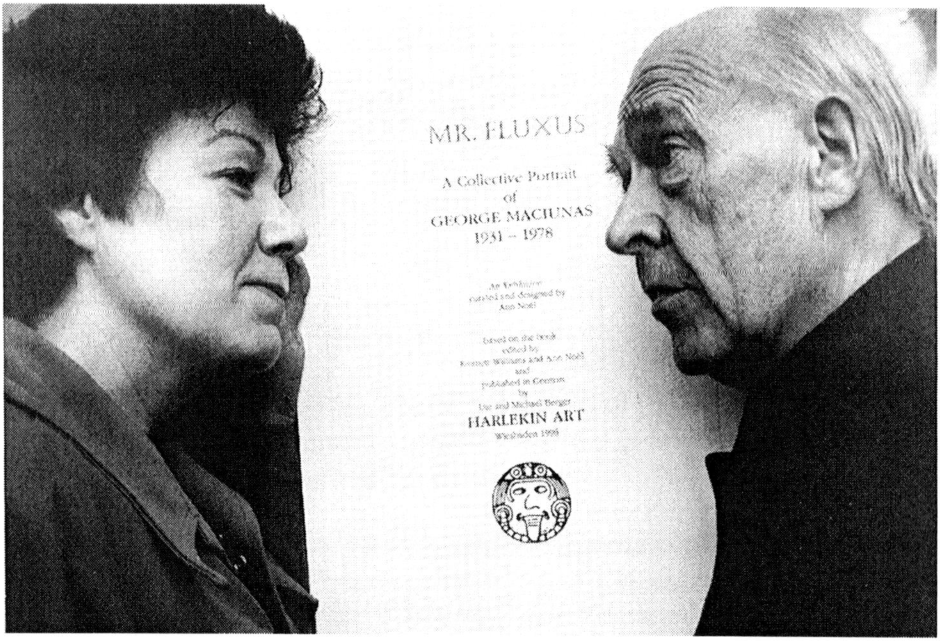

57 Ann Noël and Emmett Williams at preview event for publication of their book *Mr. Fluxus: A Collective Portrait of George Maciunas, 1931–1978*, at the Fluxeum in Wiesbaden, Germany, 1996. Photo by and courtesy of Larry Miller, © 1996.

Fluxus artists through the Darmstadt circle of concrete poets and the Kalenderrolle group discussed in Chapter 2 was already established. The timing may help to explain why he endorsed the notion of Maciunas's leadership of the group. In covering the Wiesbaden festival for *Stars and Stripes*, the U.S. Army newspaper, Williams described the moment of Fluxus's founding thus: "This confused beginning began in Europe in 1962, when George Maciunas said let there be Fluxus and there was Fluxus ever after."[42]

With the exception of the early and middle 1970s, when he lived in the United States and Canada, Williams has lived in Germany since the late 1950s. Location is extremely important here, since German reception of Fluxus tends to avoid the strict identification with Maciunas and his American base after 1963, instead privileging other types of activity and thus generating a different critical reception. There, the association of Fluxus with Maciunas functions as a point of coalescence for prior tendencies and as a launching point for contemporary production through the present moment. That take on the movement—as temporally and socially elastic, experientially open ended, and adaptable to multiple perspectives—is closer to my account of Fluxus and this remarkable group of people. As the following account suggests, however, there are problems with this model as it pertains to German history. From the point of view of German history, however, Williams's account should be seen as a welcome alternative to the dominant model.

Fluxus Europa: Productive Amnesia and the Accurate Account

Germany

> I deeply regret yr. being in Europe... For Heaven's sake, don't get pleased by that life. —Cage to Brecht, Dec. 3, 1965[43]

In 1965, George Brecht relocated from Metuchen, New Jersey, to France because he felt Europe, with its official support of the arts, was more amenable to his and his friends' work. After briefly running the Cédille qui Sourit, the art novelty store on the French Riviera that he shared with Robert Filliou (see Figs. 46 and 47), Brecht settled in the greater metropolitan area of Cologne.[44]

Four other American Fluxus artists permanently relocated to Germany: Al Hansen, like Brecht, settled in Cologne, where he spent most of the last thirty years of his life; Emmett Williams moved to Berlin; and Ben Patterson and Joe Jones ended up in Wiesbaden. At various times Philip Corner, Geoffrey Hendricks, Dick Higgins, and Alison Knowles lived in Germany as well, for periods ranging from six months to one and a half years. Since these artists constitute almost all the Americans active in Fluxus,[45] the pattern of relocation requires some analysis.

As we have seen, it is a one-sided interpretation of these artists' project, which has risen to visibility since the 1970s. In the 1990s, moreover, a nostalgic longing for the loftier ideals of 1960s radicalism fueled its further popular acceptance. In both situations, the critical reception of Fluxus reflected strongly on the needs of its audience. In Germany, in contrast, critics, supported in varying degrees either by the state press or, indirectly, by Springer Verlag (which some view as a virtual publishing monopoly), have presented Fluxus as a testimony to German tolerance and support of the prewar avant-garde tradition since the fall of the Third Reich. This continuity with a prefascist past typifies the amnesiac propaganda of the Adenauer and subsequent governments, especially their elision of the recent atrocities to further the perception of a continuous, democratic Germany.[46] Twenty years after the end of the war, Peter Weiss's play *The Investigation* parodied this attitude: "Today now that our nation has once again worked its way up to a leading position we should be concerned with other things than with recriminations. These should long ago have been banished from the law books by the statute of limitations."[47] And from cultural history as well, if we follow that logic through. Hence the strong support in the 1960s of culture that aligned with the prewar avant-garde.

Given this attitude, it is hardly surprising that many exhibitions and publications from this time endorse the avant-garde qualities of early Fluxus work as well as the movement's democratic pluralism. By 1989, the prevailing social philosophy in Germany was that of the *Kulturgesellschaft* (cultural society), out of which would "evolve a political culture that thrived on adversarial debate (*Streitkultur*) rooted in a basic social consensus"—the intention being, according to section 4 of the Basic Program of the Social Democratic Party (SPD), to provide "a new culture of mutual toleration and collaboration."[48] Given this philosophical atmosphere, favorable responses to Fluxus expound on its iconoclastic qualities (which link it stylistically to the historical avant-garde) as well as its political pluralism, or *Streitkultur.* Less sympathetic responses, rooted in similar terminology, question the potentially negative political influences of Fluxus as a practice identified with dada.

The association of Fluxus with the historical avant-garde was not limited to the German press and culture industries. Maciunas himself associated Fluxus with dada, and several Fluxus artists had personal relationships with such dada-associated figures as Marcel Duchamp and Richard Hülsenbeck.[49] The inspiration that Fluxus artists found in dada was different at different times, ranging from a primarily constructive reading in 1962 to a comparatively nihilistic one by 1963.

A key event in this evolution occurred on 9 June 1962 at one of the first European Fluxus concerts, "Après John Cage," held in Wuppertal, when Arthur C. Caspari read Maciunas's essay "Neo-Dada in Music, Theater, Poetry, Art" aloud. The text describes neo-dada not as nihilist (as the American press interpreted it), but as positioned between anti-art and the creative principle, in particular the idea of concretism, which here means a fusion of life and art, form and content.

> Neo-dada, ... or what appears to be Neo-dada manifests itself in very wide fields of creativity. It ranges from "time" arts to "space" arts; or more specifically from literary arts (time-art), through graphic-literature (time-space-art) to graphics (space-time-arts) to graphless or scoreless music (time-art), through theatrical music (space-time-art) to environments (space-arts).... Almost each category and each artist, however, is bound with the concept of Concretism ranging in intensity from pseudo concretism ... to the extreme of concretism, which is beyond the limits of art, and therefore sometimes referred to as anti-art, or art-nihilism.[50]

As the context for this reading suggests, Maciunas's early idea of neo-dada—specifically, as a model for validating the work of artists previously clustered around Cage and Stockhausen—matured in a receptive German environment. Given the standard view of dada as a rejection of German expressionism, his interdisciplinary definition of neo-dada might also reflect a desire to relate Fluxus to abstract painting.[51] In 1962, then, Maciunas made the association between Fluxus and neo-dada; however, his politics in relation to the earlier movement remained unformed. By 1963 the concretism of neo-dada would yield to the politicization of Fluxus.

The period of Maciunas's conversion toward the ideology of the 1963–64 publications described in Chapter 2 coincides with the baptism of Fluxus in 1962 and its subsequent politicization at his hands a year later. As sometime Fluxus artist Henry Flynt observed, "As of mid 1961, Maciunas' preference in art was for a reasonable, academic modernism.... [By 1963], Maciunas had shifted to a position of hostility to respectable culture—on a basis of radical unpretentiousness and [radical art] was supposed to accord with left politics."[52] Whereas in his "neo-dada" statement, Maciunas mentions many forms of concrete art, such as theatrical music and environments, that would not have been consistent with his later "hostility to respectable culture," his later perspective was exemplified by small-scale pieces and Events. Thus, in 1962 Maciunas's use of the term *neo-dada,* while it may have had some political implications, was primarily not political but philosophical, aligning Fluxus with artistic concretism and anti-expressionism and with the historic shift from expressionism to dada. By the time he wrote the Purge Manifesto in 1962 (see Fig. 28), his evolution toward the "extreme of concretism" was complete.[53]

In contrast to this narrow definition of neo-dadaism, a dissertation by the German art historian Maria Müller favors a multifaceted reading of dada in the German context:

> Consciousness [of dada in the 1950s] was not only of its will to destruction, through which the majority of dada could be characterized, but also and directly of the visual work of the dadaists[, occurring] as *a constructive alternative to art history* necessarily became valued. In reaction to the then-dominant currents of abstract expressionism..., the generation of young artists sought...a loosening from the subjective language of self-expression and a real relevance, through the integration of extra-artistic materials, of art on life.[54]

Reviews of Fluxus in Germany divide along these same lines, with critics emphasizing the destructive aspects of dadaism and proponents lauding its rejuvenating and socially reflexive elements, its constructive force. The *Neue Rheinische Zeitung* published a negative review of a Fluxus concert in 1962, targeting the most overtly iconoclastic aspect of dada's influence on Fluxus: "[At] the end senseless sentences and conversational scraps were recited, then five minutes of reading postage cancellations from the participating cities, until the audience... revolted against the dadaist, revolutionary humor."[55] At the other extreme, the *Rhein-Saar-Spiegel* supported the constructive interpretation of neo-dada and nostalgic harking back to the historical avant-garde: "Fluxus relates to all types of artistic exceptions of people, indeed it [the Fluxus concert] was also in part 'anti-art,' which in no sense should be understood as nonartistic, rather only a playful variation of artistic action.... That is exactly the situation that existed forty years ago. At that time it was called dada. Today its analogue must be called neo-dada."[56]

Elsewhere writers, tiptoeing gingerly around intolerance of the avant-garde under Hitler, demand open-mindedness toward vanguard art. Heinz Ohff, for example, in an article titled "That's Just Crazy," states that "it is the job of art historians, sociologists and philosophers to justify. Artists should not have to justify, rather they should be justified."[57] To expect the artist to engage in didactic clarification, in other words, is to compromise the principle of artistic freedom, since it requires a production of ideas for a mass audience. Considering Nazi oppression of the arts, where artists were persecuted because they did not conform to populist and nationalistic expectations for their work, Ohff's statement both reflects and rejects a historical situation. However, even in the early 1960s social and political freedom hung very much in the balance, as the erection of the Berlin Wall in 1961 makes clear. Thus, the problem of tolerance produced two lines of criticism that, even as both adhered to a historicist program, differed at the level of value, since one associates free thought with explanation and mass accessibility, and the other associates the same not with audience access so much as with free production.

For example, in a twist on the theme of tolerance, Klaus Honnef suggests that the freedom engendered by the apparent art-life mixture in Fluxus might lead paradoxically to an aestheticization, and hence a tolerance, of violence: "If... all of reality is declared an aesthetic experience, one must also take on [the] horror: it follows that atom bombs are an aesthetic sensibility and consciousness in the sense of the Happenings ideologues."[58] Free speech necessarily includes polarized ideologies—and can, Honnef seems to be saying, produce monsters. It is possible to imagine Fluxus principles applied to appalling political ends—left or right.

Significantly, a polarized situation marked both the late Weimar Republic (during the transition to National Socialism) and the early and middle 1960s, as Germans tried to comprehend the division of their country along cold war ideological lines. Specifically, there were differences of opinion between Germans in both the East and West zones, on the one hand, and the postwar occupying forces, on the other. The allies had introduced an educational policy meant to demonstrate the power of American democracy; however, since democratic tolerance of hate speech had to some extent enabled the rise of fascism, and since capitalism generated class differences that had resulted (ultimately) in communist revolution, many Germans preferred a third option, called "democratic socialism" or "socialist humanism," which would match free speech with social responsibility. Honnef's denouncement of the aestheticization of violence partakes of this debate. In the end, the allies squelched the dream of this third option as being ideologically incompatible with what some describe as "inflexible notions of German collective guilt."[59]

Given the redemptive aims of the occupying forces in Germany and the orientation in the West toward political democracy on the American model, it is not surprising that Fluxus would be introduced in the American military newspaper *Stars and Stripes.* As Emmett Williams later explained, "The way it got written sounds a bit like a conspiracy. I was working as a feature writer for the Stars and Stripes in Darmstadt. George Maciunas, the father-figure and prime mover of what was to become known as Fluxus, was working as a [graphic] designer for the U.S. Air Force in nearby Wiesbaden."[60]

In the *Stars and Stripes* articles reviewing Fluxus, which appeared on 30 August and 21 October, the writers rightly describe Germany as "a leading center for experimental music in the postwar world."[61] The *Allgemeine Zeitung* agreed: "The possibilities of existence [for Fluxus artists] . . . are apparently richer, or less poor, than in America."[62] The *Stars and Stripes* also cited George Maciunas, whom they called an "American impresario" (he was actually a Lithuanian expatriate who by 1962 had lived only briefly in New York), as saying, "In fact, some of it [Fluxus] is anti-musik."[63] Such coverage in major daily newspapers indicates mainstream support for experimental work in general, and Fluxus in particular, in Germany. It also suggests the delicacy of cold war relations, with Maciunas's origins in a country now belonging to the East Bloc being accorded little significance (or, alternatively, his association with the United States being deemed advantageous). Finally, the 30 August article noted that Maciunas would be taking "the Fluxus Festival lock, stock and barrel, plastic butterflies, stomach pump, footprints etc., etc., etc., to Paris in

December, then to Holland, Luxembourg, Italy, Austria, East Europe, Japan and eventually the United States." This ultimately unfulfilled plan suggests a potential for interpreting early Fluxus as a multicultural art enterprise. The spread of Fluxus as a form of cultural imperialism took explicit form in Joseph Beuys's altered version of the Purge Manifesto from this period, where he exchanged *Americanism* for Maciunas's *Europanism*—meaning pan-Europeanism—effectively referencing American hegemony in the postwar period as something worthy of purging.

René Block, a German who owned a gallery in West Berlin from 1964 to 1970 and then became an independent curator and director of the National Museum in Kassel, has used the German-American link in Fluxus to benefit the artists. Block is largely responsible for the high visibility of Fluxus since 1964 in Germany and the relocation of the center of Fluxus in Germany to West Berlin. He has curated Fluxus shows and festivals from a pro-avant-garde perspective that emphasizes its relevance for the present moment. As the center of a vital community of artists and informed collectors, it is fitting that Williams dedicated his book to Block.[64] One typical concert series sponsored by Block occurred at the Forum Theater in Berlin in 1966 and included work by most of the core members of the group.[65] Maciunas, who had departed for the United States in 1963, composed only one of the thirty-three Events performed, which perhaps explains his relative absence in press coverage of Fluxus from the mid-1960s in Germany.[66]

But does it really? As an East European with Marxist orientations, Maciunas had a political perspective on Fluxus that may well have exceeded the cultural tolerance even of many Germans.

In early-1960s West Germany, the Nazi past was interpreted by the Germans as the result of individual, not (as the Allies saw it) collective, guilt. Because of the Allies' fear of German nationalism, the engines of culture were decentralized: witness the autonomous radio, television, and newspaper services of Frankfurt, Munich, Stuttgart, and West Berlin. The result, according to Keith Bullivant and C. Jane Rice, was "a vibrant and uniquely decentralized cultural scene in West Germany." Until the mid-1960s, according to Bullivant and Rice, West Germans had a strong suspicion of ideology—and with good reason, having experienced the age of National Socialism and been "confronted before or after the war with the excesses of Stalinism and with the black-and-white ideological simplicities of the Cold War."[67]

By the 1970s, democratic pluralism was the defining feature of the German mainstream. Moreover, as the filmmaker Wim Wenders noted about the German politico-cultural context of 1976, "The need to forget twenty years created a hole and people tried to cover this...by assimilating American Culture. One way of forgetting the past, and one way of regression, was to accept American Imperialism."[68] Within this amnesiac context, in which German culture was made to function in parallel with American culture and German ideals of pluralism (meaning international, not national; and free, not ideological), Block was able to expand his support of Fluxus to citywide festivals and large-scale exhibitions. For example, he organized the Fluxus-intensive "New York–Downtown Manhattan: SoHo" exhibition in Berlin in 1976, which situated Fluxus and related tendencies as a SoHo-based settlement for which Maciunas and Robert Watts, as directors of Fluxhouse Cooperative, were largely responsible.[69] Later, Block's directorship of the artists program (Künstlerprogramm) within the state-run Deutscher Akademischer Austauschdienst (DAAD, which sponsors research and residencies in the arts, humanities, and sciences) allowed him to give a measure of governmental support to American Fluxus artists, including stipends to live in Berlin and funding for concerts. One typical DAAD-sponsored evening, "Musikum 1962 und neuere Fluxuskompositionen," which took place in 1983 at the Hochschule der Künste, included both new and older Fluxus work. The press release stated of Fluxus: "It was and is a spiritual position. This is clear in the differentiated, very individualistic forms of presentation."[70]

If one considers some of the artists—including Joseph Beuys, Wolf Vostell, Nam June Paik, and George Maciunas—supported directly or indirectly by Block's gallery, the success of his strategy in the German art market is apparent. In addition, Geoffrey Hendricks, Dick Higgins, Alison Knowles, Robert Watts, and Emmett Williams all had DAAD stipends at one time or another.[71]

In the postwar era, especially since the 1970s, regional support of contemporary cultural projects has been strong. As Jürgen Grabbe, cultural secretary of the Council of German Cities and Towns, commented, "It is the diversity of its cultural assets and resources which constitutes the attractiveness of a town.... Investing in culture, therefore, means investing in their future."[72] In light of this new emphasis on economic revitalization through contemporary culture, it is perhaps not surprising that present work became a rallying cry of Block's "Fluxus Da Capo" exhibition, in which artists worked at various sites around Wiesbaden from 8 September to 18 October 1992. Some of the participating artists—Dick Higgins, Alison Knowles, Nam June Paik, Ben Patterson, and Emmett Williams—had been at the first Fluxus-titled concerts thirty years earlier; they were joined by four artists representing the cardinal directions.[73] This organization is somewhat in line with Emmett Williams's hybrid Maciunas- and present-based sense of Fluxus, which emphasizes Maciunas as the origin ("there was Fluxus ever after") yet maintains the importance of continuous relationships with Fluxus artists. In the case of Da Capo, however, the movement toward a new work strategy and the conspicuous nonpresence of historical materials at this historic site shift the focus strongly toward contemporary production. Installations of new work at Da Capo included Alison Knowles's "Floor Moon," which consisted of found objects ticketed with instructions for making noninstrumental sound, placed on a white, circular ground at the Villa Clementina; Emmett Williams's series of "object portraits" of figures including Al Hansen, George Maciunas, Joseph Beuys, and Man Ray; and Geoffrey Hendricks's *Quarter* installation of moonscapes and sky images—small watercolors—and ladders and broken furniture (see Fig. 56).

The variety of experiences available in the installations mounted by Knowles and Williams illustrates the dialectic variation within Fluxus. Both works contain found objects placed on a neutral ground. In "Floor Moon," a person sitting at the edge of the circle would pick up and sound an object and then return it, thus restructuring the overall design of the piece. In contrast, the viewer standing before an object portrait would piece together the subject's name by reference to real objects associated with that person's habits and tastes. For example, the *m* in the name of Maciunas—who hated smoking—is represented by a book of matches. What results is a sort of "alphabet symphony" that arrives at an identity. As visual art, then, Williams's portraits seem to rely on a traditional viewer-object relationship, while Knowles's installation exploits the sensations of touch. In fact, hers belongs equally to the multisensory performative mode associated with music. Likewise, the portraits should be seen as poems that physically engage the viewer with language. In a manner far removed from normal letters and words, these graphic forms march in step across a page. These object poems intermediate between portraits, still lifes, and poems.

Between these two Fluxus works is dialogue: about the audience as interactive or separate, the object as temporal or static, the artist as maker or initiator, and the work as fixed or changing. Knowles and Williams offered work with very different implications, despite using strikingly similar material elements: everyday or found materials on a neutral ground. I missed this crucial point in my earlier writing on Williams's portraits.

In keeping with this view of Fluxus as a pluralistic practice involving a group of artists, the catalogue *Fluxus Da Capo 1962 Wiesbaden 1992* consists of statements written or chosen by the participating artists.[74] Selections include accounts by early Fluxus proponents, such as Jill Johnston of the *Village Voice* (chosen by Hendricks), as well as more recent authors, such as the American critic Robert C. Morgan (selected by Knowles). Henning Christiansen and Dick Higgins wrote about themselves, while Joe Jones asked Geoffrey Hendricks to write something. The book conveyed the impression of a Fluxus tree, with a historic root and branches both searching inward and reaching outward.[75]

This emphasis on discursive range reflects official German policy. By the late 1980s, as we have seen, the SPD had codified the Basic Program, section 4 of which called for " 'a new culture of mutual toleration and collaboration' which would include 'a political culture which thrived on adversarial debate (Streitkultur) rooted in a basic social consensus.' "[76] Thus in Germany, Fluxus becomes, perhaps ironically and certainly unintentionally, affirmative culture: that is, it supports official cultural policy.

Contemporary statements by Fluxus artists in the German art press likewise emphasize the pluralistic nature of Fluxus. For example, *Kunst Köln* published Ben Patterson's comments on the exhibition "Fluxus-Virus 1962–1992" in terms that move the line of origin past 1962 and toward 1960, before Maciunas knew these artists.

> The idea "Fluxus 1962" belongs incidentally to Wiesbaden, where in 1962 that well-known series of Events took place, meaning the form of art that today would be called "Fluxus"—which was designated for the first time "Fluxus".... If [however] one looks back at where all the artists lived who worked in Germany at that time and whose work helped to define the beginnings of Fluxus—namely, Cologne—then Cologne must take the position of the most important center of these subversive activities... and possibly the title of the exhibition would have had to have been "Fluxus Virus 1960–1992."[77]

The catalogue *Fluxus Virus,* despite certain problems, includes some well-written, provocative articles selected by the Fluxus artist Ken Friedman.[78] These essays offer new insights and represent a wide range of archival resources never brought together in a single publication before or since. Of particular importance for the American side of Fluxus reception are Wilfried Dörstel's "Das Atelier Bauermeister: Proto-Fluxus in Köln, 1960–1962," and Karen Moss's "Mapping Fluxus in California," both of which challenge the notion that American Fluxus was rooted exclusively in a New York avant-garde and flourished there only following Maciunas's return to the United States in 1963. The historian James Lewes, too, calls into doubt the New York–centered vision of Fluxus in a chronology and bibliography organized by both artist and group presentations. This exhibition and catalogue resemble Block's German *1962 Wiesbaden Fluxus 1982*[79] and *Fluxus Da Capo 1962 Wiesbaden 1992,* both of which likewise presented recent Fluxus work as evolving from the historical avant-garde.

The German response to Fluxus has tended toward a historically determined but elastic idea of the avant-garde principle in the present moment and at diverse locations. Opposing interpretations of neo-dada as either primarily destructive or primarily concrete grow from this response. As Heinz Ohff suggested, it is the responsibility of the art world to protect the freedom of artists. Freedom and pluralism: these ideas were in keeping with the initiatives of the democratic government of postwar Germany, initiatives that both reacted against and obscured the National Socialist cultural policy, in which free speech was curtailed and artistic dissidence, as represented by the historical avant-garde, quashed.

In the early postwar milieu, then, work was evaluated according to the standard of free speech. Following Germany's "economic miracle" in the late 1960s, however, this ideology of *Streitkultur* became codified through federal and especially regional funding resources. The abundance of festivals celebrating the thirty-year anniversary of Fluxus, as well as the success of gallery owner René Block, both as a businessperson and as an administrator, reflect this new economic and social reality.

Italy

The situation was similar in Italy. Under Mussolini, of course, Italy also underwent a period of fascism, a fact that may explain in part why Fluxus has found unofficial, yet generous, support there. However, the movement has not been commercially viable there, as it was in Germany, enjoying no major gallery or governmental support. Instead, Italian Fluxus is sustained by a system of private patronage, centered mainly in the collector-publishers Gino DiMaggio in Milan and Francesco Conz in Verona and the publisher Rosanna Chiessi (Pari/Dispari) when she lived in Cavriago, Reggio Emilia.[80]

As in Germany, Fluxus is associated in Italy with the historical avant-garde. However, in Italy the political framework tends to be spelled out in anarchic or ideologically nonspecific terms.[81] For example, the exhibition "Ubi Fluxus ibi Motus 1990–1962," coordinated by Gino DiMaggio (whose MuDiMa Museum features Fluxus) and curated by the well-known historian of the avant-garde Achille Bonito Oliva, occupied a pavilion at the 1990 Venice Biennale. Oliva's statement in the accompanying catalogue refers to the creative forces of the Italian heritage in art movements such as Fluxus: "The synthesis of the arts is an ancient aspiration of the modern avant-gardes, ranging from Futurism to Dadaism, but it was also included in the classical dimensions of the Italian Renaissance."[82] Thus Fluxus becomes part of the humanist dimension in Italian art, a perhaps awkward alignment with the historical avant-garde, when it is taken in its least egalitarian guise. In contrast to this historic interpretation of Fluxus as continuous with Renaissance humanism, the catalogue's opening statement, by Giovanni Carandente, suggests a different direction: "To push Fluxus toward the twenty-first century means to grasp the group's anti-historicist spirit. Hence the decision to invert history, the chronology, and the itinerary of the exhibition: not from 1962 to 1990, but instead from 1990 to 1962.... It is the present that becomes the point of departure."[83] This statement, while repudiating the historicity of Fluxus, reflects the "futurist" impulse of the historical avant-garde in Italy, which sought to break with the past in order to reinvent the present and, by extension, redefine the possibilities for the future. Perhaps because there was comparatively little Fluxus activity in Italy in the 1960s (and therefore no historic work to show), contemporary work dominated Ubi Fluxus ibi Motus almost entirely.

It might be imagined that DiMaggio's and the Biennale's support of a Fluxus presence at the Venice art fair would lead to major gallery representation, improving the salability both of items in DiMaggio's collection and of Italian Fluxus publications. This supposition assumes, however, that visibility is commensurate with market viability. That has not been the case for Fluxus. Rather, support seems to be largely a labor of love closely associated with DiMaggio's political outlook. As DiMaggio puts it:

> Fluxus arises as a reaction, as a renunciation and as a rejection of a reality that is the reality of superindustrialization, superexploitation, superconsumerism, superimperialism. It arises as a rejection of the reality that has left behind it the systematic carnage of Auschwitz and Hiroshima to look at the even more sophisticated carnage of Vietnam... quite sufficient to force us into deeper reflection and a memory which is not just nostalgia.[84]

Reactive and renouncing, Fluxus thus becomes an artistic reaction to a political situation. Rather than distancing us from the past by means of nostalgic yearning, Fluxus, through engagement, renders that past palpable and immediate. Ubi Fluxus ibi Motus conveys this immediacy by emphasizing present work in the exhibition and a mix of new and old work in the catalogue; the result is a historicizing of the present moment of Fluxus, even as the group's ongoing internal dialogue creates tension within the historic framework. In the catalogue, for example, whereas Fluxus artist Joe Jones seems to endorse the Maciunas-based paradigm when he states that "Fluxus = Maciunas = Fluxus = Maciunas = Fluxus," Henry Flynt comments that "late Fluxus extends through the Eighties to the present."[85]

These conflicting temporal frameworks suggest that dialogue, rather than a particular definition of Fluxus, is what unifies the Ubi Fluxus ibi Motus catalogue. Ken Friedman addresses this issue. By breaking the story of Fluxus into manageable pieces—signaled by the headings "The Birth of Fluxus," "The Twelve Criteria of Fluxus" (an "improvement on Higgins's eight"), and "Fluxus after Maciunas"—he is able to describe both the historical context and the practical diversity of Fluxus.[86] In the final section, Friedman avers: "Thinking about George is central to Fluxus, but thinking about him as the central figure in Fluxus is a mistake... he was not a leader, not a person comfortable working with people in the million unsystematic ways that people demand to work. That's why he changed his working method by the middle Sixties and brought others of us in... letting us develop Fluxus our own way."[87] (As if to counter this rather open-ended vision, however, the catalogue also reprints George Maciunas's essay "Neo-Dada in Music, Theater, Poetry, Art.")

Jackson Mac Low, however, who had been associated with Fluxus artists since the Cage class in 1958 but who split with Maciunas, recalls an entirely different situation: "What I didn't know about George's enterprise was its underlying agenda: an all out attack on 'serious culture.' . . . George was also aggressively exclusionary, George tried to dictate to the artists who worked with him, to make them call all their works 'Fluxus' works, to act only as part of his 'collective.' "[88] This account contradicts Joe Jones's statement that "Maciunas = Fluxus" as well.

The pattern in the Italian catalogue is consistent with that of German catalogues, despite the occasionally variable points of view offered. The lack of consensus can be found, for example, in *1962 Wiesbaden Fluxus 1982,* which begins with Emmett Williams's statement that "Fluxus has not been invented yet," and in *Fluxus Da Capo 1962 Wiesbaden 1992*, containing Dick Higgins's lengthy discussion of the problem of settling on definitions for Fluxus.[89]

The present-based model for exhibiting or performing Fluxus work thus tends to be given catalogue representation, but only on one continent. Notably, because only three present-based Fluxus exhibitions have been held in the United States—one at an Italian gallery (!), one at a small college in Massachusetts, and one at the ever-supportive Emily Harvey Gallery in New York City—no major catalogues embracing this orientation have been produced entirely in English. Coverage of the debate among Fluxus artists on the nature of their movement and their work is also exceedingly rare in American publications. It can be found in Smith and Stiles as well as in Eric Andersen, Estera Milman, and Stephen Foster's discussion in *Fluxus: A Conceptual Country* and in the "heckling catalogue" presented by Nancy Dwyer in *FluxAttitudes,* both of which introduce revisionist commentary on the theme of Fluxus pluralism.[90]

In summary, the pluralism, open-endedness, and internationalism of Fluxus have appealed most to the agendas of German and, perhaps to a lesser extent, Italian audiences. By treating Fluxus as a symbol of the viability of the avant-garde tradition, German critics bear witness to the tolerance of modern Germans. The situation in Italy is similar, though there extensive institutional support, as exists in West Germany thanks to its "economic miracle," does not apply. It is not surprising that in these countries, with their strong avant-garde heritage, the name Fluxus is closely bound up with ideas about the historical avant-garde and a fixed group of artists. Paradoxically, the concepts of pluralism and individuation enable the group to be understood as functioning within the frameworks of various flexible ideologies.

Fluxus by Many Other Names

The German and Italian present-based Fluxus exhibitions, all of which used the word *Fluxus* in the title, tended to emphasize the group's historic component. We might call this a "progressive retrospective" reading. As Block commented on the "spirit" of Fluxus and its diversity, this reading has led to a multifaceted interpretation of Fluxus style and ideology. At other locations and at other times, however, the artists themselves have used titles other than Fluxus to designate their group projects. Reasons for this flexible nomenclature include a desire for self-definition; disputes with Maciunas and the need to establish distance from him; and the related objective of creating space within the Fluxus group for new and diverse experiences.

The name Fluxus was first used for a magazine of experimental music notation, for which George Maciunas held a performance benefit at his AG Gallery in 1961.[91] Maciunas's organizational efforts of 1962 and 1963 likewise focused on raising funds for this magazine, with which Maciunas intended to chart the developments of the international avant-garde (such as those originating in John Cage's composition classes at the New School for Social Research during 1957–59).[92] During the past forty years in both the United States and Europe as many as one hundred festivals and concerts have been held, involving, almost exclusively, Fluxus artists collaborating on works not called Fluxus. Some names were playful and comic, such as "Yam," "Ergo Suits Festival," "Festival of Misfits," "Festival of Fantastiks," and "Games at the Cedilla," while others explored the issue of personal freedom, such as "Quelque Chose" and "Festival de la Libre Expression."[93] This flexible nominalism exists elsewhere as well; witness Dick Higgins's Something Else Press, Wolf Vostell's Cologne-based *De-Coll/age* magazine, and Milan Knizak's *Aktual Czechoslovakia*. No doubt Fluxus would never have cohered in the first place without Maciunas. However, persistent resistance to the name within the group itself indicates resistance both to Maciunas's efforts at inscription and to the idea of a specific definition for Fluxus.

The Danish artist Eric Andersen organized two major non-Fluxus-titled events, the 1985 "Festival of Fantastiks" and "Excellent '92," for this very reason: to distance

Danish Fluxus from Maciunas's Fluxus.[94] The 1985 festival presented historic and new performances—with emphasis on the latter—at various sites around the majestic city of Roskilde, including the art museum (a former palace), the city hall, and a fire engine in the town square; one piece, a wall of bricks that participants moved through the town, was even mobile. Present at the weeklong event were Andersen, Philip Corner, Geoffrey Hendricks, Alison Knowles, Jackson Mac Low, Ann Noël, Anne Tardos, Ben Vautier, Robert Watts, and Emmett Williams. Both this and the 1992 Excellent festival were well attended, even though Fluxus has minimal commercial presence in Denmark.

Andersen's distancing from Maciunas had started early. In 1965 Maciunas, as sole representative of the Fluxus editorial committee, wrote in a press release:

> It has come to the attention of the FLUXUS editorial committee that four Fluxus renegades (Eric Andersen, Arthur Køpcke, Tomas Schmit and Emmett Williams) and expelled members have been traveling through various socialist republics giving scandalous and defamatory concerts under the name of FLUXUS.... We wish to denounce these four renegades and impostors most emphatically and wish to advise that no future opportunity be given to exhibit their scandalous activities.[95]

Although he criticizes these artists for representing Fluxus behind the iron curtain, East Bloc contact was extremely important for him; his Marxist philosophy was intrinsic to his version of Fluxus's political program after 1963.

In fact, the tour was a joke played on Maciunas; it never occurred. The press release, however, makes clear the conflict that existed between Maciunas and the European community of Fluxus artists (who might be called "Fluxus absent Maciunas"), much as the Stockhausen flyer and newsletter (see Chapter 2) signaled dissent in the American context.[96]

In an article about Andersen's "Festival of Fantastiks," the critic Henry Martin provides a bridge between the Maciunas-based paradigm and contemporary Fluxus: "The standard attempt to explain the history and nature of Fluxus always begins with George Maciunas' invention of the term in the early 1960s.... But the individual artists have always used this common starting point in manifold ways, and seeing them come together again revealed just how different they can be."[97] The review, which includes colorful descriptions of each artist's work, is unusual in American criticism for its use of the predominantly contemporary work to describe what was going on in Fluxus in 1985.

American Revisions

One could say that where the political system can profit by supporting current work by Fluxus artists (as in Germany), or where a publisher (as in Italy) or a gallery (Block's gallery in Germany) has the collector base to market the work successfully, contemporary work by Fluxus artists will flourish at the institutional level.[98] This assumption may explain why this strategy has failed in the United States, where René Block's New York gallery lasted only from 1974 to 1976[99] and where the Emily Harvey Gallery, which opened in 1982, persists at a largely underground level. Further, when new work was shown at Dick Higgins's "Fluxus 25 Years" at the Williams College Museum of Art in Williamstown, Massachusetts (1987),[100] and the Emily Harvey Gallery's "Fluxus and Co." (1989), the exhibitions attracted very little critical attention. A slightly later show, "Fluxus Closing In" at the Salvatore Ala Gallery in 1990, did receive coverage from the mainstream art press, some of which reflects a shift toward the contemporary Fluxus work, particularly at the level of practice. Frances DeVuono, for example, writing for *ArtNews,* commented: "Transforming Salvatore Ala's monumentally severe place into a whirligig of wit is no small feat, but Fluxus did it with élan. According to this exhibition, Fluxus didn't end with Maciunas' death in 1978.... Judging from this show, and the one at last spring's Venice Biennale, Fluxus is still with us, challenging, changing and giggling."[101] A *New Yorker* review, in contrast, complained that the new work conflicted with Maciunas's taste for clearly identifiable, avant-garde style and materials and the anti-art position they were reputed to represent. Witness the change in tone between the two parts of the review as the reviewer shifts from historic to new work:

> There's renewed interest in Fluxus nowadays, and given today's climate, this exhilarating, tantalizing, and gently chaotic display of Fluxus' anti-establishment, devil-may-care spirit has come not a moment too soon. Fluxus, whose halcyon days were in the sixties, was about deliberately not creating art.... In fact, many Fluxians are currently pursuing the more arty art of painting—and mostly without success, as evidenced by the smattering of recent works in the show.[102]

The reviewer's clear preference for the older work, which consisted of materials from the Silverman Collection, has created a rupture in his or her perception of the show.

In contrast, a publication from 1987 treated contemporary representational strategies in Fluxus with more sympathy. A special issue of *Whitewalls* was guest-edited by Ken Friedman, the one-time "California representative" of Fluxus, as Maciunas called him. In it Friedman, in addition to providing his own definition of the movement,[103] invited artists to comment on the problem of Fluxus—a method that gives ample room for the variability within Fluxus to be expressed.

The American critic Robert Morgan, who aligns Fluxus with the origins of conceptual art, likewise avoids the political delineations normally associated with Maciunas in his analysis of Fluxus, though he does locate the movement rather narrowly in the time period when Maciunas played the greatest role.[104] A similar constraint informed the 1992 show "Fluxus: A Conceptual Country," which situated the multifaceted vision of Fluxus squarely within the cultural context of the late 1950s and early 1960s, without recourse to new material (although its New York opening was concurrent with a show of new work at the Emily Harvey Gallery).[105] Curated by art historian Estera Milman, then at the University of Iowa, the exhibition framed Fluxus as an interweaving of a group dynamic and an ideational framework, "the coalition of an international constellation of individuals into a conceptual community, a country whose geography was a figment of the communal imagination, whose citizenry was transient and, by definition, cosmopolitan"—and, somewhat less loftily, as "a strategy for the consolidation of concurrent art activity."[106] Although the show succeeded on the level of representing a broad community of artists, it was less effective in meeting its stated goal of presenting Fluxus as an international site for the exploration of ideas, a goal that was simply too large for the middle-sized exhibition and catalogue (a special issue of the journal *Visible Language*). Milman's main contribution to the catalogue describes Fluxus as a highly differentiated misreading of dada that she associates with the 1950s, when many of the artists favored the Zen principle of decentralized cohesion and concretism associated with Cage.[107]

As these shows and the resultant criticism suggest, well-informed, recent writers and curators are sensitive to the Maciunas problem. No longer routinely described as the leader, he is now often characterized as the name giver, primary organizer, and road manager of Fluxus. Nevertheless, descriptions of the group remain colored by his perspective, and the nostalgic element continues to be validated through alignment of Fluxus with earlier art movements.

At the other extreme, Fluxus itself has been considered the basis for later, better-known movements, as Milman commented about "Fluxus: A Conceptual Country": "This show might be likened to a field of acorns from which a number of more visible oaks have grown. Without Fluxus there would probably be no Conceptual art, performance art or body art; minimalism and pop would be substantially different."[108] Conversely, this influence has occasionally become the basis of a backhanded compliment, as in a 1993 comment in the *Village Voice:* "30 years later, the Fluxus spirit is fresh as a daisy—an odd contrast to the yellowing Pop behemoths upstairs."[109] The daisy, of course, is the flower of the 1960s, and as a cut flower it is very long lasting. Perhaps Fluxus *is* as fresh as the *Voice* says—as an ongoing art practice, if not necessarily as represented in the annals of American art criticism.

In conclusion, the critical response to Fluxus in the United States has been remarkably consistent since its inception, being situated largely in the Maciunas-based paradigm. This response leaves little room for recent Fluxus work, which does not correspond to the expectations of reviewers and curators. Therefore, contemporary work by Fluxus artists generally fails, or at best is misunderstood by critics.

In contrast, the public reclamation in Germany of the avant-garde tradition, both in the 1960s and today, created institutional critical support of Fluxus that has led to the production of new work, thus furthering the creative spirit of the movement. This renewal of the historical avant-garde has been the case in Italy as well, while in Denmark Fluxus festivals have served as testimonials to variety and individualism, both hallmarks of that country's liberal tradition.

These various readings all indicate ways in which Fluxus continues to matter, in diverse situations and according to multiple expectations, to critics, curators, and artists alike—this despite the fact that the discursive frameworks used to interpret Fluxus work typically ignore its experiential basis.

To preserve the experiential aspect of Fluxus it may be necessary to extend beyond the context of art—to build the cultural frame around the work, and not the other way around. There are implications for Fluxus beyond the domain of art.

What form this experiment might take is not clear, though we could perhaps learn a thing or two from the replication of the caves in Lascaux, France. Perhaps the time has come to reproduce Fluxus objects and Events for nonart purposes. Is it possible to conceive of an entire exhibition of replicas intended for multisensory interaction? Or to create Fluxus-like situations for visitors to art institutions? My modest effort in the next, and final, chapter to extrapolate a pedagogical model from Fluxus extends the lessons learned from Fluxus experience into the stratosphere of influence. At their best, after all, experiences change our perceptions.

TEACHING AND LEARNING AS ART FORMS

Toward a Fluxus-Inspired Pedagogy

5

The fact that Fluxus experience exists in the art world indicates that experience has some sort of relevance there—that primary information is a positive counterbalance to the overwhelming preference for secondary forms of information and analysis in Western culture. Fluxus experience thus has a discursive function—it means something within a framework of argument—even though, given its basis in primary information and its communal structure, it fails to mean any one thing consistently.

In what follows, I would like to address this discursive function. In particular, I will explore some possible applications of Fluxus experience and the communitarian ideal, taking them beyond Fluxus, even beyond the art world per se. To do so, I will develop a broad-based pedagogical model based on the experimental pedagogy of several Fluxus (and related) artists.[1] Not only is this strategy practical in intent, but it has historical justification: Fluxus, after all, originated to a certain extent in the college classroom of John

Cage in New York (and to a lesser degree that of Stockhausen in Düsseldorf), and several figures associated with Fluxus subsequently came to view their art through the lens of pedagogy.

The General Account

One artist, albeit not a core member of Fluxus, devoted many of his talents to education. Allan Kaprow had taken Cage's course in composition at the New School in 1957; he was already a professor at the Douglass campus of Rutgers University, where he was joined by Fluxus artists Geoffrey Hendricks and Robert Watts.[2] Kaprow later moved to Cal Arts and the University of California, San Diego. As a professor of art, he saw his role as engaging students in critical activity; in a "Manifesto" he wrote that "as art becomes less art it takes on philosophy's role as critique of life."[3] Similarly, Joseph Beuys, an artist loosely associated with Fluxus, taught art at the Düsseldorf Academy for virtually his entire artistic career; he said, "To be a teacher is my greatest work of art."[4] For both Kaprow and Beuys, teaching was not merely a way to earn a living; it was, rather, a crucial aspect of their artistic practice. This distinction is important, for it implies a highly motivated, and by extension creative, basis for their respective pedagogies.

In his introduction to *Teaching and Learning as Performing Arts,* Robert Filliou describes the applicability of Fluxus and related art forms to experimental pedagogy: "The purpose of this study is to show how some of the problems inherent in teaching and learning can be solved—or let's say eased—through an application of the participation techniques developed by artists in such fields as: HAPPENINGS, EVENTS, ACTION POETRY, ENVIRONMENTS, VISUAL POETRY, FILMS, STREET PERFORMANCES, NON-INSTRUMENTAL MUSIC, GAMES, CORRESPONDENCES, etc."[5] As Beuys puts it in part one of Filliou's book, "The enlarged conception of Art includes every human action."[6] John Dewey likewise stresses experiential engagement when he describes the artist as the creator of experiences and the audience as co-creators: "We become artists ourselves as... our own experience is reoriented."[7]

Following these ideas, Filliou, in a literal invitation for the creative reader (reading also being a form of performance, after all), leaves about a third of his book empty. The space, he explains, is intended for reader interaction. "Of course the reader is free not to make use of the writing space. But it is hoped that he will be willing to enter the writing game as a performer rather than as a mere outsider. . . . This is a long short book to keep writing at home."[8]

Of course, coproducing experiences is easier said than done. In this pedagogical project, however, Fluxus experience has particular value, promoting as it does, first and foremost, experiential learning, but also interdisciplinary exploration, self-directed study, collective work, and the nonhierarchical exchange of ideas. Finally, by fostering such freedom, it avoids the homogenizing influence of formal institutions of learning and art academies. Such an approach to education, moreover, need not be informationally weak or structurally undisciplined. Rather, in the Fluxus modality, information (including scientific and historical fact) is treated as one form of knowledge among many, all of which may enter into the production of experience through the creative mechanism called art.

A communitarian approach is important in this project as well. In an interview in Filliou's book, John Cage argues that "a greater quantity of information exchanges or experience exchanges immediately come in the more people there are, but that is exactly the situation we are now living in—one of an abundance of ideas and experiences."[9] For Cage, teaching and learning are lateral activities, with a number of people working equally to effect an active exchange within the materially diverse human environment.

His use of the phrase "abundance of ideas and experiences" to characterize what is exchanged conveys a large, accessible universe of materials for exchange. These materials are not just traditional ones like books and specialized information, but all forms of human invention: conceptual or poetic models, music, food, dance, even direct interaction with the local environment, to name but a few.[10] Ultimately, such nonliterary modes of exchange form the ontological basis of the human narrative.

The value of learning thus lies in inquiring actively—with an expanding, abundant attitude—into the materials of one's own environment. In this framework, there can be no single perspective on what constitutes the environment: the knowledge gained from active inquiry is relational, fostering an appreciation of unique as well as shared experiences, interests, and concerns.

Such learning has as its goal mutual understanding (as distinct from agreement)—a point that flies in the face of the traditional educational models where experts dictate how the world should be experienced. As the education critic

D. Emily Hicks puts it, borrowing from Gilles Deleuze and Félix Guattari's notion of the politically charged, deterritorialized subject: "'Shared decision making' is more likely to take place in an environment in which subjects with a multiplicity of perspectives are able to engage in pleasant encounters."[11] Kaprow likewise describes the emotional benefits of such an intersubjective system when he states that "everyone's experience ought to in some way be connected with everyone's love, whatever that is."[12] The community framework implied by this statement, which is at the same time celebratory of individual differences, suggests a range of possible encounters between objective and subjective realities, rational observations and emotional experiences, and personal, political, and civic identities, with a "sense of solidarity" being the desired outcome.[13]

Harvard University professor of education and neurology Howard Gardner, addressing the problem of individual difference on a cognitive level, has theorized that human beings engage with the world using at least seven fundamentally different forms of intelligence. In addition to the linguistic and logical-mathematical forms privileged by standardized tests at all levels of the first-world education system, humans also possess musical, bodily-kinesthetic, spatial, interpersonal, and intrapersonal intelligences to varying degrees.[14]

Linguistic intelligence is the ability to synthesize and play with language: it is the gift of poets. Logical-mathematical intelligence is the ability to reason, to discern abstract mathematical patterns or derive a scientific theory: it is the gift of scientists and may be the most prized form of intelligence in the West today. Musical intelligence involves tonal patterns and relationships: it is the gift of composers and songwriters. Through bodily-kinesthetic intelligence, we solve problems using our body: it is the gift of dancers and athletes. Spatial intelligence allows us to mentally and physically negotiate space: it is the gift of sailors, surgeons, engineers, sculptors, and painters. The interpersonal and intrapersonal intelligences involve the ability to understand others or oneself, respectively: the former is the gift of teachers, politicians, clerics, and salespeople, and to some degree we all possess the latter gift.

Gardner proposed effecting reform in elementary and high schools by means of individualized curricula geared to the dominant forms of intelligence found in each student, which would allow greater individual access to the world of facts through natural talents and interests. As he put it, "Intelligences are potentials or proclivities, which are realized or not realized.... Intelligence, or intelligences, are always an interaction between biological proclivities and the opportunities for learning that exist in a culture." Since these proclivities vary so widely, it follows that instruction should include many different ways of communicating: "For even if the courses themselves are mandated, there is no reason why they need to be taught in the same way at all.... A history lesson can be presented through linguistic, logical, spatial and/or personal modes of knowing, even as a geometry class can draw upon spatial, logical, linguistic, or numerical competences."[15]

And let us not forget emotions, which likewise play a key role in learning and receptivity according to Gardner's theory. As another education theorist, David Gerlenter, writes (about artificial intelligence), "Emotions are not a form of thought, not an additional way to think, not a special cognitive bonus, but are fundamental to thought."[16]

Gardner's natural proclivities and Gerlenter's observation that emotion underlies all thought give a strong thrust to Kaprow's deceptively simple "love" as a key to learning. Indeed, I have seen this repeatedly in my own students: things start to click for them when they feel passionately about the material—when they love it. Learning, in other words, involves attachments: to an evolving internal identity (whether one's own or another's), to a sense of place, both in the social world and on this planet. Education, then, is, at its best, transactional and performative for teachers and learners alike: for it is only through these transactions, these performances, that we create our subjective sense of the shared meaning of life.

According to the education theorist Danny Wildemeersch (writing about adult education),

> Learning can be understood as a process of continuous exchange between the life-world of subjects and the objective reality which is present in society as a whole. The most important agents of these exchange processes are the groups that are part of the external objective world but, at the same time, are closely linked to the subjective reality of a person. It is especially the process of interaction between individuals and the groups they belong to, that enables the *mediation between the subjective and objective world*.... The groups to which one belongs, as they are composed of several subjective realities, represent segments of objective reality which are relevant to one's subjective understanding of life.[17]

Far from the pretense toward objectivity endorsed in current models of higher education, Wildemeersch asserts the importance of an interpretive function that connects subjective and objective reality: "We may think of adult education...as a transactional dialogue between participants who bring to the encounter experiences, attitudinal sets, differing ways of looking at their personal, professional, political and recreational worlds and a multitude of varying purposes, orientations and expectations."[18] The goal of all education, indeed, should be to establish a sense of continuity between the self and the world. The opposite of this approach produces alienation, as Beuys baldly states: "Man faces his fellow man as a stranger."[19]

This model of education as a way of bringing together our (normally divided) objective and subjective selves of course poses problems for the so-called standards movement, especially as it applies to higher education and the process whereby future success is "quantified" by standardized tests (for example, SATs and GREs). "Traditional tests," notes the former journalist and economist Peter Sacks, "reinforce passive, rote learning of facts and formulas, quite contrary to the active critical thinking skills many educators now believe schools should be encouraging."[20] Thus, not only does this fixation on tests as gateways for further education reinforce the overvaluation of the logical-mathematical and linguistic forms of intelligence, but it standardizes students' minds and robs them of other critical and creative skills that they need to function in the complex world of today. The ecological psychologist Edward S. Reed puts it this way: "As our opportunities for primary experience shrink in everything from manual and social skills to learning about nature, society or work, we become increasingly unable to function in the real world."[21]

Cognitive psychologists distinguish between "surface" thought, which requires only speedy recall and repetition, and "deep" cognitive thought, "which involve[s] the synthesis and analysis of a variety of sources of information in order to interpret that information, solve a complicated problem, and possibly even create something interesting and new."[22] The culture of testing, which avoids the messy realms of experientially processed information and multiple intelligences, fosters cognitive superficiality. Given the importance to democracy of effective intellectual training, this situation is unnerving at best. Many intelligent but "nonstandard" students are alienated by, ostracized from, or drop out (are "pushed out," in Hicks's terms) of this system, and even among those who stick with it there may be little or no depth of thought.

These issues remain largely unaddressed in the academy—a situation I find particularly distressing in the humanities. How can we revere the creative production of our poets and artists, musicians and dancers, even as we fail to establish effective means of cultivating the associated forms of intelligence? Might there not be some small value in learning art history from, say, an artist, or in the reverse, in attempting to make an art history that speaks to spatial intelligence? It stands to reason that a culture as diverse as ours might benefit from training *all* the forms of intelligence. We should, as Stephen J. Gould argues, learn a thing or two from evolution and the value of biodiversity to continued life on the planet.[23]

But what of the matter of expertise, which, after all, faces a certain threat in a stronger valuation of experiential learning? Though perhaps—fear for our jobs aside—we would do better to ask, Whom do the standards of expertise really serve? Bard College president Leon Bottstein points to economic causes for the current power structure and thrust toward specialization in higher education: "The departments that are the power centers at colleges and universities will not relinquish their hold over students' time because time means enrollment and enrollment means money and faculty positions, and those two items together constitute power and influence." He continues, bringing into play Gardner's theory of multiple intelligences as well as Kaprow's notion of "love": "Colleges possess an opportunity that has civic consequences and is entirely independent of the system of specialization.... Developing discipline and self-confidence seriously beyond mere appearance often means favoring one subject over another. This means that students would follow the natural course of their own interests."[24]

And this begs another question: Is it possible to theorize Fluxus's intermedia idea as a fertile field for multiple intelligence interactions, and as a way of growing beyond one's natural talents? I would say, definitely yes.

Imagine an open-ended charting mechanism for pedagogical approaches along the lines of the "Intermedia Chart" (see Fig. 33), allowing for a sort of cognitive cross-training through exploratory creativity. I have seen an activity manual for applying the theory of multiple intelligences in the primary classroom that begins to come close to this idea. Parallels with Fluxkits and Events abound, with instructions for making smelling boxes, for example, or for measuring everyday objects by reference to logically unrelated objects (expressing the size of gloves as a number of paper clip lengths, for instance).[25] An especially strong correlation exists in a series of "sensory poem" exercises that result in poems shaped like things or expressing rich experiences involving sight, sound, touch, taste, or smell.[26] The exercises—so reminiscent of "avant-garde" genres like visual poetry—work across intelligence formations, combining literary skills with spatial and kinesthetic intelligences.

Just as the theory of intermedia can be applied in the classroom, so can the theory of multiple intelligences be used to understand Fluxus productions. For example, George Brecht's Fluxkit *Valoche/A Flux Travel Aid* (see Fig. 17) involves a clear interaction of spatial and logical-mathematical intelligences. The Event score itself—such as Philip Corner's *Piano Activities* (1962), one piece of which has the performers climb under the piano and move it across the floor—calls on musical, linguistic, spatial, and bodily-kinesthetic intelligences, as well as a sort of "cultural intelligence," in that it interacts with cultural expectations of music and performance.

The biology professor Carla Hannaford has studied the cognitive feedback mechanism behind bodily-kinesthetic intelligence, called proprioception, which "gives the feedback necessary to maintain optimal muscle contraction and relaxation for balance in our environment."[27] When proprioception is maximized through self-conscious (as opposed to incidental) movement, relaxation, centeredness, and significant increases in brain receptivity and activity occur at all the locations associated with the various forms of intelligence. By completing a series of twenty-six targeted physical exercises (bundled into a program called "Brain Gym") learning-disabled, tired, or lagging students have been able to perform well in seemingly unrelated areas.[28] This occurs because the cortex of the brain, which covers the cerebrum like an orange peel, is stimulated by movement and serves as a filter and distributor for all sensory information (except smell) to the complex of lobes that constitute the brain.[29]

The implications for education are vast: the different types of intelligences brush up against and enable one another when given the proper stimulation and interaction. Hannaford describes, for example, how the sense of touch actually increases learning potential in other parts of the brain: "My college students have commented that just having clay available to manipulate during a lecture allowed them to more easily take in information. Whenever touch is combined with the other senses, much more of the brain is activated, thus building more complex nerve networks and tapping into more learning potential."[30] Imagine a *Finger Box* (see Fig. 16) on every desktop!

At the postsecondary level, interdisciplinary study may be just as important. It goes beyond the mere sprinkling of one subject with spices from another in the hope that someone already interested in, say, literature might come to care about mathematics. Rather, interdisciplinarity, of which many Fluxus objects and Events may be understood as material expressions, creates opportunities for an expanded and interactive play of diverse cognitive functions. Indeed, multiple intelligences—especially with emphasis on interpersonal and intrapersonal intelligences—and interdisciplinarity may well allow students to apply their base of knowledge toward their lived lives. As described by Leon Bottstein, this routinely overlooked function of advanced education should be its primary purpose: "In their ideal form, the undergraduate years of college ought to be the time when an individual, as an adult, links learning to life... in that classical Freudian pairing, *love and work.*"[31]

Cage noted in 1970, in his interview in Filliou's book, that "within five years after you get a Ph.D. from a given American University in a particular field, all the things you learned in the course of your education are no longer of any use to you." Facts never stop accumulating. He continues: "One will become skeptical about what the function of education is, and ultimately, what one will have to do is to give each individual, from childhood, *a variety of experiences* in which his mind is put to use, not as a memorizer of a transmitted body of information, but rather as a person who is in dialogue A, with himself and B, with others as though they were him too." On the topic of "the brushing of information against other information," Cage states that "very often a third thing, or even a larger number of things occur in your mind. Your mind invents, or creates, so to speak, from this brushing, and it is going to be there that we need to be if we are going to be learning something that we did not yet know."[32]

Filliou, in response, imagines within all educational institutions an interdisciplinary institute that he elsewhere calls an Institute of Permanent Creation.[33] This is not merely a mixed-media program, multiplying the existing categories and eventually leading to further stagnation. Rather, Filliou proposes a "pioneer world that should be in the hands of artists" where teachers and students as well as media hierarchies are erased and "anybody might make suggestions about what kind of things might be investigated or looked at."[34] This new space cannot, and should not, be named by a specific practice, even one that is popularly understood as interdisciplinary—performance art, for example, which can be seen to combine art and theater, or computer art, which mixes technology and fine art—lest convention overtake it (as has occurred with the self-revelatory performance-art monologue).

Within an existing university structure, an open, interdisciplinary line of study (a major) might be called something like Investigative Studies and would include those creative practices appropriate to a teacher/learner's methods and questions. The course of study would by definition be unspecialized; rather than focusing on discrete job skills, it would emphasize exploration and expression of individual skills and adaptability to the ever changing job market (though some students might become more, not less, specialized, if they were fortunate enough to possess a certain form of intelligence in abundance, could identify it, and found it consistently valued by the job market). Teachers would facilitate not by transmitting information, but by offering open-ended opportunities to problematize, to look for patterns in the students' experience and meaningfully guide them through their personal concerns and interests. The teacher-as-facilitator role, which is already found in progressive elementary education—think of Marie Montessori's "observer-helpers"—as well as in the studio classrooms of artists, is neither wildly impractical nor utopian. It involves little more than the applicability of information to daily life, and as such it is time to move it into higher levels of education.

The experiential model of education does not neglect information gathering and analysis. The difference is that information is accessed on an "as needed" basis. Not only will students be on a voyage of exploration, accessing and combining information and ideas they may never have suspected existed, but teachers, no matter how "expert" in a particular discipline, cannot know everything students will need to master to grapple with what matters to them. The teacher's job, therefore, is to provide some flexible sense of the world and its history and help initiate lines of inquiry, thereby aiding the student's life passage. Reed again: "Education should be thought of as a process for integrating primary and secondary experience and should therefore be reconceptualized as a lifelong process that combines real-world problem solving with traditional school learning."[35] In our imaginary institute, for example, art students might produce in the public sphere and, in the process, learn the history of art, what it takes to create a work of art, and how to find funding, negotiate the art market, and manage the public response to the work.

In the words of education theorists Ian McGill and Susan Warner Weil, experiential learning "entails making sense of and transforming personal meaning within the social context. . . . Dialogue can replace a traditional educational emphasis on rights and wrongs, on certainty and prediction."[36] Such transformations are easier named than built, however. Reed has called the "fear of uncertainty" the defining anxiety of the Enlightenment and the various garden-variety philosophical traditions and institutions that it has produced: "There is . . . a connection between theories that treat experience as if it were a pure subjective state and the all-too-real and unpleasant situations many of us face because we are unable to use our experience to make important decisions about how we shall live."[37] Filliou extends this observation: "Each and every one of us becomes conservative as soon as he wants things to work out smoothly, whether it be trains or marriages . . . there cannot be real democracy without a 'mess.' "[38] Thus, a self-directed educational experiment that would include the lessons of experiential learning and interdisciplinarity would have to be in a constant state of reform (Filliou's "permanent creation"); yet even that process of flux, in providing endless occasions for problem solving, would be an extraordinary (if sometimes exasperating) educational tool for all involved.

As Gardner and others point out, individualized curricula are not informational islands. They merely allow information to be organized and presented in a manner appropriate to the student's needs and, in the case of more advanced students, help them to identify, work with, and communicate patterns and structures. This "self-directed" mode, based as it is on shared intellectual production of teachers and students, tends to be comparatively symbiotic, though the production in question differs for each person involved.

If we accept the idea that intelligence reflects social change, we can say further that the arts must play a central role in the educational (and civil) arena,[39] going beyond the strictures of a particular discipline. Gardner describes intellectual specialization as reflecting the functional specialization of the industrial age. In an era when the machine is the model of progress, it makes sense that logical intelligence is prized. However, as we move into a postindustrial phase flexibility of information has become a valuable asset, and what we call intelligence has itself taken on new dimensions. As Gardner puts it, "We might define intelligence primarily as the manifestation of engagements between two components: (a) individuals, who are capable of using their array of competences in various domains of knowledge, and (b) the societies that foster individual development through the opportunities they provide."[40]

In a postindustrial society, then, understanding is reached through negotiation between the individual and his or her culture. Intelligence thus becomes communal, creative, and communicational, reflecting an ability to bring relevant "knowledge to bear on a novel situation" and a context in which "understandings can only be apprehended and appreciated if they are *performed* by a student."[41] Hence, when Filliou describes teaching and learning as performance forms, he references not only performance art but also the productive exchange between teachers and learners, which, at its best, is as interactive, surprising, and challenging as the exchange between performance artists and their audiences.

It therefore becomes possible to extrapolate from performance art in general, and the Fluxus Event and intermedia concepts in particular, a performative model for all levels of education, in which schools become "learning societies" that encourage emotional and social engagement, thereby promoting knowledge acquisition and understanding.[42] In contrast to the traditional displays of skills in schools—"performances that in some way merely repeat or give back what the teacher has modeled"—we can imagine a situation where students "use the concepts and skills acquired in school to illuminate new and unfamiliar problems... in the process revealing that they have understood."[43] This understanding takes time, however, and as long as absorption of volumes of knowledge (what my well-intending colleagues call "getting it all in") is emphasized, true understanding will remain elusive.

In this performative mode of education there will be a pull toward what Gardner calls "authentic domains," those disciplines that spring from lingering social values and motives through which a person interacts with others of common interests. Insofar as these may reflect certain intelligence formations, the traditional disciplines aren't likely to go away. The institutional structure of education might, however, be more immediately impacted. When viewed in a fundamentally open system, many forms of structure—time schedules, for example, or inflexible classroom seating arrangements—can be recognized for what they are: obstacles to thinking. The effects of such structure on the prepubescent mind have been much studied; there has been relatively little attention to such matters at the university level, however. Indeed, few *publicly* challenge the culture of testing and the pyramidal standard of classroom dynamics. Hannaford is one exception; as she explains,

> Many of our educational practices derive from the unexamined assumption that people will learn best if given lots of information in either lecture or two-dimensional written form. And in order to learn they must sit still, keep their eyes forward and take notes. We have only to look at the glazed eyes and vacant stares of students in a lecture hall or classroom to know that this is a belief that needs to be abandoned.[44]

Think instead of situations that, free of bureaucracy and schedules and strict formatting, foster the free exchange of ideas—cafeteria conversations, late-night chats on the dormitory steps, casual encounters before or after a class. It is in situations such as these, I contend, that the most relevant learning happens (sparked, ideally, by an educator's input), where information is internalized, perspectives developed, and domains of interest identified.

Why not introduce such free-form interaction into the classroom environment? Enrichment could come as well from restructuring lecture methodologies to be more conversational and introducing multiple learning modes to the approach. This multiplicity of approaches would require an enriched environment. Hannaford, citing the work of Marian Diamond with rats, explains that "in enriched environments [rats] actually developed structural changes in their brains, and exhibited behavior which could be interpreted as demonstrating improved intelligence."[45] An enriched environment, then, refers to the concrete physical space which the body inhabits as the (not-so-separate)mind does its intellectual labor. The classroom might be radically reconfigured to include stimulating seating arrangements and more relaxed, comfortable furniture and writing tools, varied lighting schemes, and even organized discussion "break" areas—places where the group can convene when the discussion peters out or the discussants seem weary.

Case Studies

Our Flux-pedagogue Robert Filliou conceived of an (unrealized) utopian model for just such a program, which he called the "Poipoidrome." This model, though interdisciplinary and spatial, is unlike similar attempts at reform by such figures as Jacques Derrida and Joseph Beuys in that it does not transmogrify into a text-based structure (Derrida)[46] or a fixed model (Beuys). Instead, the Poipoidrome is architectural, consisting of four attached rooms, or learning situations, that allow physical, emotional, and psychic experiences of knowledge to be linked to various modes of pedagogical presentation and spatial awareness.[47]

The Poipoidrome, a building twenty-four meters square, is open to everyone. The term *poi* refers both to poeisis, conceived generally as a creative act of any kind, and to "whatever comes next," given its use in music to mean "then, later, or next." *Poipoi,* then, means not only subsequent creativity (the creative legacy of passing through the space) but also creative subsequence (the adjacency of all creative activity: experience). It is an Institute of Permanent Creation architecturally conceived, with specialties that simultaneously parody established universities, with their discrete disciplines, and offer an experiential alternative.

The first room contains the "Poipoidrome wheel," a five-meter wheel that affirms and then negates a particular belief about art (though its subject matter could be anything): Castro, for example, represents a person's belief that art is political (so Castro becomes an artist). The second room, the "Anti-Poipoi," is filled with proverbs and includes as well two chambers (called "Bringing up to date" and "Aspects of things to come") that exemplify the power of language to define experience. Third is the "Postpoipoi," a place "where the poipoi spirit is applied to the individualization of several disciplines," including anatomy, applied psychology, zoology, paleontology, psychoanalysis, mathematics, grammar, geography, comparative religion, modern Christianity, and history.[48] Finally, the visitor encounters the Poipoidrome as such, a giant arena containing the poiegg, an undefined feature that seems to refer to a meditation space or sacred sitting areas: "Here the circuit ends, here the visitor meditates, absorbs, conceives."[49] Filliou's description, even as it lampoons the hierarchical structure of traditional universities, emphasizes the applicability of disciplines to experiential encounters. For example, geography is presented simply as "streets and roads a man has trod on printed on his soles."

The first room, with its Poipoidrome wheel, demonstrates that many prejudices and commonplace beliefs need to be made explicit, then addressed and possibly reversed. The attitude thus conveyed about culture, historical facts, modes of analysis, and so-called objective fields of study is fundamentally critical. The wheel itself, with its cycles and evolutions that may be found in virtually every mythology in the world, turns against ideology, thus establishing a foundation for critical thinking.

The wheel is a potent symbol for our Fluxus-based pedagogical model, for it demands that we think in reverse, address topics from another point of view than our own, and approach our fundamental assumptions about the world with a mind toward change. Imagine, for example, a history classroom where the American Revolutionary War is discussed from the point of view of the victors ("America won the war") *and* the vanquished ("Native Americans, African Americans, the environment... lost the war," or even "America lost the war"). More generally, ideology (that is, belief systems) could be addressed. For example, by phrasing the statement "the nuclear family is a moral good" in opposite terms—"the nuclear family is not a moral good"—a range of social, economic, and political questions are raised: When did the nuclear family come into existence? What does this system serve? Are there other, equally viable systems?

Similarly, the Anti-Poipoi room, in which "proverbs and colloquialisms are translated in visual terms,"[50] extends the wheel's call for critical thinking to the terms of discourse itself. One might attempt to diagram the components of the "scales of justice" or the "most likely to succeed" and find that both require a specific balance of rights or materials to realize their claims. In our hypothetical classroom, the absurdity of a range of expressions associated with American history or with the virtues of family, with the American judicial system or with our modeling of success, could be explored through such visualizing means—making clear the oxymoronic quality of "home of the free," for instance, or raising questions about the proverb "Home is where the heart is" (sure, but where's the rest of me?).

The Bringing-up-to-date and Aspects-of-things-to-come chambers within the Anti-Poipoi room likewise address the coercive power of language to define the past and future for us. For the first, Filliou offers Shakespeare on a Vespa; for the second he offers apocalyptic objects, such as "the stick with which Jesus will chase the Pope from Rome."[51] The chambers, taken together, suggest that neither current social systems nor their terminologies are absolute: Shakespeare need not remain a hallowed representative of Elizabethan theater; indeed, he lives on in the contemporary experience of anyone reading Shakespeare. Likewise, the absolute authority of the Catholic church as an exemplar of divine, not human, authority is, as Filliou points out, a fallacy.

The third room, the Postpoipoi, suggests the stamp on individual disciplines of multiple perspectives based on experience. By means of maps printed on the soles of shoes, for example, he parodies expertise in a field by giving it illogical concrete form: "Applied Psychology: Shampoo bottles for brain washing"; "Sociology: Measurement and weighing of visitors, with odd objects (thus a man may find out his height in tomatoes, and his weight in books)."[52] Altogether, the arbitrary basis of our collective standards of cartography, knowledge, measurement, and weight are disclosed, while the experiential fact of primary information—length and weight themselves—is given emphasis. With the primary knowledge of how a volume of flour, say, feels relative to the same volume of corn, we can base seemingly abstract ideas concerning the quantities of these commodities traded and shipped around the world in some known, physical fact.

The fourth room, the Poiegg, where the visitor "meditates, absorbs, conceives," stresses the importance of self-awareness in the development of identity. For me, this endpoint represents downtime, an opportunity to clear one's mind before moving on (though Filliou, a Buddhist, would probably criticize this view as too pragmatic, too functionalist). Whereas creative people often seek downtime between projects, educational systems allow scant opportunity for contemplative pursuits, mistakenly assuming that they are unproductive.

The Poipoi concept developed out of the Cédille qui Sourit store for "useless" ideas (ideas lying outside the traditional productionist mode of activity; see Figs. 46 and 47), which in turn had a basis in Brecht and Filliou's 1966 proposal for a "Non-École de Villefranche" (Villefranche being the Mediterranean town where the store was located). The programmatic statement of the non-école, which would have run on the simple principles of "freedom, equality, availability to all, mindfulness," encapsulates Filliou's educational model: "CAREFREE EXCHANGE OF INFORMATION AND EXPERIENCE, NO STUDENT, NO TEACHER, PERFECT FREEDOM, AT TIMES TO TALK AT TIMES TO LISTEN."[53] This statement foregrounds a multidirectional exchange of experience and information; the boundaries between student and teacher are dissolved even as the curriculum expands to include unexpected information and behavior. This expansion of didactic roles is possible only through mutual respect, engendered by means of attentive speaking and listening, teaching and learning.

As we have seen, two of the contributors to Filliou's book, Kaprow and Beuys, worked within the traditional university system and were strongly committed to education. Beuys's *German Student Party* (originally called *The Educational Party*) was based on the idea of artistic performance as political action within the social fabric (which he called "sculpture"). Actively engaged in an interdisciplinary dialogue with students regarding social experience and the students' perspectives on religion, science, history, and so on, Beuys saw his "performances, that is, their content, . . . [as] comparable to the exemplar content [specialized disciplines] of a university academy. The content of a university academy being, at the same time, comparable to that of this student party." The free flow of expression in a performance is thus analogous to the free flow of information in an educational context and of individual expression in a political one. For Beuys, as for Filliou, these elements are fundamentally alike in their ability to express the unique needs, wants, and skills of human beings. Beuys continues by adapting these terms of expression and information to an art context, and vice versa: "All these terms which appear in the performances as pictures, appear in the discussion of a student party as terms which are related, for example, to the concept of society."[54]

Ideally, participatory art, which includes performance as well as interactive objects, has an educational component as well as a democratic political one. In addition to injecting alternative notions such as interdisciplinarity, status equality between educators and students, and self-education into the pedagogical mix, Filliou, like Beuys, advocated "participation techniques"—active engagement, as opposed to passive absorption of information—such as practitioners of Events and Happenings relied on. In this way, the role of teacher as gatekeeper to an official culture of expertise becomes obsolete. Rather, the teacher becomes a guide, helping students find information and determine how it might be adapted to their particular needs.

The open-ended nature of Filliou's exchange with many participants through a partly empty book stands in stark contrast to Beuys's charisma as a lecturer and the idolizing response of his students. Beuys acknowledged the apparent irony of this; referring to the shamanistic persona that he cultivated, replete with felt hat, safari vest, and full-length fur coat, he said that "in places like universities, where everyone speaks so rationally, it is necessary for a kind of enchanter to appear."[55] Perhaps, though, his self-presentation in fact had the opposite effect, replicating the most damaging aspects of traditional education: attendance to a leader and intentional mystification. To sidestep this difficult territory with a description of the therapeutic effect of shamanistic testimonial, as one author has done, is a thin solution.[56] In our culture, artists assert themselves over the voices of authority, at best challenging that authority or, at worst, becoming new authoritative voices themselves. While Beuys seems to have understood the desirability of participation, he was apparently unable to put it into play in the public arena. One wonders: In the presence of such a forceful personality, is real exchange even possible?

In *Teaching and Learning,* in contrast, Allan Kaprow describes a possible application for this integrated approach, an Art Corps project (like the Peace Corps but for artists) geared to an educational setting: "I have proposed that our university... should establish experimental institutes in which artists of a very interesting and advanced inclination could come to do whatever they want in a noncategorized way. Their only requirement beyond doing their artwork should be to make themselves available in some way to the artist-teachers in the lower schools, and also occasionally to bring their art to the children of the lower schools." Following this multilevel exposure to all manner of things artistic, "when these children come to college it would be very interesting to see if their attitudes and capacities to study historical art, more advanced critical problems about the arts... made them much better qualified" thinkers, problem solvers, etc.[57]

Such a project requires the teacher *and* learner (conceivably the same person) to negotiate two kinds of experience, which Edward Reed calls firsthand and secondhand:

> Firsthand experience involves using information gained autonomously. Secondhand experience typically derives from situations that also offer some form of firsthand experience, but what makes the experience secondhand is that one has to take information that has been selected by someone else.... In spite of these connections..., secondhand experience still carries an important limitation not found in firsthand experience. When one is examining the world for oneself there

is no limit to the scrutiny—one can look as carefully as one wishes, and one can always uncover new information.[58]

Thus, despite the usefulness of expert information, it is in primary experience—close perceptual rapport with an object of scrutiny—that a learner discovers or invents new levels of meaning.[59]

The educator Miriam Hutton has diagrammed the process of experiential learning, in which one obtains information even as one figures out how to use it. Her flexible system is reminiscent of the most open-ended aspects both of Kaprow's Happenings and of the more structured Events, in that the outcomes of a particular action may not be clear. As she puts it, her work "consists of identifying a process for the making of a judgement or decision, rather than focusing on the outcome expected."[60]

Hutton describes "a reflective framework for learning from action" that moves both learner and teacher-facilitator through the process. First, the "initial situation" is broken down into conditions (the pertinent facts, such as physical characteristics, history, and material characteristics) and a stance (the attitudes, values, and beliefs about the conditions). The situation is then judged as to "possible/probable alternatives or hypotheses," whereupon a decision is made that leads to choice or action, with outcomes, both expected and unexpected, being the final result. The process is then repeated. For example, the conditions of dependency on foreign oil relate to historic facts and to material characteristics such as what oil does and how it can be used. "Stance" refers to attitudes about these conditions, such as the Western "right" to access foreign oil and the perception that it is right to pay individuals for it (the Saudi royals come to mind). Possible and probable outcomes are assessed: What if we have no "right" to it? Should we expect anti-American sentiment in the region? Or, if we do have a "right" to buy it, but not from individuals, should we expect social unrest in a given region? Actions might range from a redistribution of sales to more emphasis on local reserves or alternative energy sources—each of which comes with its own conditions, stance, and hypothesis. In this system, proficiency in managing the unknown (as opposed to the known) would constitute expertise in a field.

This seemingly arcane mechanism is simpler in use than it might appear. Returning to Filliou's book, we find analogous processes applied in problem-solving situations: Kaprow describes a tire-rolling event in Central Park, Ben Patterson tells about a collage poem project undertaken at a local school, and Cage relates the story of a Zen monk and his pupil (the teacher says nothing). In each case the core problem is how to trigger a link between imagination (which moves toward the unknown) and firsthand experience. Although the conditions—art fair, poetry class, and Zen koan—vary, the stance—the need to learn a discrete skill—is more or less constant. And in each case, the student, through a process that combines firsthand information and experience, achieves self-education.

In the end, education should not be about applicability to an existing job situation, but about everything else. For it is through creative play that new solutions to problems may be found. Leisure is not antithetical to progress, just to a continuation of the status quo—a point made repeatedly in the various schools of Marxian thought. It is telling that many artists "can't distinguish between work and play. They require no vacations from this work because of their total involvement."[61]

In contrast to artistic play, Reed describes the work-related "machining of the mind," in which mental processes are subjugated to values such as predictability and certainty.[62] Filliou's "creative use of leisure" is intended to extricate us from this kind of industrial or machine-age mind control, the enslavement to a work ethic, which eradicates individualism. Witness Filliou's self-description as a "Good for Nothing. Good at Everything,"[63] wherein his freedom from the production-based model of human value as linked to work makes him paradoxically "Good for Nothing"—a bum of sorts—and "Good at Everything"—freed from the valuative mechanism that would limit him to one type of work or play.

These artists argue for learning situations that are not tied to degrees, that are liberated from the constraints of time (daily as well as academic schedules), fixed locations (especially in the sense of a study-conducive "physical plant" consisting of bolted-down desks and uniform lighting), and institutional affiliation (which too often means institutional ideas). Experiential learning goes some way toward eradicating these circumstances; after all, experience, in a sense, meanders through one's life, allowing a constant redefinition of both place and time.

The pedagogical model offered by Fluxus in general, and the Fluxkit and Event in particular, includes direct experience, conversations, collaborations, and a liberation of means. Fluxus encourages us to look at, listen to, and feel the environment, to learn from that experience and to remain open to new perceptions.

A Polemical Ending

Makers of culture and those creatively engaged with it are fortunate people. We may have somewhat more thorough access to experience, to getting outside ourselves and to getting inside something, or someone, else. These exchanges with the productions of human creativity are made possible by skills we have learned, skills that often rub against what we are taught—or rather, what we are taught to think about rationally. This is true even if these skills and the productions that respond to them are culturally or historically specific.

I believe that Fluxus offers a particularly useful means of having these transformative experiences here and now, in the Euro-American context of advanced capitalism and millenarian pathos. Fluxus is not unique in this, of course. It is, however, a particularly viable conduit for free creativity and free discourse—in part because of its ontological basis (as demonstrated in the Event and Fluxkits), but even more so because it contains multiple perspectives on itself and its relationship to the world. As such, it offers a model for a multicultural, multilingual society that is characterized by both difference and group feeling, and by a sense of connection to the physical world.

Educators are like artists insofar as it is the teacher-facilitator's job to make experiences available to students that give them a stake in the world as it is coming to be. All art *and* all education have this potential. Such actualization is in no way the unique domain of Fluxus or Happenings—or of any hypothetical pedagogy we might imagine. Still, these artistic movements do offer tools for us to create meaningful experiences on our own. They are (to greater and lesser degrees) fundamentally democratic in this regard.

As a historian, I consider it my task to learn something of human nature from what humans make as art. The mindful basis of the work I study makes this task relatively easy. This mindfulness also makes me wish I could follow Filliou's lead and end this book with a single word:

mind

Instead, I end with these words from John Dewey's *Art as Experience,* which could as easily have been written by Filliou:

> Instruction in the arts of life is something other than conveying information about them. It is a matter of communication and participation in values of life by means of imagination, and works of art are the most intimate and energetic means of aiding individuals to share in the arts of living. Civilization is uncivil because human beings are divided into non-communication sects, races, nations, classes and cliques.[64]

NOTES

Preface

1. Owen F. Smith, "Introduction," in *Fluxus: The History of an Attitude* (San Diego: San Diego State University Press, 1998), 1.
2. Ibid., 11.
3. John Dewey, *Art as Experience* (New York: Capricorn, 1934), 25.
4. Accordingly, the history of art may be understood as the history of what makes experiences possible at a given place and time.
5. For details on locations, participants, and works performed in specific concerts and festivals, see Smith, "Introduction."
6. For details on the biographical dimension of my own Fluxus experience, see "Fluxus Familias," in *Art Journal,* summer 2000.
7. See my Ph.D. dissertation, "(En)versioning Fluxus" (University of Chicago, 1994).

Introduction

1. John Cage, "Interview with Michael Kirby and Richard Schechner," *Tulane Drama Review* 10, no. 2 (winter 1965).
2. Allan Kaprow, *18 Happenings in 6 Parts,* 1959.
3. For details on this period, see Robert von Zahn, "'Refusierte Gesänge': Musik im Atelier Bauermeister," in *Intermedial, Kontrovers, Experimentell: Das Atelier Mary Bauermeister in Köln, 1960–62* (Cologne: Emons Verlag, 1993).
4. See Wilfried Dörstel, Rainer Steinberg, and Robert von Zahn, "The Bauermeister Studio: Proto-Fluxus in Cologne, 1960–62," in *Fluxus Virus,* ed. Ken Friedman (Cologne: Gallerie Schüppenhauer, 1992), 56.
5. The Fluxus experience can be ascribed to these other modes as well, but that is a project for another time and place.
6. Robert Filliou, *Teaching and Learning as Performing Arts* (Cologne and New York: Kaspar König, 1970).

Chapter 1

1. *Fluxfilm Program,* ed. George Maciunas, 1966 (available through Arthouse, Inc., New York). John Cavanaugh's film *Flicker* (1966) is sometimes called *Blink,* though the title bears no relation to the famous *Blink* image (*The Scissors Brothers' Warehouse Sale* print) described below. The film was shown at various Fluxus Festivals and reproduced in many Fluxkit multiples through the 1960s. For a list of editions and festivals, see *Fluxus Codex: The Gilbert and Lila Silverman Fluxus Collection,* ed. Jon Hendricks (New York: Abrams, 1988).
2. J. L. Austin, typical among sensory theorists that position themselves against this polarizing tradition, offers an admirably concise summary of why this is so. In *Sense and Sensibilia* (Oxford: Oxford University Press, 1962), 61, Austin says that "it is a curious and in some ways rather melancholy fact that the relative positions of [H. H.] Price and [A. J.] Ayer at this point turn out to be exactly the same as the relative positions of [John] Locke and [George] Berkeley, or [David] Hume and [Immanuel] Kant. In Locke's view there are 'ideas' and also 'external objects,' in Hume's 'impressions' and also 'external objects,' in Price's view 'sense data' and also 'physical occupants'; in Berkeley's doctrine there are *only* ideas, in Kant's only *Vorstellungen* (things-in-themselves being not strictly relevant here), in Ayer's doctrine there are *only* sense-data—but Berkeley, Kant and Ayer all further agree that we can speak as if there were bodies, objects, material things."
3. Dewey, *Art as Experience,* 25.

4. Austin, *Sense and Sensibilia,* 4.

5. Laura Mulvey's groundbreaking "Visual Pleasure and Narrative Cinema" has been especially influential in the field of art history; it can be found in *Feminism and Film Theory,* ed. Constance Penley (New York: Routledge, 1988).

6. Much recent art history complicates this myth of optical objectivity. However, that was not generally the case in the 1960s; see, for example, Ernst Gombrich's *Art and Illusion: A Study in the Psychology of Pictorial Representation* (Princeton: Princeton University Press, 1969). Similarly, mainstream modernist criticism is strongly influenced by the idea of pure opticality. Examples include the writings of Clement Greenberg, in particular "Toward a Newer Laocoön," *Partisan Review* 7 (1940); and "Modernist Painting," in Clement Greenberg, *The Collected Essays and Criticisms,* ed. John O'Brian, 4 vols. (Chicago: University of Chicago Press, [1962] 1986–1993). For analysis of the incompatibility of this objective optical premise with other forms of expression, see Michael Fried, "Art and Objecthood," in *Minimal Art: A Critical Anthology,* ed. Gregory Battcock (New York: Dutton, 1968).

7. For an overview on the changing function of the gaze within art history, see Margaret Olin, "Gaze," in *Critical Terms for Art History,* ed. Robert S. Nelson and Richard Schiff (Chicago: University of Chicago Press, 1992). Notable book-length studies on the gaze by art historians and cultural critics include Norman Bryson, *Vision and Painting: The Logic of the Gaze* (New Haven: Yale University Press, 1983); Guy Debord, *The Society of the Spectacle* (Detroit: Black and Red, 1983); and Michael Fried, *Absorption and Theatricality: Painting and Beholder in the Age of Diderot* (Berkeley: University of California Press, 1980).

8. The entire collection of *L'Optique Moderne* can be found in the privately held Gilbert and Lila Silverman Fluxus Collection in Detroit, Michigan.

9. Paul Virilio, *The Vision Machine* (Bloomington: Indiana University Press; London: British Film Institute, [1988] 1996), 15.

10. Ibid., 16–17.

11. Robert Romanyshyn, *Technology as Symptom and Dream* (London: Routledge, 1989), 33, 173.

12. Kristine Stiles, "Between Water and Stone, Fluxus Performance: A Metaphysics of Acts," *In the Spirit of Fluxus,* ed. Elizabeth Armstrong and Joan Rothfuss (Minneapolis: Walker Art Center, 1993), 65. Stiles's use of the term *performative* derives from J. L. Austin's *How to Do Things with Words* (Cambridge, Mass.: Harvard University Press, 1975); see Stiles, "Between Water and Stone," 96 n. 7. Austin is largely concerned with how words do things; Stiles expands on this to include a comparatively wide range of activities and experiences that connect thoughts with acts. See also, on the linguistic sense of performativity, Judith Butler's *Excitable Speech* (New York: Routledge, 1997).

13. In its phenomenological characteristics, its mode of production, manner of sale, and use of a Cagean organizational matrix, *Blink* is emblematic of much Fluxus work. First, and most importantly for my argument, *Blink* destabilizes vision, substituting a haptic or tactile mode of representation. Second, the imagery is at once ordinary and extraordinary. Third, *Blink* was sold through the commonplace format of a warehouse sale, except that pricing was arbitrary, thereby negating both the high cost and traditional audience of high art. Fourth, the combination of images was indeterminate—that is, each artist was free to select images at will—giving the project an air of chance operations characteristic of many Fluxus works. Fifth, as a cooperative endeavor, *Blink* signifies the collective nature of many Fluxus experiences and productions.

14. Robert Witkin, *Art and Social Structure* (Cambridge: Polity, 1995), 64.

15. See Paul J. Staiti, "Illusion, Trompe L'oeil, and the Perils of Viewership," in *William M. Harnett,* ed. Doreen Bolger, Marc Simpson, and John Wilmerding (New York: Metropolitan Museum of Art; Abrams, 1992), 38: "Viewing begins with a distanced, genteel, dispassionate sighting of an entire painting: the entire ensemble of objects in it, their shapes, formal pattern, and position in a shallow space. Response is held in check at first, but it leads to a more proximate, lively, and, finally, more troubled encounter with surrogate reality."

16. One effect of trompe l'oeil resonates with my experience of the scissors in *Blink:* "As signifiers of indeterminate signification, anxiously indicating both object and representation, these items were so deceptively painted that viewers were impelled to abandon the etiquette of passive spectatorship by actively moving near the picture or even touching it in an effort to determine what it was they were seeing" (ibid., 32).

17. It should come as no surprise that thirty years later, Fluxus artist Emmett Williams would produce artist portraits that consist of objects fixed to a red, glazed ground.

18. Svetlana Alpers, *The Art of Describing: Dutch Art in the Seventeenth Century* (Chicago: University of Chicago Press, 1983), 44.

19. David Howes, "Introduction: To Summon All the Senses," in *The Varieties of Sensory Experience,* ed. David Howes (Toronto: University of Toronto Press, 1991), 7–8.

20. George Maciunas was the most energetic and devoted organizer of Fluxus activities during the so-called heroic period (1962 to the middle 1960s). While he was responsible for the Fluxus avant-garde graphic style and organized many of the most important festivals, it is a mistake to describe him as a leader or definitive figure for Fluxus, since (even though Fluxus would probably not have existed without him) several other Fluxus styles exist, he was not always involved in the historic concerts, and the group continues its activities although he died many years ago. Overemphasizing Maciunas's role requires making arbitrary divisions within the Fluxus oeuvre. This problem is further explored in Chapter 2.

21. Henry Martin, "Fluxus and the Humanistic Tradition," lecture transcript, Jan. 1993, 5 (in my archive).

22. Dewey, *Art as Experience,* 301; emphasis mine.

23. Martin, "Fluxus and the Humanistic Tradition," 5.

24. Edward S. Reed, *The Necessity of Experience* (New Haven: Yale University Press, 1972), 2; emphasis mine.

25. For the contents of two such boxes, see Hendricks, *Fluxus Codex,* 110.

26. There are far too many Fluxkits to survey them in anything shorter than an entire book. What follows is a representative sample that may function as an invitation for further study.

27. W. Ivins, *Art and Geometry: A Study in Space Intuitions* (New York: Dover, 1964), 4.

28. See John Dewey, "Experience and Education" (1938), in *The Later Works of John Dewey,* vol. 13 (Carbondale: Southern Illinois University Press, 1988); and idem, *Art as Experience.* See also William James, *Essays in Radical Empiricism* (Cambridge, Mass.: Harvard University Press, [1912] 1984).

29. Dewey, *Art as Experience,* 22.

30. Hilary Putnam, *Pragmatism: An Open Question* (Oxford: Basil Blackwell, 1995); idem, *Renewing Philosophy* (Cambridge, Mass.: Harvard University Press, 1992); and John McDowell, *Mind and World* (Cambridge, Mass.: Harvard University Press, 1994).

31. Putnam, *Pragmatism,* 454.

32. Hilary Putnam, "The Dewey Lectures, 1994—Sense, Nonsense, and the Senses: An Inquiry into the Powers of the Human Mind," *Journal of Philosophy* 91, no. 9 (1994): 445–511; quotation from 454.

33. David Michael Levin, *The Body's Recollection of Being* (London: Routledge and Kegan Paul, 1985), 56.

34. Ibid., 145; quote is from Maurice Merleau-Ponty, *Phenomenology of Perception* (London: Routledge and Kegan Paul, 1962), 326.

35. Levin, *Body's Recollection,* 126.

36. Martin Heidegger, *What Is Called Thinking?* (New York: Harper and Row, 1968), 187.

37. Levin, *Body's Recollection,* 128, 129.

38. Lawrence K. Frank, "Tactile Communication," in *Explorations in Communication,* ed. Edmund Carpenter and Marshall McLuhan (Boston: Beacon Press, 1960), 4.

39. Constance Classen, David Howes, and Anthony Synnott, "Introduction," in *Aroma: The Cultural History of Smell* (London: Routledge, 1994), 4–5.

40. Although Saito is best known for her smell chess works, over the past thirty-five years she has also produced tactile, grinder, sound, weight, and fruit chess games. Maciunas proposed related works, such as the *Good Smell Eggs* and *Bad Smell Eggs,* which would have consisted of blown eggs filled, respectively, with spices and perfumes and with rotten egg or food. Like the chess works, the eggs would look the same.

41. Letter from Miller to Maciunas in Hendricks, *Fluxus Codex,* 570.

42. Classen, Howes, and Synnott, *Aroma,* 132.

43. Putnam, *Pragmatism,* 454.

44. Alfred Gell, "Metamorphosis of the Cassowaries: Umeda Society, Language, and Ritual," in Classen, Howes, and Synnott, *Aroma,* 26.

45. Classen, Howes, and Synnott, *Aroma,* 135.

46. Diane Ackerman, *A Natural History of the Senses* (New York: Random House, 1990), 6.

47. Howard Gardner, *Frames of Mind: The Theory of Multiple Intelligences* (New York: Basic Books, 1983), 61.

48. Rudolf Arnheim, *Visual Thinking* (Berkeley: University of California Press, 1969), 19.

49. *Fluxnewsletter,* 31 Jan. 1968; Silverman Collection, Detroit.

50. Photographs of these Events can be found in the Silverman Collection, Detroit, and in several of the artists' personal photo collections.

51. I had the extreme good fortune to attend a black meal organized by Geoffrey Hendricks and a rainbow meal organized for a reunion in 1988 and 1992, respectively. My descriptions here are based on those experiences.

52. Joel C. Kuipers, "Matters of Taste in Weyéwa," in Howes (ed.), *Varieties of Sensory Experience,* 117.

53. See Philip Corner, *The Identical Lunch: Philip Corner's Performances of a Score by Alison Knowles* (San Francisco: Nova Broadcast Press, 1973); and Alison Knowles, *Journal of the Identical Lunch* (San Francisco: Nova Broadcast Press, 1971). Kristine Stiles has written extensively on the lunch; see, for example, "Tuna and Other Fishy Thoughts on Fluxus Events," in *Alison Knowles: Notes toward Indigo Island* (Saarbrücken, Ger.: Stadtgalerie Saarbrücken, 1995).

54. Postcard in the Silverman Collection, Detroit.

55. This work was reassembled by the Gilbert and Lila Silverman Fluxus Collection for the *In the Spirit of Fluxus* exhibition at the Walker Art Center, Minneapolis, in 1992.

56. For example, the Japanese Fluxus artist Hi Red Center organized a Fluxclinic (1966) that measured visitors' height, weight, volume, head strength, finger length, etc. Clinical cards were printed up and included in later Fluxkits. See Hendricks, *Fluxus Codex.*

57. This occurred in 1993 at the "A la Carte" evening of Fluxus Festival Chicago at the Arts Club of Chicago.

58. Marshall McLuhan, *Verbi-Voco-Visual Explorations* (New York: Something Else Press, 1967). See also Marshall McLuhan, *The Gutenberg Galaxy* (Toronto: The University of Toronto Press, 1962).

59. Walter J. Ong, "The Shifting Sensorium," in Howes (ed.), *Varieties of Sensory Experience,* 25.

60. More details may be found in my doctoral thesis, "(En)versioning Fluxus."

61. Ken Friedman, ed., *The Fluxus Performance Workbook* (Verona, Italy: Editions Conz; New York: Emily Harvey Gallery, 1990), 16, 114.

62. Levin, *Body's Recollection,* 153.

63. Martin Heidegger, *Being and Time* (New York: Harper and Row, 1962); emphasis mine.

64. With the exception of Robert Filliou, no Fluxus artist has been publicly committed to Buddhist doctrine, though Philip Corner, Alison Knowles, and Willem de Ridder, to name a few, did follow Buddhism sporadically. It is for this reason that I look to the Western philosophical tradition to help explain the significance of chance and indeterminacy in Cage and Fluxus.

65. David Michael Levin, "Decline and Fall: Ocularcentrism in Heidegger's Reading of the History of Metaphysics," in *Modernity and the Hegemony of Vision,* ed. David Michael Levin (Berkeley: University of California Press, 1993), 203; my emphasis. I am deeply indebted to Levin for his analysis of Heidegger.

66. Ibid., 212. This argument underlies Levin's *The Listening Self* (London: Routledge, 1989). See also Martin Heidegger, *An Introduction to Metaphysics* (New York: Doubleday, 1961), 109–11, 123.

67. Jacques Derrida, *Of Grammatology,* trans. Gayatri Spivak (Delhi, India: Motilal Banarsidass, 1994), 60.

68. Ibid.

69. W. J. T. Mitchell, *Iconology* (Chicago: University of Chicago Press, 1986), 59.

70. Derrida, *Of Grammatology,* 60.

71. Ellen Dissanayake, *What Is Art For?* (Seattle: University of Washington Press, 1988), 6.

72. Ibid., 90, 95.

73. Martin, "Fluxus and the Humanistic Tradition," 5.

74. Dissanayake, *What Is Art For?* 101.

75. Martin, "Fluxus and the Humanistic Tradition," 4.

76. Ellen Dissanayake, *Homo Aestheticus* (New York: Free Press, 1992), 38, 54 (emphasis mine), 63.

77. James Hillman, "When You're Healed, Send Me a Postcard," in *Conversations before the End of Time,* ed. Suzi Gablik (London: Thames and Hudson, 1995), 196.

78. See James Hillman and Michael Ventura, *We've Had a Hundred Years of Psychotherapy and the World's Getting Worse* (New York: Harper Collins, 1992).

79. Jerry Mander and Edward Goldsmith, eds., *The Case against the Global Economy: And for a Turn toward the Local* (San Francisco: Sierra Books, 1996).

Chapter 2

1. George Brecht, "Something about Fluxus," *Fluxus Newspaper,* no. 4, June 1964; Silverman Collection, Detroit.

2. Jean-Yves Bosseur, "The Eye and Musical Notation," in *Sound and the Visual Arts: Intersections between Music and Plastic Arts Today,* ed. Jean-Yves Bosseur (Paris: Dis Voir, 1993), 22.

3. Maciunas to Bauermeister, n.d., Archiv Mary Bauermeister, Historisches Archiv Köln (HAStK), inv. 1441, no. 25.

4. Stockhausen was to include the score for *Originale* and other works in *Fluxus* no. 2, Western European issue no. 1; George Maciunas, "Notes for Projected Issues," 1962, Archiv Sohm, Staatsgalerie Stuttgart.

5. Maciunas ("Notes," 1962) initially conceived of the festivals as financial engines for the projected Fluxus magazine, which explains in part why he included Stockhausen in his festival projections, publicity, and programs.

6. Paik to Maciunas, n.d., Archiv Sohm.

7. John Cage, "Indeterminacy" section of "Composition as Process" in *Silence: Lectures and Writings* (Hanover, N.H.: Wesleyan University Press, [1961] 1973), 36. This should not be confused with the lecture "Indeterminacy," which is found in the same volume.

8. Original program located at Archiv Sohm.

9. Author's notes from public conversation between Alison Knowles, Allan Kaprow, and Dick Higgins, "Fluxforum," at the Wexner Center for the Arts, Columbus, Ohio, 25 February 1994.

10. Allan Kaprow, "The Real Experiment" (1983), in Kaprow, *The Blurring of Art and Life,* ed. Jeff Kelly (Berkeley and Los Angeles: University of California Press, 1993), 202–3.

11. Brecht, "Something about Fluxus," 144.

12. "Avant-Garde: Stuffed Bird at 48 Sharp," *Time,* 18 Sept. 1964.

13. Foubion Bowers, "A Feast of Astonishments," *Nation,* 28 Sept. 1964.

14. Though adamant that he is not part of Fluxus, at key moments, such as at *Ubi Fluxus ibi Motus* in Venice in 1990, Flynt has appeared in the context of Fluxus as both an artist and a writer, and he has had intermittent yet often significant contact with Fluxus artists.

15. George Maciunas, *Fluxus News-Policy Letter,* no. 6 (Apr. 1963); located in the Silverman Archive, New York (distinct from the Gilbert and Lila Silverman Fluxus Collection in Detroit). The paper is one of a series of newsletters that Maciunas began publishing in Wiesbaden on 21 May 1962; by the time number 6 was published, Maciunas had returned to New York City and was producing the paper there.

16. This is admittedly a gross simplification of dadaism. Many dada artists work in affirmative modes of many kinds, as pointed out by Dawn Ades in her book *Photomontage* (London: Thames & Hudson, 1986); nevertheless, at the time relatively little was known about dadaism, and the myth of dada in America focused primarily on its destructive aspect. Regarding this manifesto, because no consensus was reached on its representativeness for the movement, I will use the less proprietary term *Purge Manifesto* in what follows, taken from the directive in the document that Fluxus should "purge the world of bourgeois sickness, 'intellectual,' professional & commercialized culture, PURGE the world of dead art, imitation, artificial art, abstract art, illusionistic art, mathematical art,—PURGE THE WORLD OF 'EUROPANISM'!"

17. George Maciunas, *Fluxus News Letter,* no. 7, 1 May 1963; Silverman Archive, New York.

18. Ibid.

19. Brecht to Maciunas, 18 Apr. 1962, Archiv Sohm.

20. Mac Low to Maciunas, 25 Apr. 1962, Archiv Sohm.

21. Letters located at Archiv Sohm.

22. Maciunas to Higgins and Knowles, 1963, Archiv Sohm.

23. See Peter Bürger's *Theory of the Avant-Garde,* trans. Michael Shaw (Minneapolis: University of Minnesota Press, 1984), 22–23. Bürger states that "with the historic Avant-Garde movements, the social subsystem that is art enters the stage of self-criticism.... As institution and content coincide, social ineffectuality stands revealed as the essence of art in Bourgeois society, and thus provokes the self-criticism of art."

24. Maciunas to Williams, Spoerri, and Filliou, 1963, Archiv Sohm.

25. Maciunas's notebooks from New York University (Silverman Archive, New York), which date from the 1950s, show a great fascination with the history of ethnographic and popular art forms; his often took the form of graphs or time lines, resembling the Fluxus genealogies he would construct many years later.

26. Stephen Jay Gould, *Full House: The Spread of Excellence from Plato to Darwin* (New York: Three Rivers Press, 1997).

27. See, for example, Jürgen Habermas, "Modernity: An Incomplete Project," in *The Anti-Aesthetic: Essays in Postmodern Culture,* ed. Hal Foster (Port Townsend, Wash.: Bay Press, 1983); Andreas Huyssen, "The Search for Tradition: Avant-Garde and Postmodernism in the 1970s," *New German Critique* 22 (1981); and Matei Calinescu, *Five Faces of Modernity: Modernism, Avant-Garde, Decadence, Kitsch, Postmodernism* (Durham, N.C.: Duke University Press, 1987.)

28. Calinescu, *Five Faces of Modernity,* 96.

29. Ibid.

30. Bürger, *Theory of the Avant-Garde,* 22–23.

31. Renato Poggioli, *The Theory of the Avant-Garde* (Cambridge, Mass.: Harvard University Press, 1968), 25.

32. Bürger, *Theory of the Avant-Garde,* 22.

33. These critiques are surveyed admirably by Ann Gibson in "Avant-Garde," in *Critical Terms for Art History,* ed. Robert Nelson and Richard Schiff (Chicago: University of Chicago Press, 1996), 156–69.

34. An early draft of this manuscript was rightly criticized by the ever vigilant and insightful Kristine Stiles for failing to offer a viable alternative to the Maciunas-based linear history of Fluxus. What follows, though provisional, attempts to work toward a model for Fluxus as an interpenetrative and flexible group of mutually interested artists, a social matrix.

35. Martin, "Fluxus and the Humanistic Tradition" (lecture). Martin accepts the risk in his lecture when he states that "radical self-awareness" and "radical self-awakening" are central to Fluxus.

36. Daisetz Teitaro Suzuki, *Essays in Buddhism,* 3d ser. (London: Luzak, 1934); and idem, *Living by Zen* (London: Rider, 1991).

37. For details, see David Revill, *The Roaring Silence: John Cage—a Life* (New York: Arcade, 1992), 107–125; quotation, 108.

38. Friedman (ed.), *Fluxus Performance Workbook,* 56.

39. John Cage, *A Year from Monday* (London: Marion Boyars, 1967), 107.

40. John Cage, "Music Lovers Field Companion," in *Silence,* 276.

41. John Cage, "Experimental Music," address given to the Music Teachers National Association, Chicago, winter 1957; the address was printed in a brochure accompanying the

recording of the famous Town Hall performance, New York, 1958; and reprinted in *Silence,* 8.

42. John Cage, "Lecture on Nothing," in *Silence,* 109.

43. John Cage in *New York Post,* 10 June 1958.

44. There may have been as many as a hundred festivals and concerts in the United States and Europe since the 1950s that involved Fluxus artists almost exclusively but that are called something else because of an overrestrictive sense of the Fluxus name. Examples include the Ergo Suits Festival and Festival of Misfits (1962), Festival of Fantastiks (1992), Games at the Cedilla (1966), and Excellent Festival (1992). Significantly, the Cologne-based Fluxus artist Wolf Vostell published *De-Coll/age Magazine* in the 1960s, which routinely disseminated scores, texts, and photographs of work by Fluxus artists. He later relocated to Berlin. In France, Ben Vautier, Robert Filliou, and George Brecht had shops that distributed Fluxus objects: Ben Vautier's store, in Nice, sold primarily his own work and a few Fluxkits; La Çédille qui Sourit, run by George Brecht and Robert Filliou, was also on the Riviera, in Villefranche-sur-Mer. Milan Knizak's Group Aktual Czechoslovakia published samizdat materials and organized performances of Fluxus works by Eastern European artists throughout the 1960s and 1970s.

45. According to Peter Frank, *The Something Else Press: An Annotated Bibliography by Peter Frank* (New York: McPherson and Co., 1983), 3: "the set copy languished for almost a year as Maciunas became involved with other activity. Finally, like Young and *An Anthology* before, Higgins lost patience and retrieved the copy. . . . Higgins returned home and recounted to Knowles that he was starting his own press."

46. Higgins revived the term in "Intermedia," *Something Else Newsletter* 1, no. 1 (1966): 1; reprinted in Dick Higgins, *Horizons: The Poetics and Theory of the Intermedia* (Carbondale: Southern Illinois University Press, 1984), 18–21. The Coleridge citation dates to 1812, but I have not located it in a specific work. On the basis of Higgins's description, the Norwegian art historian Ina Blom produced an excellent analysis of Fluxus as an intermedial practice; see "The Intermedia Dynamic: An Aspect of Fluxus" (Ph.D. diss., Universitetet i Oslo, 1993).

47. Blom, "Intermedia Dynamic."

48. Higgins, "Intermedia," in *Horizons,* 18.

49. Blom, "Intermedia Dynamic," 40.

50. In the United States, the art aspect of the intermedia was emphasized, suggesting synonymity with mixed media, action theater, or total art. Use differed in other countries, where the avant-garde tradition was different. The term was adopted for the art festival Intermedia '69, held in Heidelberg and organized by Jochen Goetze, Klaus Staeck, and

Friedrich Gerling; participants included Fluxus associates Albrecht D., Eric Andersen, Joseph Beuys, Henning Christiansen, Dick Higgins, and Milan Knizak. This festival and its catalogue (published in Heidelberg by Edition Tangente) presented the pared-down, subtractive form of intermedia as exemplified by these concrete poets and Event artists. Finally, Udo Kulturmann's *Leben und Kunst* (Tübingen: Studio Wasmuth, 1970) popularized the term for an increasingly general audience. By 1980, the Experimental Intermedia Foundation had published *Theoretical Analysis of the Intermedia Art Form* (Buenos Aires: Centro de Arte y Comunicación, 1980).

51. Reviewed by Ross Wetzsteon in "Theatre Afield; Intermedia and Skiing," *Village Voice,* 17 August 1967. Wetzsteon criticized intermedia work on the grounds that the public needed access to difficult critical formulas to understand it, and this compromised the work's radical potential.

52. Jill Johnston, "Intermedia '68," *Village Voice,* 14 Mar. 1968.

53. See Carolee Schneemann, *More than Meat Joy: Complete Performance Works and Selective Writings* (New Paltz, N.Y.: Documentext, 1979).

54. Howard Junker, "Mixed Bag," *Newsweek,* 18 Mar. 1968, 112. The author went on to provide analysis of progressive art at *Rolling Stone.*

55. George Maciunas, advertisement in the *Village Voice,* 5 Aug. 1965, n.p., a call for participants in a Carnegie Recital Hall concert: "Instrumentalist wanted by Fluxorchestra... No skill needed"; see also the ad for the same concert in the *Village Voice,* 23 Sept. 1965, n.p. (Archiv Sohm). The concert would take place in the Carnegie Recital Hall on 25 September, according to the statement of forthcoming events in *Fluxus Vaudeville TouRnamEnt,* ed. George Maciunas, July 1965 (Silverman Archive, New York). The name of this newspaper changed with each publication but always included the letters VTRE capitalized in the title, which is how the paper appears in Fluxus lists, publications, and archives.

56. Catherine Liu, "Fluxus: Selections from the Gilbert and Lila Silverman Collection," *Artforum* 27 (May 1989).

57. Thomas Crow, *The Intelligence of Art* (Chapel Hill: University of North Carolina Press, 1999), 5; my emphasis. In this book, Crow suggests possible solutions to the problem of overdetermined, method-driven analysis, citing studies by Meyer Shapiro, Claude Lévi-Strauss, and Michael Baxandall.

58. Ibid., 103.

59. In its acceptance of the uniformity of the cycles of modernism as the basis for a pluralistic reaction, recent (postmodern) art is not fundamentally different from art that came before it. Witness the shift from Italian Renaissance to mannerist art.

Chapter 3

1. The print he made, of a house, traveled in the "Spirit of Fluxus" show in 1993–94.

2. Philip Jackson, *John Dewey and the Lessons of Art* (Chicago: University of Chicago Press, 1998), 1–67.

3. Photocopy of artist's statement, n.d., collection of the artist.

4. Dewey, *Art as Experience,* 110; my emphasis. Joseph Kupfer, shifting Dewey's argument into nonart situations, reverses Dewey's terms: "The basic importance and pervasiveness of the aesthetic and various spheres of life [lie] not just in the obviously aesthetic"; see Joseph Kupfer, *Experience as Art* (Albany: State University of New York Press, 1983), 2.

5. Martin, "Fluxus and the Humanistic Tradition," 6.

6. See, for example, Fredric Jameson, *Postmodernism; or, The Cultural Logic of Late Capitalism* (London: Verso, 1991); Hal Foster, *Return of the Real* (Cambridge, Mass.: MIT Press, 1996); Jean Baudrillard, "Pop—an Art of Consumption," in *Post–Pop Art,* ed. Paul Taylor (Cambridge, Mass.: MIT Press, 1989); and Arthur Danto, *The Philosophical Disenfranchisement of Art* (New York: Columbia University Press, 1986). In these interpretations, pop art is treated as a cipher for a wide range of transformations: late capitalism (Fredric Jameson), a fragmented psychology in search of the real (Hal Foster), semiotic simulacra (Jean Baudrillard), and a shift in the historically self-referential narrative of art (Arthur Danto), to name but a few. With the notable exception of Danto, whose experience with Warhol's *Brillo Box* was clearly transformative, no one finds the power of art within art itself. Indeed, even Danto can be said to base his logic primarily within the modern art movements up until pop, after which he describes art as posthistoric.

   Warhol's signifying a paradigm shift is a by-product of his aloofness from modern, painterly aesthetics. Put differently, *apparently* lacking an invested, painterly intelligence, Warhol has been particularly vulnerable to hyperliteralization.

7. In *Into the Light of Things: The Art of the Commonplace from Wordsworth to John Cage* (Chicago: University of Chicago Press, 1994), George A. Leonard argues that Cage's silence functions negatively against objects. It is in negative terms, then, that Leonard establishes Cage as a model for the so-called anti-art dimension of art from the past thirty years. Leonard's insight in choosing Cage as an alternate paradigm marker is therefore overdetermined by negative dialectics.

8. The Emily Harvey Gallery, New York, press release, "Fluxus and Co.," 2 Dec. 1989–13 Jan. 1990; author's collection.

9. Allan Kaprow, quoted in Michael Kirby, *Happenings* (London: Sidgewick and Jackson; New York: Dutton, 1965), 44–46.

10. Allan Kaprow, *Assemblage, Environments, and Happenings* (New York: Abrams, 1966).

11. Harold Rosenberg, "The American Action Painters," *Art News* 51 (Dec. 1952), 22; emphasis mine.

12. Clement Greenberg, "How Art Writing Earns Its Bad Name," *Second Coming* 1, no. 3 (Mar. 1962): 58–62.

13. Hilton Kramer, "The New American Painting," *Partisan Review* 20, no. 4 (July–Aug. 1953): 421–27.

14. John Wilcock, "What's Happening with Happenings," *Village Voice,* 21 Jan. 1965, 2.

15. Mariellen R. Sandford, ed., *Happenings and Other Acts* (London: Routledge, 1995), offers an excellent overview through primary source materials.

16. Ibid., 197–98.

17. Hans Robert Jauss, *Toward an Aesthetic of Reception,* trans. Timothy Bahti (Minneapolis: University of Minnesota Press, 1982), 25.

18. In about 1970, Kaprow moved away from self-identification as an artist on the art side of the art/life matrix toward a description of himself as an "Un-Artist" creatively engaged with life itself. For details of his transition, see "The Education of the Un-Artist, Part I (1971)" and "The Education of the Un-Artist, Part II (1972)," in Jeff Kelley, ed., *Essays on the Blurring of Art and Life: Allan Kaprow* (Berkeley: University of California Press, 1993), 97–126.

19. Jauss, *Toward an Aesthetic of Reception,* 35.

20. Allan Kaprow, "The Real Experiment" (1983), in Kelley (ed.), *Essays on the Blurring of Art and Life,* 203.

21. Allan Kaprow, "Participation Performance," ibid., 182.

22. Ibid., 194.

23. Ibid., 173.

24. Jean-Jacques Lebel, *Le Happening* (Paris: Denoël, 1966), 78. Lebel lists European artists who had been active in Happenings since 1959, including Ben Vautier, Joseph Beuys, and Wolf Vostell. Kaprow's various lists of artists active in Happenings since 1959 in the United States would add Nam June Paik, George Brecht, Dick Higgins, and Carolee Schneemann.

25. Günther Berghaus recounts these points of contact in "Happenings in Europe," in Sandford (ed.), *Happenings and Other Acts,* 351.

26. Henry Martin citing Jean-Jacques Lebel in "Happenings or Dance Happenings . . . ," in *Ubi Fluxus ibi Motus, 1990–1962,* ed. Gino DiMaggio (Milan: Mazzotta, 1990), 63–64.

27. George Brecht, *Chance Imagery: A Great Bear Pamphlet* (New York: Something Else Press, 1966), 6–7.

28. Dick Higgins, "Something Else about Fluxus," *Art and Artists* 7 (Oct. 1972): 18.

29. Tomas Schmit, "If I Remember Rightly," *Art and Artists* 7 (Oct. 1972): 39; emphasis mine.

30. Tomas Schmit, "Zyklus," in Friedman (ed.), *Fluxus Performance Workbook,* 45. This piece was performed in several of the 1962 concerts.

31. Allan Kaprow, "18 Happenings in Six Parts," in *Happening and Fluxus,* ed. Hans Sohm (Cologne: Kölnischer Kunstverein, 1970), n.p.

32. Kaprow, "Nontheatrical Performance," in Kelley (ed.), *Essays on the Blurring of Art and Life,* 170.

33. Ibid.

34. Several pages of Event scores like this were published in Allan Kaprow's watershed collection of performance documentation, *Assemblage, Environments, and Happenings.*

35. "A Theater Whatzit," *Village Voice,* 30 Mar. 1960, 11.

36. Henry Flynt, "Concept Art," in *An Anthology,* ed. LaMonte Young and Jackson Mac Low (New York: LaMonte Young, 1962/3), n.p. Flynt gave "Concept Art" in lecture form in the summer of 1961. His essay anticipates the critical justifications of word-based artists such as Joseph Kosuth, Les Levine, Tom Marioni, and the British group Art and Language; yet the standard histories of these artists give Fluxus short shrift, if it is mentioned at all.

37. John Cage, ed., *Notations* (New York: Something Else Press, 1968).

38. Lucy Lippard, "Introduction," in *Six Years: The Dematerialization of the Art Object from 1966 to 1972* (Berkeley: University of California Press, [1973] 1997), ix.

39. Ibid., x.

40. Ibid.

41. Peter Frank, *George Brecht: Works, 1957–1973* (New York: Onnash Galerie, 1973), 1.

42. Robert Morgan, "Idea, Concept, System," *Arts* 64 (Sept. 1989): 64–65.

43. Seth Sieglaub, in *Conceptual Art,* ed. Ursula Meyer (New York: Dutton, 1972), xiv.

44. Joseph Kosuth, "Art after Philosophy," *Studio International* 178 (Oct.–Dec. 1969), 134–37, 160–61, 212–13; reprinted in *Art in Theory, 1900–1990,* ed. Charles Harrison and Paul Woods (Oxford: Basil Blackwell, 1992), 843.

45. Ibid.

46. Ibid.

47. In recent years, the term *concept art* has shifted significantly in meaning. Whereas references to Fluxus as conceptual art were relatively rare in the 1960s and 1970s, by 1988 Fluxus artist Robert Watts was described in his *New York Times* obituary (4 Sept. 1988, sec. C) as a "conceptual artist and designer."

48. John Cage, "Music as Process" ("Indeterminacy" section), in *Silence,* 35.

49. This statement is quoted on a one-page broadside by Lawrence Alloway of New York's Billy Apple Gallery and called "Addendum to Pop Art." I have seen several versions of this document. One is dated 1971 and is housed at the Jean Brown Archive, Getty Research Institute for the History of Art and the Humanities, Santa Monica.

50. Watts to Jacob, 20 Nov. 1964, Robert Watts Studio Archive, New York.

51. Young's static-music concept has been realized in a yearslong taped version at his Dreamhouse on West Broadway in New York City.

52. Mac Low to Maciunas, 8 Dec. 1968. Jean Brown Archive. Later in this letter, Mac Low notes that his concept of the static film derives directly from LaMonte Young's static states in music.

53. Howard Junker, "Johnny One-Note," *Newsweek,* 4 Mar. 1968.

54. According to Dick Higgins, "John Cale played piano originally, and included work by Cage and I think La Monte Young in a New Departures concert probably in 1961; soon afterwards he came to New York, in part, I think, to work with LaMonte. Possibly he knew LaMonte earlier, maybe from Darmstadt?" (letter to the author, 16 Aug. 1994).

55. John Cale, quoted in Gerard Malanga and Victor Bockris, *Die Velvet Underground Story* (Augsburg: Sonnentanz Verlag, 1988), 42.

56. Letter from Wilcock to Maciunas, 1968; Archiv Sohm.

57. John Rockwell, *All American Music* (New York: Knopf, 1983), 237–38.

58. Jauss, *Toward an Aesthetic of Reception,* 25.

59. Christin J. Mamiya, *Pop Art and Consumer Culture: American Super Market* (Austin: University of Texas Press, 1992), 147.

60. Dore Ashton in "A Symposium on Pop Art," Museum of Modern Art, 13 Dec. 1962; proceedings printed in *Arts* 37 (Apr. 1963): 37–39, 41–42.

61. Thomas Kellein, "Fluxus—an Addendum to Pop?" in *Pop Art: An International Perspective,* ed. Marco Livingstone (London: Royal Academy of Arts, 1991), 224.

62. Emmett Williams in Williams and Claes Oldenburg, eds., *Claes Oldenburg's Store Days: Documents from the Store (1961) and Ray Gun Theatre (1962)* (New York: Something Else Press, 1967), cover notes.

63. Ibid., 51.

64. The Wiesbaden collectors Michael and Uta Berger, owners of Harlekin Geschenke, were responsible for the mass production of these multiples. Robert Watts opened his Supermarket at the Paul Bianchini Gallery in New York on 20 November 1964.

65. "Then, once Maciunas had shipped a crate of additional materials in 1964–65, de Ridder set up a mass of Fluxus works in his livingroom. Dorothea Meijer posed provocatively in its midst and a photograph was taken. That evening a movie, Its Harem Time, was filmed in the same location where the Fluxshop had been" (Hendricks [ed.], *Fluxus Codex,* 237).

66. In 1984, the photograph was used to produce a detailed reconstruction of the scene at the Contemporary Arts Museum in Houston, Texas.

67. Evelyn Weiss, "Pop Art and Germany," in Livingstone (ed.), *Pop Art;* emphasis mine.

68. Adrian Glew, *Fluxbritannica* (London: Tate Gallery, 1994), 1; and documentation in the Tate Gallery's Fluxshoe archive.

69. Programs in Archiv Sohm. The Reuben Gallery was an important forum for Happenings and pop art in New York.

70. *New Forms—New Media,* Martha Jackson Gallery, New York, 6–24 June and 27 Sept.–22 Oct. 1960.

71. W. C. Seitz, *The Art of Assemblage* (New York: Museum of Modern Art, 1961).

72. "The Popular Image," which opened at the Washington Gallery of Modern Art on 18 April 1963, was organized by Alan Solomon and Alice Denney. Artists included Vern Blosum, George Brecht, James Dine, Jasper Johns, Roy Lichtenstein, Claes Oldenburg, Robert Rauschenberg, James Rosenquist, Andy Warhol, Robert Watts, John Wesley, and Tom Wesselman. See Alan Solomon, *The Popular Image Exhibition* (Washington, D.C.: Washington Gallery of Modern Art, 1963).

73. Robert Watts, Notebooks 1964–1966, Robert Watts Studio Archive, New York.

74. Several of these objects were produced and offered through mail-order advertisements in the *Village Voice* and at Multiples, a store on 57th Street.

75. In the tradition of the surrealist game "exquisite corpse," a kind of collective collage of words or images that exploits the mystique of accident, the Scissors Brothers print included images chosen by each artist and assembled at random. *Blink,* whose bold three-part graphic, reminiscent of commercial signage practices, looks much like Warhol's silkscreen work, was included in the exhibition and catalogue *Pop Art: An International Perspective* and is also part of the pop art holdings of the Museum Ludwig in Cologne.

76. Alison Knowles, conversation with the author, 5 Apr. 1993.

77. Several of these exist at the Getty Center. They are about the size of a business card with letters carefully hand-rendered in sans serif characters.

Chapter 4

1. See Amelia Jones, *Body Art/Performing the Subject* (Minneapolis and London: University of Minnesota Press, 1998).

   See also Laurel Fredrickson, "A Good for Nothing Huguenot: Robert Filliou's Upside-Down World," master's thesis, University of Illinois, Chicago, 1998, which is essential to my discussion.

2. I attended this festival during the time of my DAAD grant. In my dissertation, I neglected to acknowledge Pedersen's efforts at organizing this festival; see Knud Pedersen, *Kampen mot borgermusik,* trans. Anne-Charlotte Weimarck (Kristianstad: Kalejdoskop Forlag, 1983) for significant coverage of such projects.

3. Another precursor can be found in Robert Watts's Supermarket at the Paul Bianchini Gallery in New York, which opened on 20 November 1964. There may well have been others.

4. Peter Frank, "Art for Life's Sake," in DiMaggio (ed.), *Ubi Fluxus ibi Motus,* 435.

5. All three Wiesbaden evenings followed this format; the Copenhagen festival, however, featured only one à la carte evening. For other Nikolai Church evenings, organizers tried two other formats: Hire an Artist, where the audience could hire an artist by the minute or hour to perform with or for them; and a twelve-hour marathon concert consisting largely of extremely long Event pieces, in which, for example, a single note was played on the organ for an hour (Philip Corner) or notes were played alone and then simultaneously (Eric Andersen). Insufficiently acquainted with the artists to make confident hiring choices, the audience wandered aimlessly to the work stations looking for artists to hire. This aimless quality also characterized the marathon, except that there, aimlessness functioned positively: because people felt free to come and go, or to eat lunch outside while listening to the sounds within the performance space, the pieces blended with all other features of the day. Especially successful on this day was Ben Vautier's piece. Sitting on top of a pillar high above the audience, he spent the afternoon writing on cardboard signs that rested on an easel. These read, for example, "Look at me"; "Don't look at me"; "Forget me"; and "Sometimes I think Fluxus is boring."

6. Alf Collins, "Hey Seattle, Get Ready to Be Fluxed," *Seattle Times,* 18 Sept. 1977.

7. Deloris Tarzan, "Fluxus Demystifies Art," *Seattle Times,* 27 Sept. 1977.

8. R.M. Campbell, review, *Seattle Post-Intelligencer,* 30 Sept. 1977.

9. Barbara Cavaliere, "Flux-Concert: The Kitchen," *Flash Art International* 92/93 (1979): 49.

10. "The Kitchen" program, 24 Mar. 1979, Archiv Sohm.

11. Milan Knizak, "Snowstorm No. 1 (1965)," in Friedman (ed.), *Fluxus Performance Workbook,* 29.

12. Yoko Ono, "Wall Piece for Orchestra to Yoko Ono" (1962), ibid., 43.

13. Elin von Spreckelsen, "Zen Vaudeville," *SoHo Weekly News,* 5 Apr. 1979, 32; emphasis mine. Subsequent quotes are from this article.

14. Tom Johnson, "Paper Airplanes and Shattered Violins," *Village Voice,* 9 Apr. 1979, 71–72.

15. Barbara Moore, "George Maciunas: Finger on Fluxus," *Artforum* 21 (Oct. 1982): 38. The article is accompanied (on pages 33–37) by a photographic essay by Peter Moore, "Fluxus Focus: Fluxmaster George Maciunas." Following several vertical-format formal portraits of Maciunas (all from 1978) in drag, as a military man, and as a white-suited Chaplinesque gentleman are several photographs of very early Fluxus concerts, called "Disconcerting Concerts." Then comes a section titled "Hyperactive Activities" with several pictures of Events from the Maciunas-organized Flux Game Fest in front of and inside 80 Wooster Street in New York in 1973. The final image is of an outdoor marching Event in the snow at Maciunas's farm in New Marlborough, Massachusetts, in 1977.

16. Dick Higgins, in a letter to the author of 5 May 1994, described Maciunas's efforts to maintain a consistent style in the face of utilitarian obsolescence: "Maciunas's IBM typewriter was IBM News Gothic. But News Gothic was the third most popular sans serif font in the sixties, after Helvetica and Futura. When he got his changeable font machine, he hoped to get News Gothic, but the rights problems connected with the decline of Intertype made the font all but unavailable, and now it is seldom used."

17. Others include Archiv Sohm, Staatsgalerie Stuttgart (public); Fluxus Archive, Tate Gallery, London (public); Hermann Braun Fluxus Collection, Remscheid, Germany (private); Museum DiMaggio, Bologna, Italy (private); Editions Conz, Verona, Italy (private); Jean Brown Collection, Getty Center, Santa Monica, California (public); and René Block Collection, Berlin, Germany (private).

18. Jon Hendricks, "Aspects of Fluxus from the Gilbert and Lila Silverman Collection," *Art Libraries Journal* 8, no. 3 (autumn 1983): 8–13.

19. In chronological order they are Jon Hendricks, ed., *Fluxus Etc.: The Gilbert and Lila Silverman Collection* (Bloomfield Hills, Mich.: Cranbrook Academy of Art Museum, 1981); Hendricks et al., eds., *Fluxus Etc., Addenda I: The Gilbert and Lila Silverman Collection* (New York: Ink and Press, 1983); Hendricks, ed., *Fluxus Etc., Addenda II: The Gilbert and Lila Silverman Collection* (Pasadena: Baxter Art Gallery, California Institute of Technology, 1983); and Hendricks and Clive Phillpot, *Fluxus: Selections from the Gilbert and Lila Silverman Collection* (New York: Museum of Modern Art, 1988); and Hendricks (ed.), *Fluxus Codex* (1988).

20. Jon Hendricks, in conversation with the author on 25 April 1994, stated that the earliest Silverman shows reflect a "non-interferal curating" policy, in which work by almost any Fluxus artist could be admitted under the rubric "etc." By 1984 the exhibitions had

become unwieldy, and a narrower curatorial policy, which omitted the "etc." option, was instituted.

21. Jon Hendricks, "Fluxus, Etc." (flyer), Cranbrook (Michigan) Academy of Art.

22. Thomas Kellein, *Fluxus* (London: Thames and Hudson, 1995). The book contains texts by Kellein ("I Make Jokes! Fluxus through the Eyes of 'Chairman' George Maciunas," 7–27) and Hendricks ("Uncovering Fluxus—Recovering Fluxus," 119–39).

23. Jon Hendricks, "What Is Fluxus?" exhibition flyer for Neuberger Museum, State University of New York, Purchase, 1983.

24. Grace Glueck, "Some Roguish 60's Art Achieves Museum Status," *New York Times,* 13 Feb. 1983, sec. C.

25. Review, *Los Angeles Times,* 23 Oct. 1983, sec. E.

26. Clive Phillpot, "Fluxus: Magazines, Manifestos, Multum in Parvo," in Hendricks and Phillpot (eds.), *Fluxus,* 11.

27. Hendricks to Castleman, 3 Nov. 1987; Silverman Archive, New York.

28. Catherine Liu, "Fluxus: Selections from the Gilbert and Lila Silverman Collection," *Artforum* 27 (May 1989): 89.

29. Robert C. Morgan. "Fluxus, Museum of Modern Art," *Flash Art International,* no. 146 (May–June 1989): 14.

30. Hendricks (ed.), *Fluxus Codex,* 15.

31. Bruce Altschuler, "Fluxus Redux," *Arts* 14 (Sept. 1989): 66–70.

32. In an oral-history interview with Richard Candida Smith, Jean Brown stated about the beginnings of her collection: "If I was going to do Fluxus, I would have to have lots of objects, because George made them all"; see "The Fluxus Movement: Jean Brown, Art History Oral Documentation Project" (Oral History Program, University of California, Los Angeles, and Getty Research Institute for the History of Art and the Humanities, 1993), 41.

33. Eric Vos, "A Checklist of Archival Material for the Jean Brown Collection" (Getty Research Institute for the History of Art and the Humanities, Santa Monica, Sept. 1990), 6.

34. Brown said that she "wanted their records. I just wanted those records someplace on earth... which might not have been kept by anyone else. Because I wanted the history, the background, very good archival material.... I don't think I was rigid about that at all" (ibid., 57–61).

35. Vos, "Checklist," 6.

36. Michael Mattison, "In the Spirit of Fluxus," *Art Paper,* June 1993, 18.

37. Elizabeth Armstrong and Joan Rothfuss, eds., *In the Spirit of Fluxus* (Minneapolis: The Walker Art Center, 1993).

38. The reason live performance is usually excluded from Fluxus exhibitions in the United States, I believe, is that if an exhibition is based on the Maciunas paradigm, and Maciunas is dead, then live performance is antithetical to the operative definition of the show.

39. Emmett Williams, *My Life in Flux—and Vice Versa* (London: Thames and Hudson, 1991).

40. Emmett Williams and Ann Noël, eds., *Mr. Fluxus: A Collective Portrait of George Maciunas* (Wiesbaden, Ger.: Harlekin Art, 1996).

41. Young to Williams, n.d. [1962], Jean Brown Archive.

42. Williams, *My Life in Flux,* 28.

43. Located at Archiv Sohm.

44. The shop was in an old candy store in Villefranche-sur-Mer. An exhibition and book, *Games at the Cedilla,* were produced, featuring correspondence with and contributions from Fluxus friends as well as miscellany (notes, journal materials, word and pen games, Events, etc.) created by the proprietors while they minded their shop. See George Brecht and Robert Filliou, *Games at the Cedilla; or, the Cedilla Takes Off* (New York: Something Else Press, 1967). Today Brecht is a complete recluse: he sees no one, answers no mail, and responds only to the phone calls of his patron, Hermann Braun.

45. The most notable exceptions are Larry Miller and Robert Watts, who, to the best of my knowledge, made only brief visits to Germany.

46. These governments of the 1960s were themselves populated by ex-Nazis, including President Heinrich Lübke and Chancellor Kurt Georg Kiesinger. See Keith Bullivant and C. Jane Rice, "Reconstruction and Integration: The Culture of West German Stabilization, 1945–1968," in *German Cultural Studies: An Introduction,* ed. Rob Burns (New York: Oxford University Press, 1995), 241.

47. Peter Weiss, *The Investigation: Oratorio in 11 Cantos,* trans. Alexander Gross (London: Calder and Boyars, 1966), 203.

48. Bullivant and Rice, "Reconstruction and Integration," 241, 260.

49. Richard Hülsenbeck published a facsimile of the *Dada Almanach* (1920) with Something Else Press in 1966 and made occasional appearances at the annual New York Festival of the Avant-Garde. Somewhat tangentially, Duchamp was a guiding spirit for many Fluxus artists; he lived in New York during this period (the 1950s–60s) and in 1968 worked with Alison Knowles and Emmett Williams on a Something Else Press reprint of his *Floating Hearts* (*Coeurs volants,* 1936).

50. George Maciunas, "Neo-Dada in Music, Theater, Poetry, Art," read by Arthur C. Caspari at the Fluxus concert "Après John Cage," Wuppertal, West Germany, 9 June 1962. Manuscript can be found in Archiv Sohm, Staatsgalerie Stuttgart; reprinted in DiMaggio (ed.), *Ubi Fluxus ibi Motus,* 214–25.

51. To a greater or lesser degree, there was precedent for this association in the highly influential Düsseldorf-based Zero Group (Heinz Mack, Otto Piene, and Günther Uecker), who performed art actions and launched group exhibitions in the late 1950s. For background on these activities and the magazine produced by the group, see Heinz Mack and Otto Piene, *Zero* (Cambridge, Mass.: MIT Press, 1973).

52. Henry Flynt, "Mutations of the Vanguard: Pre-Fluxus, During Fluxus, Late Fluxus," in DiMaggio (ed.), *Ubi Fluxus ibi Motus,* 99.

53. Maciunas's correspondence (in Archiv Sohm) with Paik, Brecht, and Watts, all artists who consider themselves apolitical, does not discuss partisan politics explicitly even long after this point.

54. Maria Müller, "Aspekte der Dada-Rezeption: 1950–1966" (Ph.D. diss., Albertus-Magnus-Universität, Cologne, 1986), 3–4; my translation and emphasis.

55. Gunter Schab, "Zuviel Klamauk mit Neo-Dada," *Neue Rheinische Zeitung,* 19 June 1962, n.p., Archiv Sohm; my translation. (In the following, all sources are clippings [without page numbers] located in Archiv Sohm and translations are mine, unless otherwise noted.)

56. "Brief aus Wiesbaden," *Rhein-Saar-Spiegel,* 7 Sept. 1962.

57. Heinz Ohff, "Das ist ja absurd!" *Tagesspiegel,* 18 Apr. 1966. Ohff later wrote an important book on pop art and related tendencies.

58. Klaus Honnef, "Das Feuilleton: Bewußtsein von trivialen Dingen," *Aachener Nachrichten,* 27 Sept. 1966, 4.

59. Bullivant and Rice, "Reconstruction and Integration," 237.

60. Williams, *My Life in Flux,* 22.

61. Richard O'Reagan, "There's Music and Eggs in the Air," *Stars and Stripes,* 21 Oct. 1962, 11. O'Reagan covered the events themselves, while Williams and Patterson wrote publicity and inside accounts.

62. "Musik und Anti-Musik: Konzert der 'Fluxus'—Festspiele in Wiesbaden," *Allgemeine Zeitung: Mainzer Anzeiger,* 3 Sept. 1962.

63. Emmett Williams, "Way Way Way Out," *Stars and Stripes,* 30 Aug. 1962; in Williams, *My Life in Flux,* 23–24.

64. Williams, *My Life in Flux,* 7.

65. René Block, poster, "Galerie Block im Forum Theater: MUSIKFESTIVAL 16. und 17.4.1966," Archiv Sohm; pieces by Eric Andersen, George Brecht, Stanley Brouwn, Ludwig Gosewitz, Dick Higgins, Toshi Ichiyanagi, Addi Køpcke, Jackson Mac Low, George Maciunas, Robin Page, Benjamin Patterson, Terry Riley, Diter Rot, Gerhard Rühm, Tomas Schmit, Robert Watts, Emmett Williams, and LaMonte Young.

66. René Block, program, "Galerie Block im Forum Theater: MUSIKFESTIVAL 16. und 17.4.1966," Archiv Sohm.

67. Bullivant and Rice, "Reconstruction and Integration," 221, 233.

68. Wim Wenders, quoted in Jan Dawson, *Wim Wenders* (New York: Zoetrope, 1976), 7; cited in Rob Burns and Wilfried Van Der Will, "The Federal Republic, 1968 to 1990: From Industrial Society to the Culture Society," in *German Cultural Studies: An Introduction,* ed. Rob Burns (New York: Oxford University Press, 1995), p. 317.

69. Poster for "New York–Downtown Manhattan: SoHo," Akademie der Künste, Berlin, 5 Sept.–17 Oct. 1976, Jean Brown Archive; and catalogue, Silverman Archive, New York.

70. René Block, press release, "Eine kleine Geschichte von Fluxus in drei Teilen" (Berlin: DAAD, Berliner Künstlerprogramm, 12 Jan. 1983); my translation.

71. Documented in conversations with the artists, 1992. Indeed, while Block is no longer running the program, my own DAAD grant, awarded in 1992, attests to the continued official expenditure on behalf of Fluxus, as does the purchase of Hans Sohm's Fluxus collection by the prestigious Staatsgalerie Stuttgart. Sohm, a dentist who attended several early Fluxus festivals in Germany, collected Fluxus works and editions (some of which predate 1962) as well as documentation and reviews of Fluxus exhibitions and festivals. Artists would often stuff an envelope with whatever detritus a situation produced and send it to Sohm, who then catalogued the contents and envelopes. He later sold the materials to the Staatsgalerie Stuttgart, which augmented the collection considerably. He was the primary contributor to the exhibition and catalogue *Happening and Fluxus* (Cologne: Kölnischer Kunstverein, 1970), the first document containing primary materials and a Happenings and Fluxus time line.

72. Quoted in Karla Fohrbeck and Andreas Wiesand, *Von der Industriegesellschaft zur Kulturgesellschaft? Kulturpolitische Entwicklungen in der Bundesrepublik Deutschland* (Munich: C.H. Beck, 1989), 78; cited in Burns and Van Der Will, "The Federal Republic, 1968 to 1990," 259.

73. Henning Christiansen, from Denmark, represented north; Geoff Hendricks, from New York, west; Joe Jones, from his expatriate homes in Wiesbaden-Erbenheim and Italy, south; and Milan Knizak, from Czechoslovakia, east.

74. René Block, ed., *Fluxus Da Capo 1962 Wiesbaden 1992* (Berlin: Ludwig Vogt, 1992).

75. Similarly, on the occasion of "Fluxus Virus," an anniversary exhibition held in Cologne in 1992, the magazine *Kunst Köln* said this about the ghost of Maciunas, "The Miracle of Cologne": "The spirit of the great boy... felt comfortable in this stimulating atmosphere, so that he, cautiously at first, and then with other such Fluxpop people, blew his spirit through the space and let all the candles flicker out" ("George Maciunas: The Miracle of Cologne," *Kunst Köln* 2 [1992]: 60; my translation). Maciunas's "comfort" and

"stimulation," albeit imaginary, reflect the author's attempt to retain the historic reference and internal dynamics of Fluxus as well as the fresh spirit of new Fluxus work.

76. Cited in Burns and Van Der Will, "The Federal Republic, 1968 to 1990," 260.

77. Ben Patterson, "Fluxus-Virus 1962–1992," *Kunst Köln* 3/4 (1992): 62–63; my translation.

78. Friedman (ed.), *Fluxus Virus.* The title page of this book misattributes the editorial effort to Christel Schüppenhauer, who confused copyediting and translation with editing proper; Friedman deserves credit as concept editor.

79. René Block, ed., *1962 Wiesbaden Fluxus 1982* (Berlin: Berliner Künstlerprogramm des DAAD, 1982).

80. Although very few Fluxus editions sell in Italy, each of these benefactors is a publisher; moreover, the artists receive payment for the published editions not in cash, but in copies of the books, print portfolios, and multiple objects, which the artists are free to sell independently. As printer assistant to my parents in various capacities in Italy, I have witnessed the exchange of labor for editions. My understanding of the process was corroborated in conversations with Philip Corner at Fluxus Virus (1992) and with Eric Andersen at Fluxus Festival Chicago (1993).

    Chiessi has relocated to Capri, where she continues to publish editions but on a greatly reduced scale.

81. It remains to be seen whether the rhetoric of freedom and tolerance works the same way in Italian texts with regard to Italy's past as I have inferred from German texts.

82. Achille Bonito Oliva, "Ubi Fluxus ibi Motus," in DiMaggio (ed.), *Ubi Fluxus ibi Motus,* 26.

83. Giovanni Carandente, "Opening Statement," ibid., 12.

84. Gino DiMaggio, "Fluxus Art as a Private Form of Subversion," ibid., 39–40.

85. Joe Jones, "Fluxus," ibid., 15; Henry Flynt, "Mutations of the Vangarde," ibid., 99.

86. Ken Friedman, "Fluxus and Company," ibid., 328.

87. Ibid., 332.

88. Jackson Mac Low, "Fluxus, Maciunas, Mac Low," ibid., 208–9; emphasis mine.

89. Emmett Williams, "Introductory Statement," in Block (ed.), *1962 Wiesbaden Fluxus 1982,* 1; Dick Higgins, "Fluxus Then, Fluxus Now, and Fluxus Next," in Block (ed.), *Fluxus Da Capo,* 88.

90. See Estera Milman, ed., *Fluxus: A Conceptual Country,* special issue of *Visible Language* 26 (1992); and Nancy Dwyer, "Heckling Catalogue," in *FluxAttitudes,* ed. Cornelia Lauf and Susan Hapgood (Gent, Bel.: Imschoot, 1991).

91. The flyer for this concert is in the Jean Brown Archive.

92. Hannah Higgins, "Naming Change and Changing Names: Fluxus as a Proper Noun," in Friedman (ed.), *Fluxus Virus,* 68–90. Information on the proposed magazine is derived from flyers, posters, and announcements located at Archiv Sohm.

93. James Lewes, "Chronology," in Friedman (ed.), *Fluxus Virus,* 333–56, provides an almost comprehensive list of Fluxus festivals titled something other than Fluxus.

94. Conversation between the author and Eric Andersen, Chicago, Nov. 1993.

95. George Maciunas, press release, n.d. [1965], Archiv Sohm.

96. Conversation with Andersen, Nov. 1993.

97. Henry Martin, "Roskilde: The Zetetics of Zealous Zambians," *Art News* 7 (Sept. 1985), 125–26.

98. This accords with the art-historical paradigm that the market alone determines artistic practice, exhibition, and scholarship. While the market certainly influences whether a strategy meets with success or failure, ideology, practice, and desire also play important roles. Had Block's agenda been determined entirely by the marketplace, he would have abandoned Fluxus as a group and focused exclusively on his better-known artists.

99. René Block, "Chronology, Gallerie René Block, 1964–1979," Archiv Sohm.

100. The exhibition was team-curated by Higgins and the students in his Fluxus seminar while he was a guest lecturer at Williams; the resulting catalogue is Dick Higgins, *Fluxus 25 Years* (Williamstown, Mass.: Williams College, 1987).

101. Francis De Vuono, "Fluxus—Closing In," *Art News* 90 (Jan. 1991): 157.

102. "Fluxus Closing In," *New Yorker,* 29 Oct. 1990.

103. Ken Friedman, in *Whitewalls* 16 (spring 1987): 50.

104. Robert Morgan, "Idea, Concept, System," *Arts* 64 (Sept. 1989), 61–65.

105. "Fluxus: A Conceptual Country" started out at the Franklin Furnace in Manhattan (18 Sept.–14 Nov. 1992), then continued on to Madison, Wisconsin; Iowa City, Iowa; Montgomery, Alabama; and Evanston, Illinois.

106. Estera Milman, "Introduction," in *Fluxus: A Conceptual Country,* 13.

107. Estera Milman, "Historical Precedents, Trans-Historical Strategies, and the Myth of Democratization," ibid., 17–35.

108. Milman, "Introduction," 13.

109. "Voice Choice," *Village Voice,* 27 July 1993, 17.

Chapter 5

1. There are historical bases for this as I have already sketched out the history of Fluxus particularly in America—Beuys, Brecht, Cage, and Patterson all have ties to Fluxus in America and Europe.

2. The years 1957–63 were very active at the Douglass campus. The "Rutgers Group" also included artists associated with pop art, such as Roy Lichtenstein, George Segal, Lucas Samaras, and Robert Whitman.

3. Allan Kaprow, "Manifesto," in *The Discontinuous Universe: Selected Writings in Contemporary Consciousness,* ed. Sallie Sears and Georgianna W. Lord (New York: Basic Books, 1972), 292.

4. Willoughby Sharp, "An Interview with Joseph Beuys," *Artforum,* Dec. 1969, 44. Joseph Beuys had a long and often contested relationship with Fluxus. He was present at the first Fluxus-titled concerts in Düsseldorf in 1962 and produced work with Maciunas after that time. However, he had limited creative contact with other Fluxus artists after the early 1960s. To the best of my knowledge, although Beuys produced many wonderful performance works and objects, he never completed a Fluxkit or wrote an Event. Therefore, it is most accurate to describe him as an artist who had a significant, if short-lived, relationship with Fluxus, but not as a Fluxus artist in the communitarian sense.

5. Robert Filliou, *Teaching and Learning as Performing Arts by Robert Filliou and the READER if he wishes, with the participation of JOHN CAGE, BENJAMIN PATTERSON, GEORGE BRECHT, ALLEN KAPROW, MARCEL, VERA AND BJOESSI AND KARL ROT, DOROTHY IANNONE, DITER ROT, JOSEPH BEUYS* (Cologne and New York: König Verlag, 1970), 12.

6. Beuys in ibid., 12.

7. Dewey, *Art as Experience* (New York: Milton Balch, 1934), 334.

8. Filliou, *Teaching and Learning,* 1.

9. Ibid., 114.

10. This point has been made as well by D. Emily Hicks in *Ninety-five Languages and Seven Forms of Intelligence* (New York: Peter Lang, 1999), who argues that the multicultural, and by extension multilingual, classroom benefits from diversity when that diversity is expressed as cultural pride and sharing.

11. Ibid., 39.

12. Kaprow in Filliou, *Teaching and Learning,* 127.

13. Hicks, *Ninety-five Languages,* 4.

14. Howard Gardner, *Multiple Intelligences: The Theory in Practice* (New York: Basic Books, 1993), 8–9. See also his *Frames of Mind: The Theory of Multiple Intelligences* (New York: Basic Books, 1983).

15. Gardner, *Multiple Intelligences,* 221, 73.

16. David Gerlenter, *The Muse in the Machine: Computerizing the Poetry of Human Thought* (New York: Free Press, 1994), 46–47.

17. Danny Wildemeersch, "The Principal Meaning of Dialogue for the Construction and Transformation of Reality," in *Making Sense of Experiential Learning,* ed. Susan Warner Weil and Ian McGill (Philadelphia and Milton Keynes, Eng.: Society for Research into Higher Education and Open University Press, 1989), 64; emphasis mine.

18. Wildemeersch (ibid., 65) is quoting S. Brookfield, "A Critical Definition of Adult Education," *Adult Education Quarterly* 1 (1985): 41.

19. Beuys in Filliou, *Teaching and Learning,* 170.

20. Peter Sacks, *Standardized Minds: The High Price of America's Testing Culture and What We Can Do to Change It* (New York: Perseus Books, 1999), 9.

21. Edward S. Reed, *The Necessity of Experience* (New Haven: Yale University Press, 1996), 5.

22. Sacks, *Standardized Minds,* 209.

23. Stephen J. Gould, *The Mismeasure of Man* (New York: Norton, 1981), 15.

24. Leon Bottstein, *Jefferson's Children: Education and the Promise of American Culture* (New York: Doubleday, 1997), 204.

25. *The Best of Multiple Intelligence Activities* (workbook) (Westminster, Calif.: Teacher Created Materials, Inc.), 43, 95, 181, and 331, respectively.

26. Ibid., 331.

27. Carla Hannaford, *Smart Moves: Why Learning Is Not All in Your Head* (Arlington, Va.: Great Ocean, 1995), 43.

28. Ibid., 108–31.

29. Ibid., 70–95.

30. Ibid., 41.

31. Bottstein, *Jefferson's Children,* 186; emphasis mine.

32. Cage in Filliou, *Teaching and Learning,* 115–16; emphasis mine.

33. Ibid., 42.

34. Ibid., 116.

35. Ibid., 134.

36. Ian McGill and Susan Warner Weil, "Continuing the Dialogue: New Possibilities for Experiential Learning," in Weill and McGill (eds.), *Making Sense of Experiential Learning*, 249.

37. Reed, *Necessity of Experience*, 61.

38. Filliou, *Teaching and Learning*, 18–19.

39. Antonio Gramsci makes the distinction between the political and civil society in *Selections from the Prison Notebooks*, trans. Quintin Hoare and Geoffrey Nowell Smith (New York: International Publishers, 1992).

40. Gardner with co-authors Mindy Kornhaber and Mara Kreschevsky, in Gardner, *Multiple Intelligences*, 236.

41. Ibid., 188, 190.

42. Hannaford, *Smart Moves*, 56.

43. Gardner, *Multiple Intelligences*, 229.

44. Hannaford, *Smart Moves*, 48.

45. Ibid.; see also Marian Diamond, *Enriching Heredity: The Impact of the Environment on the Anatomy of the Brain* (New York: Free Press, 1998.

46. Gregory Ulmer, in *Applied Grammatology: Post(e)-Pedagogy from Jacques Derrida to Joseph Beuys* (Baltimore: Johns Hopkins University Press, 1995), undertakes a comparative analysis of the pedagogical formations of Jacques Lacan, Joseph Beuys, and Sergei Eisenstein to arrive at an applied version of Derrida's grammatology. The study is exemplary in its broad-based coverage of Derrida's use of grammatology, modeling, mnemonics, and speculation.

47. Filliou, *Teaching and Learning*, 192–97.

48. Ibid., 193–96.

49. Ibid., 197.

50. Ibid., 193.

51. Ibid.

52. Ibid., 194, 195.

53. Ibid., 198, 200. While Filliou's Poipoidrome and his school with Brecht remained unrealized, Fluxus artist Al Hansen cofounded a similar institution in Cologne with Lisa Cieslik in 1987. The Ultimate Akademie, as it was called, became an ongoing context for

the presentation and discussion of new art problems. It thrived until Hansen's death in 1995 but today struggles to survive.

54. Beuys in ibid., 169.

55. Beuys in Ulmer, *Applied Grammatology,* 238.

56. Ibid., 239.

57. Kaprow in Filliou, *Teaching and Learning,* 128.

58. Reed, *Necessity of Experience,* 93–94.

59. Ibid., 104.

60. Miriam Hutton, "Learning from Action: A Conceptual Framework" in Weil and McGill (eds.), *Making Sense of Experiential Learning,* 52.

61. Cage in Filliou, *Teaching and Learning,* 117.

62. Reed, *Necessity of Experience,* 69.

63. Filliou, *Teaching and Learning,* 79.

64. Dewey, *Art as Experience,* 336.

ILLUSTRATIONS

46. George Brecht and Robert Filliou, La Cédille qui Sourit (Store of useless knowledge), Villefranche-sur-Mer, France, 1967. Double exposure with Robert Filliou, [unknown], and George Brecht (pointing). Photo by Jacques Strauch and Michou Strauch-Barelli; courtesy of the Gilbert and Lila Silverman Fluxus Collection, Detroit. *132*

47. George Brecht and Robert Filliou, La Cédille qui Sourit, Villefranche-sur-Mer, France, 1967. Interior. Photo by Jacques Strauch and Michou Strauch-Barelli; courtesy of the Gilbert and Lila Silverman Fluxus Collection, Detroit. *133*

48. Geoffrey Hendricks, *Flux Relic No. 4,* 1992; produced for Good Buy Supermarket, Nikolai Church, Copenhagen, organized by Michael Berger, Knud Pedersen, and Eric Andersen. "Last Bottle of Wine from the Cedilla Store." Courtesy of the artist. *134*

49. Daniel Spoerri, *Meal Variation No. 4, Jack Youngerman,* from *Twenty-nine Variations on a Meal,* 1964. The original mounted meal, from which Maciunas made an edition printed on linen, 21 × 25 in. Photo by Nancy Anello; courtesy of the Gilbert and Lila Silverman Fluxus Collection, Detroit. *136*

50. Robert Filliou with George Maciunas, Peter Moore, Daniel Spoerri, and Robert Watts, photograph intended for projected edition, *Monsters Are Inoffensive,* 1967. Edition would have consisted of photo laminate, vinyl surface tabletop, 36 × 36 in. Photographer unidentified; courtesy of the Gilbert and Lila Silverman Fluxus Collection, Detroit. *137*

51. Alison Knowles, *The Identical Lunch,* 1970 (2d ed., 1990). Four-color silk-screen graphic on canvas, 17 × 17 in. Courtesy of the artist. *139*

52. Robert Watts, shown with materials for *Implosions, Inc.,* 1967. Photographer unidentified; © 1988 Robert Watts Estate. Courtesy of the Robert Watts Studio Archive, New York. *141*

53. Robert Watts, *Female Underpants,* 1965. Photo by the artist; © 1988 Robert Watts Estate. Courtesy of the Gilbert and Lila Silverman Fluxus Collection, Detroit. *142*

54. Robert Watts, *Stamp Dispenser,* 1963 (remade 1982). Commercial stamp dispenser, offset on gummed paper, cardboard folders, 17½ × 8¼ × 6⅝ in. Photo by Brad Iverson; courtesy of the Gilbert and Lila Silverman Fluxus Collection, Detroit. *143*

55. Robert Filliou, *Galerie Légitime,* 1962–63. Wool beret with mixed media. Photo by Paul Silverman; courtesy of the Gilbert and Lila Silverman Fluxus Collection, Detroit. *149*

56. Geoffrey Hendricks, *Quarter,* 1992. Mixed-media installation at Fluxus Da Capo Festival, Kunsthaus, Wiesbaden, Germany. Photo by Iosif Kiraly; courtesy of the artist. *152*

57. Ann Noël and Emmett Williams at preview event for publication of their book *Mr. Fluxus: A Collective Portrait of George Maciunas, 1931–1978,* at the Fluxeum in Wiesbaden, Germany, 164. Photo by and courtesy of Larry Miller, © 1996. *164*

INDEX

Page numbers appearing in italics refer to illustrations.

TEXT 10.5/13 ADOBE GARAMOND **DISPLAY** AKZIDENZ GROTESK **DESIGNER** NICOLE HAYWARD
COMPOSITOR IMPRESSIONS BOOK AND JOURNAL SERVICES, INC.